Planning Effective Instruction

Planning Effective Instruction

Diversity Responsive Methods and Management

Kay M. Price
Western Washington University

Karna L. Nelson
Western Washington University

Australia • Brazil • Canada • Mexico • Singapore
Spain • United Kingdom • United States

Planning Effective Instruction: Diversity Responsive Methods and Management, **Third Edition**
Kay M. Price, Karna L. Nelson

Publisher: *Vicki Knight*
Acquisitions Editor: *Dan Alpert*
Development Editor: *Tangelique Williams*
Editorial Assistant: *Ann Lee Richards*
Marketing Manager: *Terra Schultz*
Marketing Communications Manager: *Tami Strang*
Project Manager, Editorial Production: *Catherine Morris*
Creative Director: *Rob Hugel*
Executive Art Director: *Maria Epes*
Print Buyer: *Rebecca Cross*

Permissions Editor: *Kiely Sisk*
Production Service: *Sara Dovre Wudali, Buuji, Inc./ Interactive Composition Corporation*
Compositor: *Interactive Composition Corporation*
Text Designer: *John Edeen*
Copy Editor: *Heather McElwain*
Illustrator: *Interactive Composition Corporation*
Cover Designer: *Lisa Delgado*
Text and Cover Printer: *Thomson West*

Printed in the United States of America
1 2 3 4 5 6 7 10 09 08 07 06

Library of Congress Control Number: 2005936706

ISBN 0-495-00757-9

Thomson Higher Education
10 Davis Drive
Belmont, CA 94002-3098
USA

For more information about our products, contact us at:
Thomson Learning Academic Resource Center
1-800-423-0563

For permission to use material from this text or product, submit a request online at **http://www.thomsonrights.com.** Any additional questions about permissions can be submitted by e-mail to **thomsonrights@thomson.com.**

To our sisters and brothers
Gail Vandermay, Larry Vandermay, Curtis Kerce,
Randi Nelson, and Richard Nelson

Contents

Preface

To the Instructor

We wrote this book for *general education* and *special education* teachers to use in a variety of ways. Those just learning how to teach can use this book to provide or supplement initial instruction on planning and delivering inclusive lessons and activities. Experienced teachers can use it as a tool for reviewing essential elements of planning for the diverse classroom. With this versatility, this text is appropriate for use in either undergraduate or graduate courses, for both *preservice* and *in-service* teachers.

We have made many changes to the third edition and have retitled the book to reflect these changes. The first two editions were called *Daily Planning for Today's Classroom: A Guide for Writing Lesson and Activity Plans*. The third edition still provides guidance for writing plans. But we have expanded our discussion of curriculum, instruction, and management as a foundation for making thoughtful decisions about what to include in lesson and activity plans. And we have provided more information and examples to help teachers plan for the success of all students.

Something that hasn't changed in this edition is that we take a very practical, applied approach and incorporate many examples, including examples of plans. In this edition we also include plans with commentary that makes clear the planner's thinking process.

Many teachers work with students from cultural backgrounds very different from their own. They also have students who are English language learners. Many general educators, as well as special educators, teach students with disabilities who are included in their classrooms. Novice and experienced teachers recognize the need every day to plan instruction and create an environment to meet the needs of many different students. Students need diversity responsive teachers and teacher preparation programs are trying to fill that need. We believe that developing attitudes and skills in responding to diversity must begin with the first courses that teachers take. And we believe that planning for diversity must be part of all of the lessons and activities we write.

In the third edition, we have substantially reorganized the information included in previous editions in order to place an even stronger emphasis on Diversity Responsive Teaching (DRT). We introduce a new conceptual framework for DRT that will be used throughout the book. It conceptualizes three areas of daily planning for addressing diversity, that is, in deciding *how* to teach, *what* to teach, and the *context* for teaching and learning. This organization is meant to provide teachers with a structure for thinking about and planning for meeting the needs of a diverse student population within their classrooms, but also to help teachers prepare their students to be responsive to diversity in the world. The book concludes with chapters about the specifics of writing lesson and activity plans that incorporate diversity responsive ideas and strategies. We have expanded on many of the ideas that we presented in previous editions and we have added significant portions of new information as well.

The changes we have made in this edition are in response to our continued observations of teachers in classrooms, as well as feedback from our reviewers, from teachers and principals in the public schools, university supervisors and other faculty, and our students themselves. These changes target several challenges that teachers experience.

One problem we have found is that teachers sometimes struggle with developing plans because they have not thoroughly thought through what they want to teach. They have trouble answering questions along the lines of, "What's the key idea you're trying to get across?" or "What exactly do you want your students to know how to do?" The new organizational structure of this book more explicitly emphasizes the importance of carefully considering the content you will teach before planning the methods of teaching to use. Because planning the curriculum is beyond the scope of this book, Part 1 on planning what to teach is relatively brief. Although the focus remains on daily planning rather than long-term planning, we offer suggestions on making decisions about objectives, content analyses, and responding to diversity through content in "Planning What to Teach." We hope this will help teachers make thoughtful and clear choices.

Another problem teachers may have is a difficulty with managing behavior that sometimes sabotages great lessons and activities. In this edition we have expanded and reorganized information on classroom management. We believe that it is almost impossible to discuss effective instruction separately from effective management. In the third part of the book, "Planning the Context for Teaching and Learning," we focus on using universal interventions for preventing behavior problems and on building thorough management planning into every lesson and activity. We also stress creating an environment that sets the stage for learning and truly includes and supports all students.

The third challenge that teachers face—and the most important one in our view—is the diversity in classrooms and the multitude of diversity strategies. We know that preservice and in-service teachers strive to be diversity responsive, to leave no child behind, but so much information is available about how to meet the needs of diverse learners, that knowing where to start can be very confusing and overwhelming. We address this problem through the conceptual framework that we present and the organization of the book. We present and apply many specific techniques for responding to diversity. Although our prior editions emphasized planning for skill diversity, our third edition places more emphasis on planning for cultural and linguistic diversity as well.

Our reasons for writing this book in the first place still hold. We wrote the first two editions because we noticed that many of the hundreds of practicum students and student teachers with whom we worked experienced some common problems. First, just like young students, preservice teachers cannot automatically transfer what they have learned in classes to real-life situations. In the real classroom, their focus is on survival, and beginning teachers seem to forget what they learned from their training. For example, as they try to figure out how to teach division of fractions to a particular group of fifth graders tomorrow at two o'clock, they may forget much of what they learned about making instructional and management decisions. Beginning teachers can plan more effective lessons and activities when they have forms that prompt the decisions they need to make.

We also noticed that novice teachers sometimes forget to teach. They like to use exciting and creative approaches and are eager to involve their young students in learning. However, they can have trouble distinguishing between those occasions when students need the opportunity to practice and develop what they know and when students need to be directly taught new facts, concepts, and strategies. In their eagerness to be innovative, they plan fun activities but are unable to express what they want students to learn. Frequently, when they plan and teach lessons, they advance to providing student practice before they have taught enough to enable students to be successful with the practice. Novice teachers may select teaching methods based on their own interests or emerging styles rather than on the needs of their students. For these reasons, we distinguish between activities and lessons, based on their purposes, and suggest different types of planning decisions for each. We also focus on clear objectives and evaluation of learning to emphasize the accountability of teaching so that students learn.

Finally, teachers often say they are overwhelmed by the diversity of their students' needs. They routinely find themselves writing plans and then trying to modify and adjust them to meet these diverse needs. Teachers need a more efficient and effective way to design lessons and activities. We stress the inclusion of universal design and differentiated instructional principles, and of critical teaching and management strategies during the initial stage of planning. Building in these strategies can result in the completion of a more effective plan in a shorter amount of time. We feel that we clearly address these three issues in this edition.

The following are some of the highlights provided in our new edition:

- A conceptual framework designed to help readers understand and apply the key components of diversity responsive teaching
- Specific strategies and ideas that teachers can use to respond to various types of diversity, such as skill diversity, cultural diversity, and linguistic diversity
- Directions for editing written lessons for management and diversity planning, with sample annotated plans
- Explanations for using the DRT framework for brainstorming and reflection, with extensive narrative examples
- Lesson and activity plan examples designed for various grade levels, content areas, and group sizes
- New information about connecting lesson and activity objectives to the state standards for general education and special education teachers
- New information about universal instructional interventions, such as the use of universal design for learning and critical teaching skills
- New information about universal behavioral interventions, such as establishing and teaching rules, routines, and social skills
- The use of critical management skills, including ideas for integrating classroom management with effective instruction planning to prevent behavior problems
- Lists of additional resources

Our book has been used in a variety of ways. We know that principals and teacher in-service providers have used our book as a tool for working with and helping practicing teachers in their buildings or district. University instructors have used it at both the undergraduate and graduate levels. University students have used it at both ends of their teacher preparation programs, during their student teaching, and when planning in their own classrooms. Novice teachers in alternative certification programs have used it. We are confident that our revisions make our third edition even more flexible and responsive to classroom diversity.

Acknowledgments

Thank you to our students and practicum supervision colleagues (Bridget Kelley, Heather Cochran, Jenny Parker, and Beth Stickley), who contributed whether they realized it or not. Thanks to Linda Schleef and LeAnne Robinson for their willingness to be consulted.

We would also like to acknowledge our extremely supportive families. Each member has provided us with encouragement during all phases of our project. We give many, many thanks to Walter, Steve, Jerell, and Leah.

Thanks also to Vicki Knight for getting us started, and Dan Alpert for keeping us going.

A special thanks to Lyn Dyson, Gail Vandermay, and Wendy Brown who provided valuable editing and proofreading assistance.

We are grateful for the useful feedback we have received from public school personnel in both general and special education. And we would also like to thank the following reviewers: Fran Baumgartner, Roosevelt University; Carol Briscoe, University of West Florida; Katherine G. Fralick, Plymouth State University; Diane Marvin, Newman University; and Florette Reven, Tarleton State University.

Introduction

This book addresses how to plan lessons and activities that are effective in classrooms made up of highly diverse individuals. Every teacher's goal is to teach so that all students are successful. With the diversity in today's classroom, however, it often seems an unreachable goal. A one-size-fits-all approach to instruction is clearly ineffective.

Writing separate lesson plans for each student in a class is definitely not realistic. So, what can teachers do to help all students be successful? They can design lessons and activities that incorporate diversity responsive practices as they plan *what* to teach (the curriculum), *how* to teach (instructional methods), and the *context for teaching and learning* (classroom environment). More specifically, they can incorporate universal interventions designed for all students in the class, and selected interventions to meet the needs of an individual or small group of students. In this book, you will learn how to be a diversity responsive teacher, that is, one who can design lessons and activities that meet the needs of a whole classroom of diverse learners.

Today's Diverse Classroom

Before we talk about how to respond to classroom diversity, we would like to discuss the students for whom you will plan lessons and activities. The diversity in today's classroom includes factors of culture, language, ethnicity, race, ability, gender, socioeconomic background, religion, age, and sexual orientation (Gay 2002; Gollnick and Chinn 1998; Mercer and Mercer 2005; Sobel, Taylor, and Anderson 2003). You can see that the concept of diversity is broadly defined here; this is how we will apply this concept throughout this book.

Several large, steadily growing groups of students are impacting classroom diversity. First, schools have increasingly larger numbers of students from diverse cultural and linguistic backgrounds. The number of English language learners for example, has increased by 84 percent between 1992 and 2003 (NCELA 2004). Making a successful transition to school can be especially challenging for these students who are trying to learn English as well as subject matter content. Many of them experience "culture shock" as well, when their personal preferences for learning and performing do not match the expectations of their school setting. The presence of these students has created wonderful opportunities for teachers and students to learn about customs, beliefs, and traditions that may be outside of their own personal experiences. Note: It is not unusual to find several different languages spoken as primary languages by different students within one classroom.

Next, students with disabilities have significantly contributed to the diversity of the general education classroom. Special education law provides most students with disabilities the opportunity to spend their time in both special education and general education settings. Students with mild learning problems, who are commonly taught in general education at least part of their day, are increasing in number. The number of students in the learning disability category in special education has more than doubled since 1976. Both special and general education teachers typically provide services to students with disabilities with Individualized Education Programs (IEPs) (Hallahan and Kauffman 2003). Although they have presented unique challenges, they have added a rich dynamic to the classroom.

Finally, students who are considered "at risk" for school failure make up another group of students who contribute to classroom diversity. Factors that put students at risk can be found both within our society at large and within our schools. Drug and alcohol use and abuse, poverty, teen pregnancy, physical and emotional abuse, homelessness, and lack of supervision are only some of the societal problems that can lead to students coming to school unprepared to learn. Failure to recognize and address student learning problems, irrelevant curriculum, and poor teaching can significantly interfere with student progress in school. Mercer and Mercer (2005) write that 15 percent to 25 percent of the school population experience risk factors that lead to low academic achievement without intervention. Although these students have learning and behavioral problems that can interfere with school success, they often do not qualify for special education services.

Increasing diversity has heavily influenced classroom dynamics. Sobel, Taylor, and Anderson (2003) suggest that issues of equity and diversity are two of the most critical issues that challenge teachers on a daily basis. We concur with their assessment. Here are some examples of the challenges that today's teachers encounter because of this diversity: (1) the need to develop a cohesive, well-functioning group from a diverse group of students within a supportive, welcoming environment; (2) the need to present content in multiple ways; (3) the need to help some students learn English as well as learn subject matter content; (4) the need to teach students how to get along with others and/or how to learn and study, as well as teaching important academic content skills; and (5) the need to find ways to honor and accommodate individual student needs and preferences in addition to the needs of the group. Teaching really is more complex today than it was in years past, for teachers in both general and special education. It can be hard to know where to start when trying to meet the needs of so many different students.

Diversity Responsive Teaching

Diversity Responsive Teaching (DRT) has emerged as an important approach to the challenges of classroom diversity. In this type of teaching, teachers implement a set of practices to increase the probability that all students will learn. By design, DRT also promotes mutual respect among class members and provides valuable lessons for life by empowering students with accurate information about diversity. Teachers deliver this type of teaching by responding to issues of diversity with understanding, opportunity, and equity for all (Sobel, Taylor, and Anderson 2003). In addition to teaching so all students can learn, they address diversity directly and teach the students the skills they need to respond appropriately to differing perspectives, lifestyles, and ways of being. They also teach their students to celebrate the differences among people and perhaps even more importantly, to recognize their similarities. Clearly, diversity responsive teachers teach attitudes and skills that have direct application to life after school, where diversity abounds in society at large.

A Framework for Diversity Responsive Teaching

The literature is filled with specific techniques and strategies that make up diversity responsive teaching. We find, however, that for many teachers (preservice teachers especially), the sheer number of ideas available makes the task of selecting strategies an overwhelming one. We have developed a three-component framework for helping teachers implement DRT in a classroom setting. Following are summaries of the key components of this framework:

- The first component provides a structure for planning curriculum *content* that is relevant and representative of diversity, while providing P-12 students with opportunities to increase their knowledge about diversity. An additional consideration within this component is making sure that the content taught includes varying perspectives and is an accurate representation of all groups involved. This section is about *what* to teach.

- The second component helps teachers address diversity when planning *instruction*. Universal interventions such as the principles of universal design for learning, differentiated instruction, and evidence-based teaching strategies are part of this component, as are selected interventions to meet the needs of individuals. This component addresses *how* to teach.

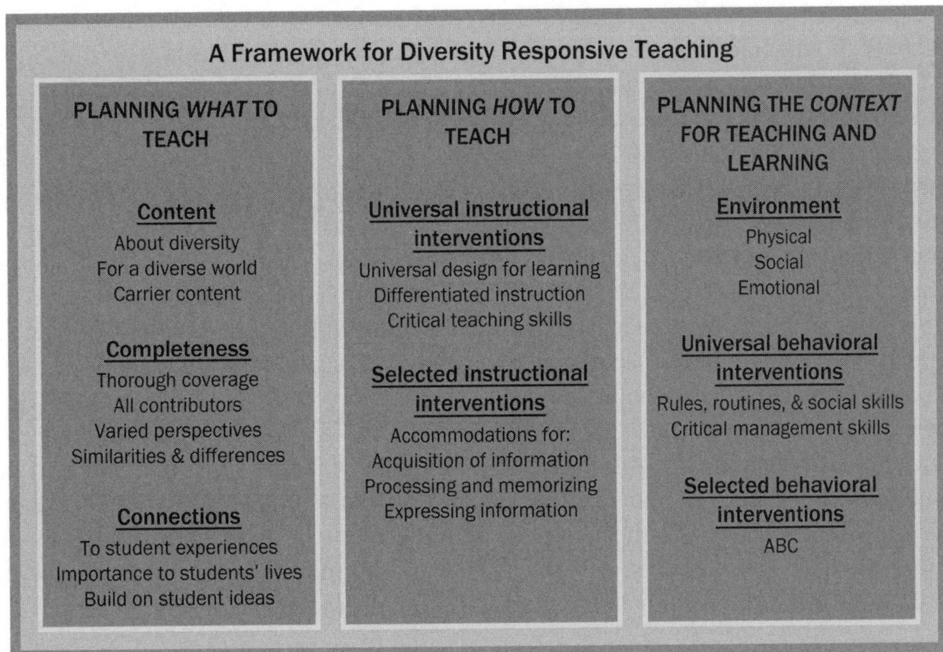

- The final component structures ideas for creating an inclusive *classroom environment,* one in which all students are supported and accepted. We include aspects of the physical environment, the social environment, and the emotional environment. This component helps teachers arrange the *context for teaching and learning.*

This diversity responsive teaching framework offers a way to think about providing for the needs of diverse learners. In other words, it is very important to respond to diversity when you plan the content to teach, the way in which you will teach, and the setup of your classroom. This framework can also help you manage the large amount of information available on the topic of teaching diverse learners. The first three parts of this book are designed around this framework.

Goals of Diversity Responsive Teachers

Diversity responsive teachers strive to teach so that all students can learn by implementing diversity responsive teaching. Teachers who help all students be successful are most likely those who make the following their personal goals:

- *To know students as individuals.* DRT teachers have the interest and therefore take the time to learn their students' likes and dislikes, strengths and challenges, and life situations and experiences.

- *To appreciate similarities and differences among students.* Although these teachers notice and respect student variation, they find and appreciate the commonalities among students as well.

- *To connect with families and community.* Diversity responsive teachers seek out opportunities to get to know their students' families. They also learn about and participate in the community in which their students live.

- *To teach so that all students are challenged and successful.* Diversity in classroom activities and objectives is an idea common to diversity responsive teachers. These teachers take into account what they know about their students as individuals to appropriately challenge them. They work hard to help ensure student success.

- *To prepare students for diversity in the world.* Diversity responsive teachers look beyond the classroom walls to determine what their students ought to learn. They identify and teach important skills that have broad real-life applications for understanding and tolerance.

Diversity responsive teachers examine their own beliefs as well as their students' circumstances and experiences. They learn how their own cultural background affects their beliefs, values, and expectations and in turn impact their choices of subject matter, models, methods, management procedures, rules, and so on. Learning about the particular cultures of their students helps teachers understand how the students' cultural backgrounds impact preferences and reactions to the methods and management used in the classroom. Note that it is extremely important to see students first as individuals. The importance of cultural background must be recognized of course, but it is essential to avoid stereotyping. Culturally aware teachers are more effective decision makers or problem solvers, as they are able to generate more ideas or options when planning. These actions will likely result in positive outcomes for students.

Universal and Selected Interventions

Diversity responsive teachers also find it helpful, particularly when planning how to teach and manage behavior, to think in terms of universal and selected interventions. These general categories of interventions can be broken down as follows: universal and selected *instructional* interventions, and universal and selected *behavioral* interventions. You will learn more about these interventions in Parts 2 and 3 of this book.

Universal Interventions

A *universal intervention* is a strategy, technique, or method designed to promote the success of all students and to prevent learning or behavior problems. These techniques and strategies are *built in* as part of your initial planning. This means they are standard procedure, routinely included, something you always do. Many varied universal interventions can be used when planning how to teach and manage student behavior. Examples of universal instructional interventions include presenting information in a variety of ways, using visual supports, and keeping students actively involved during instruction. Examples of universal behavioral interventions include connecting with each student, establishing classroom rules and routines, and teaching social skills. Universal interventions provide needed support for many students.

Selected Interventions

Even when a teacher includes numerous universal interventions in a particular lesson, one or a few students will typically need additional support. This is where selected interventions come into play. A *selected intervention* is an accommodation or modification designed to solve specific individual learning and behavior problems. It is included in a lesson or activity for an individual student or a small group of students. It is often more costly to implement in terms of time, money, or effort, and it is *added on* to initial planning.

Built-Ins and Add-Ons

Although universal interventions are built in and selected interventions are added on, the line between the two is not always a clear one. Some strategies and techniques would probably always be considered universal interventions, such as communicating clear expectations for behavior, putting directions in writing as well as saying them, and monitoring student progress. Also, some interventions would generally always be considered selected interventions, such as text in Braille and individual behavior plans. Many strategies could be considered either universal interventions or selected interventions, depending on how they are used.

The Challenging Class

Let's suppose that you are designing a plan for a social studies lesson to be used with your very challenging, diverse group of students. Once you have selected the universal interventions that you think are appropriate, you begin thinking about the selected interventions that could be helpful for your three students who have fairly significant problems with reading. You decide that providing a graphic organizer of key ideas in the textbook chapter would help them. However, you realize that this intervention could benefit many of your students. So, you decide to build it in rather than add it on. What you thought was going to be a selected intervention is now a universal intervention. Remember that by definition, if an intervention is built in, it is a universal intervention; if it is added on, it is a selected intervention. Planning for a challenging class may result in increased use of universal interventions that, in a less challenging class, might be considered selected interventions.

We suggest that you strive to build in as many interventions as possible up front to make your job easier. Remember that it often takes more time and effort to incorporate specialized strategies for one or more individuals than it does to build in a strategy that will benefit everyone. So again, build it in if it will benefit many; add it on if it will only benefit certain students and would not be appropriate for the whole class. As the number of built-in strategies increases, the number of needed add-ons decreases.

An Example of Diversity Responsive Teaching

As we mentioned earlier, the most efficient way to meet the needs of all students is to consider those needs up front—as you design lessons and activities—rather than trying to adjust for individuals after the fact. Start by incorporating best practices and building in alternatives that will allow all students access to your instruction. Include other accommodations and modifications based on the makeup of your class. The following example shows how one teacher built in universal interventions and added on selected interventions to help all of her students be successful.

Mrs. Hakim has planned an activity in which her students are asked to create an ending to a story. The intention is to provide additional practice on predicting and making inferences after lessons on these topics. After hearing or reading the first half of the story, students are asked to produce their own endings and justify them.

When Mrs. Hakim selects the story for which the students will create endings, she chooses a story by a Mexican American author. She wants her students to identify with authors so she chooses stories written by people with ethnic backgrounds similar to those of her students.

Mrs. Hakim helps students connect their prior knowledge and experience to this activity, an effective teaching strategy that she considers important for the learning of all students. She connects their use of inferences and predictions in everyday situations by asking questions such as, "You see pork, onions, green chilies, and tortillas on the grocery list. What do you think you'll have for supper? Why? What is another possibility?"

She plans to pre-teach key vocabulary using pictures and demonstrations. This is helpful to many of her students and very important for the English language learners.

At the beginning of the activity, Mrs. Hakim communicates behavior expectations to her students. This is an effective management strategy.

She plans to review the previously taught skills of predicting, finding clues in the story, and making inferences. Reviewing is an effective teaching strategy.

Mrs. Hakim passes out a written copy of the first half of the story. She then reads the story out loud. Presenting information in these two ways (multiple methods of presenting) will allow more of her students to be successful.

During her initial planning of this activity, Mrs. Hakim automatically decides to provide both written and oral directions for producing the story endings. She knows that this effective teaching strategy is essential for several of her students and that many of them find it helpful. (She also finds that the process of writing directions results in clearer directions and saves instructional time.)

Quite a few of Mrs. Hakim's students have difficulty completing tasks. Therefore, when planning the activity, Mrs. Hakim makes explicit the steps for completing this story ending assignment. She decides to list these on the blackboard: finish ending, proofread ending, put name on paper, place in box on back table. She has built this conspicuous strategy technique into her initial planning, rather than as a separate accommodation, because the makeup of her class makes this sensible.

One student needs more support to complete tasks. Mrs. Hakim plans to give him a personal list of steps, tell him to check off each step when completed, and to acknowledge his success enthusiastically ("You must be very proud of yourself. . . .").

Some of the students in Mrs. Hakim's class are more productive when they have the opportunity to work with peers; others prefer to work alone. This may be related to cultural background. Mrs. Hakim decides that the students may consult peers when writing their story endings, if they choose.

Two of Mrs. Hakim's students have very serious writing problems. She plans to have them dictate their story endings to a teaching assistant as an accommodation for them. The other students may choose to hand write or to type their assignments. She provides sentence patterns to several other students who need more support or scaffolding to be successful in writing (for example, I think Carlos will______at the end because . . .).

She modifies the content of the activity for one student. He is working on a different comprehension objective, recalling factual information. Mrs. Hakim creates questions that a parent volunteer asks him, while recording his responses.

You can see that Mrs. Hakim used both universal and selected interventions. She built in numerous techniques to provide options for all of her students. She then added on selected interventions that she thought would be appropriate for a few of her students. Due to the makeup of her class, Mrs. Hakim decided that at least one of the selected interventions she thought to use would benefit all of her students, so she build it in also, rather than adding it on. Through careful planning, Mrs. Hakim most certainly prevented potential learning problems.

Attitude of the Diversity Responsive Teacher

Your ability to be successful in working with a diverse student population begins with a belief that you have a responsibility to do so. If you believe that your job is to teach *all* students, then you will start off much better equipped to meet the challenge. If you believe that your job is to teach only those students who are easy to teach, then your ability to be effective is questionable. You will definitely spend a great deal of your time feeling frustrated.

Equally important, you must believe that you can make a difference in teaching a diverse student population. Beliefs about making a difference may have a significant impact on a teacher's success or lack thereof. We encourage you to examine your beliefs in this area. There is no question that the diverse classroom of today requires a special kind of teacher.

Regardless of age and experience level, effective teachers view teaching as an important and exciting profession. They feel a responsibility to teach all students and see student diversity as a fascinating challenge. Effective teachers plan with the needs of all students in mind. These teachers have a strong desire to learn, and stay current in the field by reading professional journals and taking courses and workshops. These teachers develop an ever-growing repertoire of teaching strategies and methods to use with challenging students. These teachers also believe they can be effective and, therefore, are very effective in diverse classrooms. We hope you are or will become one of these teachers.

Summary

Building in the ideas that are suggested in Parts 1, 2, and 3 of this book will result in classrooms that have a new look. This is important because diversity is the norm in today's classrooms, rather than the exception. To be responsive to that diversity, teachers must do things differently. They must provide options and opportunities in what they teach, in how they teach, in a setting that is safe and inviting.

The Content and Organization of This Book

This book is about diversity responsive teaching. It is designed to help you plan so that your students will learn. We focus heavily on making your lessons and activities relevant and meaningful for a diverse group of students, including those who vary in language, ethnicity, race, socioeconomic circumstances, and learning and behavior needs. This book includes information about the various components of the planning process, and it is organized to provide various levels of planning assistance. This makes it a versatile resource to utilize in methods courses, practica, and student teaching. It is also a good resource for practicing teachers in both general and special education.

The following is a review of the four sections of our book:

- *Part 1: Planning What to Teach* This section of the book starts out with a review of types of content and with ideas for addressing diversity through the content being taught. It concludes with how to organize content for teaching. A chapter on writing objectives follows.
- *Part 2: Planning How to Teach* This is the largest section of the book and it emphasizes universal instructional interventions. We present general approaches as well as specific strategies. The last chapter in this section discusses ideas for selected instructional interventions.
- *Part 3: Planning the Context for Teaching and Learning* Here you will learn about many interventions for classroom management. This section begins with a chapter on universal behavioral interventions for supporting appropriate student behavior and examples of selected interventions. Following it is a chapter on critical management skills crucial for successful lessons and activities.
- *Part 4: Writing Your Plan* This section begins by helping you learn how to decide which type of plan to write (lesson or activity). Next, you will learn about specific types of lesson plans and then how to write effective lesson and activity plans. Finally, you will learn how to put the finishing touches on your plan.

The organizational structure of this text is intended to enable you to select the specific content and the level of detail in planning, teaching, and management assistance that you need. The following may guide you in searching for specific material within this text:

1. To understand the differences between lessons and activities, see Chapter 12.
2. To learn how to write measurable objectives, see Chapter 2.
3. To review the basics of lesson planning, read the information in Chapter 13 and Chapters 15 through 17.
4. To learn or review universal instructional interventions, see Chapters 3 through 8. Universal behavioral interventions are found in Chapters 10 and 11.
5. To locate ideas for selected behavioral interventions, see Chapter 10. Selected instructional interventions are found in Chapter 9.
6. To focus on identifying or implementing critical teaching skills (planning lesson openings, presenting information effectively, planning for students to work in groups, for example), you may benefit from the detailed information available in Chapters 4 through 8.
7. To review strategies that are essential for setting up a positive learning environment, see Chapter 10.
8. To locate ideas for building preventive management techniques into lessons and activities, see Chapter 11.
9. To learn or review the key ideas that make up various lesson models, see Chapters 15 through 17.
10. For learning how to teach specific content (social skills, strategies, and concepts), see Chapter 18.
11. To learn how to think about the content you will be teaching, see Chapter 1.
12. For practicum students practicing certain models or methods of teaching, you can select the appropriate chapters or sections.

References and Suggested Readings

Bowe, F. 2005. *Making inclusion work*. Columbus, OH: Merrill, an imprint of Prentice-Hall.

Gay, G. 2002. Preparing for culturally responsive teaching. *Journal of Teacher Education* 53 (2): 106–116.

Gollnick, D. M., and P. Chinn. 1998. *Multicultural education: Education in a pluralistic society.* 5th ed. Columbus, OH: Merrill.

Hallahan, D. P., and J. M. Kauffman. 2003. *Exceptional learners.* 9th ed. San Francisco, CA: Allyn and Bacon.

Irvine, J., and B. Armento. 2001. *Culturally responsive teaching: lesson planning for elementary and middle grades*. Boston: McGraw-Hill.

Mercer, C. D., and A. R. Mercer. 2005. *Teaching students with learning problems.* 7th ed. Upper Saddle River: Pearson/Merrill Prentice Hall.

National Clearinghouse for English Language Acquisition. 2004. *The growing numbers of limited English proficient students.* http://www.ncela.gwu.edu/policy/states/reports/statedata/2002LEP/Growing_LEP0203.pdf (accessed May 22, 2005).

Salend, S. J. 2005. *Creating inclusive classrooms—Effective and reflective practices for all students.* 5th ed. Columbus, OH: Merrill, an imprint of Prentice Hall.

Sobel, D. M., S. V. Taylor, and R. E. Anderson. 2003. Shared accountability: Encouraging diversity-responsive teaching in inclusive contexts. *Teaching Exceptional Children* 35 (6): 46–54.

Planning What to Teach

A Framework for Diversity Responsive Teaching

PLANNING *WHAT* TO TEACH	PLANNING *HOW* TO TEACH	PLANNING THE *CONTEXT* FOR TEACHING AND LEARNING
Content About diversity For a diverse world Carrier content	**Universal instructional interventions** Universal design for learning Differentiated instruction Critical teaching skills	**Environment** Physical Social Emotional
Completeness Thorough coverage All contributors Varied perspectives Similarities & differences	**Selected instructional interventions** Accommodations for: Acquisition of information Processing and memorizing Expressing information	**Universal behavioral interventions** Rules, routines, & social skills Critical management skills
Connections To student experiences Importance to students' lives Build on student ideas		**Selected behavioral interventions** ABC

Teachers make important decisions about the content to teach their students. These decisions need to be made before deciding how to teach. In the first part of this book, we will focus on thinking generally about what to teach, how to analyze content, and then how to write specific and measurable objectives. When thinking about content, it's helpful to begin by thinking about what students need to learn—what subjects and what types of knowledge (for example, declarative and procedural knowledge). It is also important to carefully think about diversity so that you teach content about diversity, content that is complete and inclusive, and content that is connected to students' lives.

We will also discuss resources that teachers use when planning what to teach. One of the most important resources is state standards. Teachers must be skilled at using state standards in long-term planning and in developing short-term objectives from those standards. Teachers must also be cognizant of the important generalizations or big ideas in the various subject areas and use those in organizing content in a meaningful way.

An important final step in planning what to teach is deciding the level of understanding you want your students to achieve. It's also essential to know how to conduct content analyses, such as task and concept analyses, and determining key vocabulary and prerequisite knowledge for the content to be taught. These analyses help in determining important and clear objectives and in beginning to plan the actual lesson or activity plan.

This book is primarily about how to teach. We begin our book by discussing curriculum however, for a variety of reasons.

- It is not possible to talk about how to teach until you know what to teach. The content itself directly influences how you should teach, for example, certain types of content lend themselves to particular models of instruction.

- School districts and state offices of public instruction are paying more attention to curriculum because of mandates such as the No Child Left Behind Act and the Individuals with Disabilities Education Act (IDEA). Educators have been prompted to look carefully at the curriculum used in their schools and to attempt to more clearly define learner outcomes in relation to various content areas.

- Increasing diversity in the schools has resulted in careful evaluation of the effectiveness of curriculum in meeting the needs of diverse learners. Further, schools have struggled with ideas regarding the best ways to create curricula that are inclusive in nature and accessible to all students.

- A student's ability to learn is impacted by how teachers organize and present curriculum content for learning.

In the chapters that follow, you will learn how teachers determine what to teach, and how they describe what their students need to know and do.

CHAPTER 1 Thinking about Content

Introduction

Planning for instruction begins with thinking about content. Before making decisions about how to teach, instructors need to decide what to teach. We'll begin by considering content in terms of the wide variety of subject matter taught in schools, the types of knowledge, and the importance of considering diversity. In addition we'll focus on standards that guide teachers in selecting what to teach their students. Finally we'll talk about preparing to teach content, deciding what levels of understanding you want students to achieve, and how to organize content for teaching.

Thinking about What Students Need to Learn

We'll begin by examining the types of subjects that are typically taught in schools.

Subject Matter

Students in our public schools need to learn various subjects. Certainly everyone agrees that they need to learn reading, writing, and arithmetic. We also teach science and social studies in school. Often art, music, and health and fitness are taught, although they seem to be cut first during budget crunches. Teachers today also teach a wide assortment of additional subjects including social and emotional skills, cognitive behavioral skills, vocational skills, and technology. Another perspective teachers need to consider is emphasizing critical thinking skills and learning strategies so that students become lifelong learners. You'll make decisions about what your students should learn based on standards, district guidelines, and individual needs.

The following are some examples of skills and knowledge by subject area that are taught routinely in schools today:

- Academics—recognizing letters, knowing the structure of plant cells, finding the circumference of a circle
- Learning strategies—completing an assignment calendar, reading for comprehension
- Social and emotional skills—taking *no* for an answer, joining in activities, dealing with embarrassment
- Arts—appreciating baroque music, drawing faces
- Health and fitness—bandaging a cut, understanding the effects of drugs, exercising aerobically
- Life skills—making a bed, riding the city bus independently, budgeting
- Cognitive behavior skills—interpersonal problem solving, controlling angry outbursts
- Vocational skills—finding a career interest, fixing car engines, using the want ads
- Technology skills—evaluating Web sites for bias, creating spreadsheets, keyboarding

Societal pressures sometimes overwhelm teachers, as they feel compelled to teach everything from responsible credit card use and safe sex to healthy eating and honesty.

Types of Knowledge: Declarative and Procedural

We can think about content in terms of types of knowledge as well as in types of subject matter. Knowledge can be categorized as knowing *about* something and knowing *how to do* something. These types of knowledge are called declarative knowledge and procedural knowledge, respectively. Naming the parts of a lawn mower is an example of declarative knowledge, whereas knowing how to start a lawn mower is an example of procedural knowledge. Knowing the history of the development of the scientific method is declarative knowledge and knowing how to use the scientific method is procedural knowledge. Understanding the concept of standard units of measurement is declarative, and measuring objects is procedural. Both types of knowledge are important and complement each other. Your students need to learn both.

Declarative Knowledge

Three kinds of information are considered declarative knowledge: facts, concepts, and principles.

The first category of declarative information is **facts.** For example, it is fact that red and yellow make up orange; 10 is a multiple of 5; and 18-year-olds may vote. Other examples of factual information include labels (the parts of a volcano), names (of states and capitals), and words and their definitions (Smith and Ragan 2004).

Concepts is a second category of declarative knowledge. Howell, Hosp, and Hosp (forthcoming) define concepts as objects, events, actions, or situations that share a set of defining characteristics. Concepts are categories in which all examples of a concept share certain characteristics. Furniture and democracy are both concepts. Triangle is also a concept. All triangles have three sides and three angles. Examples of triangles include isosceles, equilateral, right, and so on. (See Chapter 18 for more information on concepts.)

The final category of declarative knowledge is **principles,** relational rules that prescribe the relationship between two or more concepts. They are often described in the form of if–then, cause–effect, or "rule of thumb" relationships. Principles can be very simple or highly complex. The following are examples of principles: round up numbers five or higher; voting is both a right and a responsibility; and thunder is caused as air heats and expands to varying degrees along the path of lightning.

Procedural Knowledge

Whereas declarative knowledge means to know or know about something, procedural knowledge refers to knowing *how to do* something. Knowing the steps or methods to follow, processes, strategies or specific skills to use are all procedural knowledge. Knowing how to change a flat tire, to cut with scissors, to proofread, to multiply fractions, to write a five-paragraph essay, to resist peer pressure, or to register to vote, are all examples of procedural knowledge. This type of knowledge involves bringing together various subtasks to complete a whole procedure (Howell, Hosp, and Hosp, forthcoming).

Obviously, both types of knowledge are extremely important and they are directly connected. Typically one must know basic facts before using them. For example, students need to know the steps of the reading comprehension strategy before they use them in their content reading. However, it is possible to memorize and use the steps to divide fractions, for example, without understanding the underlying concepts. It is very important to determine in advance what type of knowledge you are asking the students to learn. This is key in determining how to best organize the content for teaching.

Diversity and Content

When thinking about what students need to learn, you also need to consider content that reflects the diversity of the world and the diversity in your classroom. You may find it helpful to use the content section of the diversity responsive teaching framework (see Part I: Planning What to Teach) as you think about what you want to teach your students. This information is intended to support teachers in creating a diversity responsive curriculum, that is, one that is inclusive and engaging. When working toward creating a diversity responsive curriculum, consider the following three goals to help structure your decisions: (1) teach content about diversity; (2) teach content that is complete and inclusive; and (3) connect the content taught to students' lives (Irvine and Armento 2001). We'll discuss each of these three in turn, with a focus on cultural diversity. Then we'll focus briefly on skill diversity.

Content about Diversity

Teachers can teach directly about individuals, groups, cultures, traditions, beliefs, issues, events, and so on, that reflect diversity. These topics can be made the content of lessons, activities, and units. For example, teachers can select diversity responsive content by teaching lessons and activities on any of the following: deaf culture; the art, music, and literature of Mexico; the civil rights movement; female athletes; or different kinds of families.

Teachers can also select objectives that focus on developing skills for a diverse world. For example, when you plan to have students work in small groups or with a partner, you can write objectives for the skills they need to work together effectively. Some examples of important skills for a diverse world are social action skills, perspective taking, recognizing stereotypes, empathy, cross-cultural communication including sign language, collaboration, conflict resolution, and so on. All of these skills are designed to help students respond to diversity inside and outside of school in a respectful, accepting manner.

Teachers can also consider using *carrier* content related to diversity when teaching any subject matter. Incorporating diversity content while teaching other knowledge or skills helps to engage or inform students. For example, if you are teaching reading comprehension skills, you could choose a story about a family that is homeless. Reading comprehension is your primary objective. The content about homelessness is carrier content. As another example, when fishing is an important aspect of the culture of the community in which you teach, write math problems with content about fishing (If you caught 300 pounds of cod per day . . .). This material carries the knowledge or skills you are teaching, informs students about a diversity-related topic, and, potentially, engages students in your class who are from the same background (in these examples, those who are also homeless or those whose families fish).

Content That Is Complete and Inclusive

A second goal to help structure decisions about curriculum is providing completeness (Irvine and Armento 2001). Make sure to include all contributors, voices, and perspectives when teaching subjects such as history, literature, art, and music. Include all important, relevant contributors such as historical figures, writers, artists, and so on from all backgrounds: different genders, races or ethnicities, abilities, classes, and sexual orientation.

This doesn't mean including a Central American author because you have Latino students in your class this year. Rather, when teaching about environmental issues, logging, fishing, whaling, or hunting, bring in various points of view. Include Native American and European settler perspectives when teaching U.S. history. When teaching about governing, investigate a variety of ways, such as by the wisdom of elders, by consensus, and by majority vote.

Also, emphasize similarities. Avoid focusing only on differences. Look for common themes in folk tales, such as wise animal stories or children who do not obey their parents. Combine folk tales from different cultures. Point out commonalities like caring and sharing among different types of families. Show similarities in the occasions for celebrations (spring, harvest, independence) among cultures.

The most important thing to remember is to be thorough in your coverage of topics. The idea is to teach completely for everyone's benefit, so that all students can be fully educated.

Content That Is Connected to Students' Lives

The third thing to think about when planning topics is how to make connections between the topics and the students. Select examples, images, and metaphors connected to students' experiences and cultural backgrounds (Irvine and Armento 2001). Use examples that show the importance of the content to students' lives. Build on student ideas and examples. For example, when teaching the topic of discrimination, connect with the students by having them discuss their experiences of discrimination, as young people, people with disabilities, or people of color. If teaching fractions, begin by creating an experience in sharing, perhaps half a cookie with a friend. When teaching poetry, connect with nursery rhymes, jump rope chants, song lyrics, or raps.

To find these connections, you will need to learn about your students' cultural backgrounds and about the community in which you teach. You may use books, articles, and Internet sites to gain general information. To learn specifically about your students and community, spend time with student families, read the local newspaper, attend community events, and get to know everyone at school. To summarize, considering these three categories related to curriculum (content, completeness, and connections) will help you be a diversity responsive teacher in *what* you teach.

When planning what to teach you'll also want to consider skill diversity. To begin with, be sure that you are teaching important knowledge and skills. If students have fallen behind in the curriculum, there is no time for fluff and filler. Teach what is most generalizable. Consider the possibility that you need to teach more lessons and fewer activities. Reexamine the rationale for the planned activities.

In addition, engage students by using content based on their interests. Offer choices to students when possible. For example, allow students to read articles from the sports pages to practice reading skills. Teach students to take charge of their learning by setting and monitoring their own learning goals.

Help students learn the skills that will allow them to learn more efficiently. Teach learning strategies along with teaching content areas, such as working on active reading strategies in the social studies textbook. Teach school survival and task-related skills, such as study skills, test-taking skills, problem-solving skills, and organizational skills. Teach students the skills they need to be successful in various teaching models and methods such as discussion or peer interaction skills, and skills for staying focused and for dealing with challenges and frustration.

In summary, when thinking about content, consider what your students need to learn in terms of subject matter, types of knowledge, and diversity. The possibilities of what to teach seem nearly endless. Obviously, you want to teach the most important content to your students. Fortunately there is help in selecting what to teach.

Guidance in Choosing What to Teach

Teachers aren't expected (or allowed) to make all decisions about what to teach. They receive guidance in selecting content from a variety of sources. These include state standards and standards developed by professional organizations. In addition, teachers are guided by district curricula and, in the case of students with disabilities, individual education programs (IEPs).

State Standards

State standards are a valuable source for giving direction to teacher planning. Most states have adopted a set of standards that provide a description of what students across the state will learn as they progress through the K–12 public school system. The standards are meant to guide the general curriculum. They were developed in an attempt to raise student achievement levels and to standardize the learning expectations for all students in the state. The standards appear as sets of goals in content areas such as reading, mathematics, and the arts, and describe what students will accomplish in each area. State tests, given at various grade levels, measure student progress in relation to these standards.

The special education law, Individuals with Disabilities Education Act (IDEA 04), was developed to ensure that special education also connected with state standards. Therefore, students with disabilities also have access to the higher standards of the general curriculum. This allows teachers to plan programs for these students with the state standards in mind.

State standards and goals provide focus in schools in several ways. First, they help describe the general curriculum and provide a guide for planning the content of teaching (King-Sears 2001). These standards ensure that students, including those with disabilities, have opportunities to prepare for the state tests and learn the content considered important enough to appear in state standards. They also serve as tools around which students, teachers, principals, and parents can communicate about learning.

Example of a State Standard

State Standard Mathematics #1:
The student understands and applies the concepts and procedures of mathematics.

Component 1.1: Understand and apply concepts and procedures from number sense.

- Benchmark 1 (Grade 4): Identify, compare, and order whole numbers and simple fractions.
- Benchmark 2 (Grade 7): Compare and order whole numbers, fractions, and decimals.

- Benchmark 3 (Grade 10): Explain the magnitude of numbers by comparing and ordering real numbers.

Note that all examples of state standards in this chapter come from Washington State.

These standards identify accomplishments in a given content area that are considered important for all students in the state. Generally, all lessons and activities taught will be linked to these standards. (See Chapter 2 for how to use state standards when writing objectives.)

Professional Organization Standards and Big Ideas

Other important sources in the development of classroom curriculum are professional organizations such as the International Reading Association, National Council of Teachers of Mathematics (NCTM), National Council of English Teachers, National Council of the Social Studies, and the National Science Teachers Association. Many of these organizations have developed standards and/or have described the important generalizations or "big ideas" in their subject areas. These are meant to help teachers choose the most important content to teach and to connect and organize knowledge and skills with essential understandings for that discipline. Following are some examples of big ideas:

- Economic systems are influenced by supply and demand.
- Patterns are everywhere.
- Geographical features affect where people settle.
- Writers try to persuade their readers to believe or act in certain ways.
- People have created different forms of government to meet their needs.

School district curriculum guides can also aid teachers as they plan what to teach. A group of teachers within the district often develops these guides. The guides can include long- and short-term objectives and activities that teachers who helped write the guide have tried. These guides can help teachers plan lessons and activities that are related to the state standards.

Published programs can also be purchased for reading, math, social studies, social skills, study strategies, and so on. These programs usually include long- and short-term objectives and all needed materials. Teachers must be sure that such program objectives meet the needs of their students. If not, they will want to make appropriate adjustments. School district or university curriculum libraries, as well as the Internet, can be good places to start your search for published programs.

It's clear that teachers must make important decisions about what to teach. If you are a practicing teacher, you know that part of your responsibility is to figure out what your students need to learn. If you are a practicum student or student teacher, a classroom teacher who makes these curricular decisions is probably directing you. Important decisions about what to teach must ultimately be based on the learning and behavioral needs of individual students.

When teaching students with disabilities, refer to the IEPs, the most important sources of information to help teachers decide what to teach. The IEP provides teachers with a look at the individualized goals and objectives that the IEP team determined to be most important for particular students to learn. This information can help provide a focus for planning how to best facilitate the learning of students with disabilities.

Once you have consulted the standards and other sources and have selected the content to teach, you are ready for the next step in planning to teach.

Preparing to Teach

Now that you know what content you need to teach your students, you still have work to complete before you begin actual lesson planning.

Levels of Understanding

As you begin to transition from planning what to teach to planning how to teach it, you'll need to decide the level of understanding that you want your students to obtain at this time. Will you introduce the content, teach it thoroughly, or strengthen previously taught information? Determining this will influence whether you teach in the form of an activity or a lesson, among other things (see Chapter 12).

One level of understanding is introductory knowledge. Teachers introduce content when they want to build background knowledge, to expose students to the content, to build interest or motivation, to prepare students for a series of lessons and activities on a topic, or to introduce a topic or skill that will be taught completely in a future grade. On the other hand, teachers may intend that their students develop a thorough understanding of important knowledge and skills. They want them to remember the information, comprehend it, and be able to apply it.

A third possibility is that teachers want to strengthen their students' understanding of previously learned information. Therefore, they may provide a review, additional practice, or opportunities for generalization. They may integrate content from different subject areas.

Deciding the level of understanding you want your students to gain is essential in planning an appropriate lesson or activity.

Organizing Content for Teaching

Once you know what subject matter and kind of knowledge (declarative or procedural) you will be teaching, you need to determine how to best organize and teach the content. Preparing a thorough content analysis will really pay off in the long run.

Content Analysis

In the beginning stages of planning a lesson or activity, you need to think through the specifics of what you are teaching and how it is best taught by preparing a content analysis. A thorough content analysis could contain one or more of the following: a *subject matter outline,* a *concept analysis,* a *task analysis,* or a *principle statement,* definitions of *key terms and vocabulary,* and a list of *prerequisite skills and knowledge.*

ORGANIZING DECLARATIVE KNOWLEDGE

The following are ways to organize declarative knowledge information:

Subject matter outlines are standard outlines of the specific content to be covered in the lesson. They are most always written for lessons designed to teach specific declarative information (for example, an informal presentation lesson on the causes of the civil war). The body of the informal presentation lesson consists of a subject matter outline and is used to guide the teacher's delivery of information.

Example of a Subject Matter Outline

Malignant Melanoma

1. Three Types of Skin Cancer
   a. Basal Cell Carcinoma
   b. Squamous Cell Carcinoma
   c. Malignant Melanoma—can be fatal
2. Risk Factors of Malignant Melanomas
   a. Sun exposure (repeated sunburns; 80 percent of damage is done during childhood)
   b. Fair complexion (Caucasian, redheads and blonds)
   c. Family history (increased risk if parents or siblings have melanoma)
3. Detection: Know the A, B, C, and D of Melanoma
   a. Asymmetrical (A line through the middle would not create equal sides. Most moles and freckles are symmetrical.)
   b. Borders (uneven: scalloped or notched edges; normal mole: smooth, even border)
   c. Color (begins with varied shades of brown, tan, or black; progresses to red, white, or blue; normal moles are an even shade of brown)
   d. Diameter (larger than normal moles: 6 millimeters or ¼ inch in diameter; normal mole is smaller)

A *concept analysis* is used for teaching concepts. It is important to do a concept analysis prior to teaching concepts. This type of content analysis helps teachers think through and write down exactly how they will explain the essential elements of the concept. A concept analysis includes: (1) a definition of the concept, (2) a list of the critical attributes that are distinguishing features or characteristics found in all examples, (3) a list of noncritical attributes that are nonessential characteristics not found in all examples, (4) a list of examples, (5) a list of nonexamples, and (6) a list of related concepts, if helpful. Following is an example of a concept analysis:

Example of a Concept Analysis

Concept Name: Proper Nouns

- *Definition:* A proper noun is a noun that names a particular person, place, or thing.
- *Critical attributes:* A proper noun, which names a particular person, a particular place, or a particular thing, is capitalized.
- *Noncritical attributes:* The position in the sentence and the number of words are noncritical.
- *Examples:* Seattle Mariners, Golden Gate Bridge, Harriet Tubman, Amsterdam, Curtis Kerce, Orcas Island, Washington State, UW Huskies
- *Nonexamples:* baseball team, bridge, woman, city, man, island, state, football team
- *Related concepts:* Common noun

A third type of content analysis is a *principle statement*. Principles are relational rules that show the relationship between two or more concepts. They are often described in the form of if–then, cause–effect, or "rule of thumb" relationships. All content areas have examples of principles.

Examples of Principles

- When water reaches 32 degrees Fahrenheit, it freezes.
- If your payment arrives late, then you will need to pay a late fee.
- When a wasp's food supply dwindles toward the end of the summer it is more likely to sting without provocation.
- If a pregnant mother has little or no prenatal care, then the risk of a premature birth increases.
- When effective memorization strategies are used for studying, then retention of information is usually greater.

Be sure that you plan in advance how you will explain the principle to your students. It can be difficult to correctly or accurately explain the principle spontaneously during a lesson or activity. Begin by writing out the complete principle statement; include the condition and the result or the action that needs to be taken. Next, consider carefully which words are best used as part of your explanation. Finally, be sure that you plan many and varied examples to illustrate the principle. It is important for your students to be able to *apply* the principle to unknown examples, not just state them (Smith and Ragan 2004).

A SPECIAL NOTE ABOUT MEMORIZING INFORMATION

Memory tasks need special planning. Generally you would not use a single lesson when planning for students to memorize significant amounts of information (for example, a long list of steps to follow for a reading strategy or to solve math story problems, a list of states and capitals, chemical symbols, math facts, and so on). This type of information is often initially introduced in a lesson, but needs to be followed by a variety of activities designed to aid memorization. Follow frequent and distributed opportunities to practice with an evaluation.

When you plan your lesson or activity, determine what new information (steps, vocabulary words, content facts) students will need to know to meet the lesson objective. Ask yourself this question: Do my students need to memorize this information? If you answer *yes,* then you may need or want to revise your objective and plan memory devices (mnemonics, for example) as appropriate, with an adequate number of practice opportunities within the lesson. If your answer is *no,* then plan which visual supports are needed to give students access to the information (posters, transparencies, and so on).

ORGANIZING PROCEDURAL KNOWLEDGE

Use a *task analysis* when you plan to teach a how-to lesson, that is, you want your students to do something at the end of the lesson that they cannot presently do. The procedures or strategies you want your students to learn to do are best organized using a task analysis. A procedure is a series of steps that leads to the completion of a task (Smith and Ragan 2004). Procedures can be academic (how to convert degrees Celsius to degrees Fahrenheit), social (how to join in a group), or describe a classroom routine (what to do with a late assignment).

Strategies are a subcategory of procedures. Howell, Hosp, and Hosp (forthcoming) define strategies as procedures that students follow to combine subtasks into larger tasks. Strategies are techniques that help students learn (how to take notes from a lecture), study (how to memorize lists of items), or organize (how to maintain an assignment calendar).

A task analysis can be written in two ways, depending on the specific content to be taught. It can be written as a list of sequential steps that must be followed in order (how to do long division, for example). It can also be written as a list of various subskills that must be completed but not necessarily in a certain order (how to write out a check, for example). The following examples illustrate how to write task analyses:

How to Alphabetize to the First Letter

1. Underline the first letter of each word in the list.
2. If all letters are different:
   a. Say the letters of the alphabet in order.
   b. As you say each letter, scan the underlined letters.
   c. Stop each time you say the name of an underlined letter.
   d. Write the word that contains the letter you said.
   e. Continue until all words are used.

How to Proofread Sentences

1. Skim the work and check that:
   a. all sentences begin with a capital letter.
   b. all sentences have an appropriate end mark (period, exclamation point, or question mark).
2. Fix any errors.

The most efficient way to conduct a task analysis is to perform the task yourself while writing the steps, including the thinking process you follow. However, you may encounter cases where the process you follow may be different from the process a child or beginner will follow. Preparing a task analysis will help you plan a presentation of information and a demonstration.

KEY TERMS AND VOCABULARY

Identifying and writing out the definitions of key terms or specialized vocabulary words to be used in a lesson is another form of content analysis. The definitions need to be written in words that the students will understand. It is important to do this in advance to avoid incorrect or incomplete definitions. Terms are not as easy to define on the spot as they would seem.

Student dictionaries and textbook glossaries can be good places to start when trying to write a clear definition for a particular term. Generally, though, this is only the first step. Suppose you are preparing a list of vocabulary words as part of a reading lesson, and one of the words is *myth.* You locate a dictionary definition that says a myth is "a story rooted in the most ancient religious beliefs and institutions of a people, usually dealing with gods, goddesses, or natural phenomena." Suppose that you write this definition into your lesson plan. When you introduce the word *myth* to your second graders the next day, you suddenly realize that, not only do they not understand the entire definition, they do not even understand some of the words that make up the definition. All definitions need to be reviewed and stated in words the students will understand.

PREREQUISITE SKILLS AND KNOWLEDGE

One part of a content analysis is determining prerequisite skills and knowledge that students must have to be ready for a particular lesson. Sometimes these are broad skills: being able to read is a prerequisite skill for using encyclopedias as a resource when writing reports. Sometimes the prerequisite skills are more specific: for example, long division requires skills in estimating, multiplying, and subtracting; using adjectives is dependent on understanding nouns; and being able to prepare food from recipes is contingent on being able to measure ingredients. It is certainly not necessary, nor desirable, to list all prerequisites. However, it is important to consider these factors.

Choosing the Analysis

The following guidelines will help you choose the type of analysis to prepare:

- Write a *concept analysis* when you plan to teach a concept.

- Include a *task analysis* when the point of the lesson is to teach a procedure or strategy, that is, a how-to lesson.
- When teaching about a topic (that is, declarative knowledge), a *subject matter outline* will be most beneficial.
- Write a complete *principle statement* (the condition and the result or action to be taken) when the objective of the lesson is to teach a principle.
- *Key terms and vocabulary words* are important to consider in every lesson or activity. Be sure that words are defined in terms that the students will understand.
- It is always important to consider *prerequisite skills and knowledge* as part of a content analysis. This will help you write the objective and determine whether the content is appropriate for the students you are teaching.

Summary

You will find it beneficial to spend time analyzing the subject matter you plan to teach. It is impossible to get a good result from teaching when you are not sure exactly what you want your students to learn. This knowledge links directly to what you will learn in the next chapter on writing objectives. A thorough content analysis helps you organize the content you will teach into a clear framework that benefits both you and your students. Preparing this framework also helps strengthen your understanding of the material. As you communicate the analysis to your students, you provide them with a structured way to consider the content. This can have a very positive impact on student learning and retention.

References

Green, T., A. Brown, and L. Robinson. n.d. *The World Wide Web in the classroom: Learning content and meeting standards through the use of Web-based projects.* Forthcoming.

Howell, K. W., J. L. Hosp, and M. K. Hosp. n.d. *Curriculum-based evaluation: Teaching and decision making.* 4th ed. Belmont, CA: Wadsworth/Thomson Learning. Forthcoming.

Irvine, J., and B. Armento. 2001. *Culturally responsive teaching: Lesson planning for elementary and middle grades.* New York: McGraw-Hill.

King-Sears, M. E. 2001. Three steps for gaining access to the general education curriculum for learners with disabilities. *Intervention in School and Clinic 37* (2): 67–76.

Smith, P. L., and T. J. Ragan. 2004. *Instructional design.* 2nd ed. Columbus, OH: Merrill.

Writing Objectives

 Introduction

An effective activity or lesson plan begins with a specific objective. We are going to teach you a format for writing objectives in a clear and measurable form. Writing those objectives will enable you to match your activity or lesson with the intended learning outcome, and you will be able to tell if your teaching was effective (whether your students learned). It is essential, however, to remember that objectives can be well written in terms of form and yet not be appropriate or important for your students.

 Definition and Purpose

Objectives describe where we want students to go and how we'll know if they got there. Objectives pinpoint the destination—not the journey. Well-written objectives help teachers clarify precisely what they want their students to learn, help provide lesson focus and direction, and help guide the selection of appropriate practice. Using objectives, teachers can evaluate whether or not their students have learned and whether their own teaching has been effective. Objectives also help focus and motivate students, and are important communication tools to use with other teachers and families.

 Process

Backward planning or *backward design,* terms that Wiggins and McTighe (2005) used are good descriptions of the process that teachers should use in developing lesson or activity objectives. The sequence of planning objectives is very important. First, decide on the learning outcomes. Second, break down general outcomes into more specific goals or objectives. Next, figure out how you'll assess the outcomes or, as Wiggins and McTighe (2005) express it, what evidence you'll accept that students have achieved the understanding. Then, and only then, plan the lessons and activities that will help students achieve those outcomes. For the first step, deciding what you want students to learn, look to state standards.

 State Standards: A Source of Objectives

States have developed sets of standards that provide descriptions of learning outcomes for K–12 students across each state. Standards are written as goals in the various content areas: reading, writing, mathematics, science, social studies, and so on. These standards establish priorities in what should be taught to students. They give teachers focus for long-term curriculum planning.

Examples of State Standards

Reading 1. The student understands and uses different skills and strategies to read.
Reading 2. The student understands the meaning of what is read.
Reading 3. The student reads different materials for a variety of purposes.
Reading 4. The student sets goals and evaluates progress to improve reading.

Note that all examples of state standards in this chapter come from Washington State.

The previous standards for reading are very general and long term. They guide teachers in deciding what their students need to learn. The second step in developing objectives is to make general outcomes more specific.

From General to Specific

In some cases, teachers are provided with state standards that are broken down into more specific components and benchmarks. This is true for the following reading standard:

Reading 1. The student understands and uses different skills and strategies to read (state standard).

1.1. Use word recognition skills and strategies to read and comprehend text (component).

1.1.1. Understand and apply concepts of print (kindergarten benchmark)

Grade-level expectations (GLE), which are more specific descriptors of components and benchmarks, provide even more specificity. Here is an example:

Reading 1. The student understands and uses different skills and strategies to read.

1.1. Use word recognition skills and strategies to read and comprehend text.

1.1.1. Understand and apply concepts of print (kindergarten benchmark)

- Use directionality when listening to or following text (GLE).
- Identify front cover, back cover, and title of books (GLE).
- Recognize that print represents spoken language, such as environmental print and own name (GLE).
- Recognize letters and spaces between words (GLE).

In other cases, state standards are kept much more general. For example, for writing:

2. The student writes in a variety of forms for different audiences and purposes.

2.1 Write for different audiences.

2.1.2 Show some awareness of audience needs.

Although state standards provide direction, teachers must develop their own very specific objectives for lessons, activities, and units. This is also true in special education where teachers help develop individual education programs (IEPs) that include specific goals and objectives intended to enable students to progress in the general curriculum based on the state standards. A teacher's task is to translate the standards into useful, specific objectives that are used to guide instruction. In this way, the learning outcomes included in the objectives will link to the state standards.

Writing specific objectives from standards and goals begins with an understanding of how standards, goals, and objectives differ. The following are some of the main differences:

- *Specificity* Specific learning outcomes are described in objectives whereas standards include more general outcome statements. Goals may be general (understand the concept of fractions) or specific (write fractions to describe relationships).
- *Long-Term or Short-Term* Objectives are considered short-term because they describe the learning outcome expected in days, weeks, or months. Goals and standards describe learning outcomes expected to occur at the end of a longer period of time—weeks, months, or years, thus they are long-term outcome statements.
- *Uses* Objectives are used in lesson and activity plans and in IEPs. Measurable annual goals are included in IEPs. Goals are also found in units of instruction. Standards are used in state or district curricula or are set by professional organizations.

Following are two examples of developing a specific objective more suitable for a lesson or activity from a state standard.

Reading 1. The student understands and uses different skills and strategies to read.

1.1. Use word recognition skills and strategies to read and comprehend text.

1.1.1. Understand and apply concepts of print.

- Recognize letters and spaces between words.

Objective: Student will identify first and last letters of words in context.

Civics 2. The student analyzes the purposes and organization of governments and laws.

2.1. Understand and explain the organization of federal, state, and local government including the executive, legislative, and judicial branches at, and among, the three levels of government.

2.1.3. Analyze problems and solutions related to the distribution of authority.

Objective: Students will understand how branches of the government check and balance each other.

Measurable Objectives

The third step in backward planning is to decide how you'll know if students have achieved the learning outcome. This is the process of making objectives measurable.

Objective: Student will identify first and last letters of words in context.

Measurable objective: Student will circle the first and underline the last letters of each word in a given five-word sentence.

Objective: Students will understand how branches of the government check and balance each other.

Measurable objective: Given the power of the legislative branch to enact laws, students will name the other two branches and describe in two sentences how this power is checked and balanced by each.

Notice in the previous measurable objectives that the assessment or evidence of learning is built into the objective. These are what we mean by "measurable" objectives. You begin with the desired learning outcome (apply writing conventions), make the outcome specific (capitalize proper nouns accurately), and define what evidence you will accept that students can do that (correct capitalization errors in a list of nouns and proper nouns). Only then do you plan your lesson or activity. Special educators are very familiar with this process—first come measurable goals, then specially designed instruction.

Multiple Objectives

Teachers sometimes design lessons or activities for the achievement of more than one objective. They do this for a variety of reasons. One such reason is for efficiency and another is to be responsive to diversity.

Because of the many valuable learning outcomes for students, teachers have tough decisions to make on what to teach and what to leave out. Sometimes teachers can develop dual-purpose lessons or activities. They might plan class discussions designed to help students develop a deeper understanding of a historical event and to learn to disagree politely. They might plan a math game activity designed to help students achieve a math objective (fluency with multiplication facts) and a social skills objective (showing good sportsmanship in winning and losing). They might plan a lesson in which they present information to help students learn the planets of the solar system and information on how to use a learning strategy to memorize items in order. It can be more efficient to use one lesson or activity to teach toward multiple objectives.

Another purpose for multiple objectives is to be responsive to diversity. Many classrooms today include students who are English language learners. Teachers can respond to linquistic diversity by designing lessons or activities that can be used to help students achieve objectives in subject areas (such as science or social studies) while also meeting language objectives for speaking, listening, reading, and writing. For example, you might plan a lesson designed to help students achieve a science objective such as "comparing types of wetlands," as well as helping students meet language objectives such as "using count nouns (as *many* plants as) and noncount nouns (as *much* water as) in comparison sentences" and "following three-step oral directions for completing tasks."

Teachers can also be responsive to diversity using multiple objectives by creating activities designed to provide instruction or practice for several students who are working on individual objectives. For example, in a special education preschool setting, students may be working on color and shape identification, physical skills, and language skills objectives. Teachers may use one activity, such as snack time, to provide different students with practice on different objectives: One student may work on naming the shape and color of a plate (producing shape and color names) and another may point to the green or blue plate (identifying colors). One student may be expected to ask for more by saying, "more juice please" (using three-word phrases), while another student signs the word *juice* (increasing sign vocabulary). One student's objective may be to grasp the handle of an adaptive spoon and take three bites (fine motor skill), whereas the objective of another student is to sit in a chair without arms at the table (balancing skill).

The same three-step backward planning process is used to develop objectives whether or not multiple objectives will be taught through one lesson or activity. Note that it is our intention to concentrate on specific short- and long-term objectives throughout this book. This means that when we talk about writing objectives for activity plans, for example, we mean writing specific long-term objectives. When we talk about writing lesson objectives, we mean specific, short-term objectives.

The Four Components of Objectives

The easy way to write a measurable objective is to include four components: content, behavior, condition, and criterion (Howell, Hosp, and Hosp, forthcoming). Including these four components will help ensure that your objectives represent a clear, specific learning outcome and a description of how that learning will be measured. Following an example objective are descriptions of each of the four components with examples and nonexamples. Common errors are noted and suggestions for writing each objective component are included.

Example Objective

Students will write answers to 20 subtraction problems (two-digit numbers from three-digit numbers with regrouping) on a worksheet, with no errors.

Content

This component describes the specific subject matter to be learned. In the example objective, the content is "subtraction problems, two-digit numbers from three-digit numbers with regrouping."

Suggestions When Writing the Content

1. Be specific enough that anyone reading the objective will understand the subject matter.

2. Be sure the description of content can stand alone, that is, be "materials-free." The reader should be able to understand the content of the objective without tracking down specific materials.

3. Be generic enough that the emphasis is on knowledge and skills that are important and applicable in a variety of contexts.

Examples of Content

The content component is italicized in the following examples and nonexamples:

- Add *unlike fractions with common factors between denominators.*
- Write *two-syllable spelling words with -ing endings (for example, hoping, hopping).*
- Compare and contrast *fables and fairy tales.*

Nonexamples of Content

- Add *fractions* (not specific); answer *fraction problems 1–7 on p. 42* (not materials-free).
- Write *spelling words* (not specific); complete *Unit 4 in spelling book* (not materials-free).
- Compare and contrast *"The Lazy Princess" and "Lost in the Woods"* (not generic or materials-free).

Common Errors When Writing Content

A common error teachers make is to include content appropriate for an activity or assignment rather than a learning outcome. The following are examples of errors in writing content:

1. Write *adjectives for 10 animals and plants from the rain forest unit.*

Are you looking for knowledge of the rain forest or knowledge of adjectives? This may be a good integrated practice activity, but it is not a clear objective.

2. Present *five facts about a bird of your choice.*

The content is unclear. We do not know what facts are to be learned. Is the real content using reference books to find facts, making presentations, or summarizing from the unit on birds? Do not confuse an instructional theme with content.

Examples of Measurable Objectives

- Given a chapter in a content text, students will construct a *concept map* that includes all main headings and subheadings, and three facts for each subheading.
- From memory, students will list the six *steps for treating a burn* as recommended by the American Red Cross.

Behavior

This component states what students will do to demonstrate their learning. Write the behavior or performance as an observable verb so outcomes can be measured.

In the example objective on p. 15, the behavior is "write." The student will demonstrate knowledge of subtraction by writing the answers to 20 problems.

Examples of Behavior

say	write	list
draw	diagram	paraphrase
operate	throw	volunteer
circle	complete	copy
label	predict	calculate
add	design	select
name	hit	laugh
choose	initiate	put in order
define	compare	contrast

Notice that some of these verbs can be made more specific, for example, one could "define" in writing or orally. You must judge how much specificity is needed, but when in doubt be more specific rather than less. For example, the commonly used verbs "identify" and "recognize" often need further specifics, such as "identify by underlining."

Nonexamples of Behavior

know	realize	comprehend
understand	experience	discover
memorize	believe	appreciate
learn	value	be familiar with

Notice that these verbs may be appropriate when writing general goals, aims, outcomes, or standards. They are not appropriate for measurable objectives because you cannot know that a student "knows" or "comprehends" or has "learned" something unless she does something overt. For example, you may have a goal that your students appreciate poetry. You cannot tell if that objective has been reached unless your students do something (voluntarily check out poetry books from the library or write poetry without being assigned to do so, for example).

Suggestions When Writing the Behavior

1. Decide whether you want students to "identify" or "produce" as you write the behavior component in objectives (Howell, Hosp, and Hosp, forthcoming). A lesson for teaching students to produce or write metaphors will be quite different from a lesson for teaching students to identify or recognize metaphors someone else has written.

2. Include only one or two required behaviors in an objective. Objectives that include many behaviors (for example, students will research, write, draw, and present) make evaluation confusing and often end up being descriptions of activities or assignments rather than learning outcomes.

3. Consider including alternate behaviors (write, type, or say, for example) to provide the flexibility to allow all students, including those with disabilities, to be successful. This is an excellent way to incorporate the principles of universal design for learning.

4. Leave out nonessential or redundant behaviors.
   - "Students will copy the sentences and circle all nouns." Omit "copy the sentences." It has nothing to do with the skill of identifying nouns.
   - Omit "locate" in an example such as, "Students will locate and point to. . . ." If the student is pointing to something, then you can assume he has located it.

5. Omit "be able to" as in the example, "The student will be able to make a speech. . . ." The phrase adds words but no meaning. Remember that the performance is important, not an assumed ability or inability.

6. Do not use the phrase, "Student will pass a test on. . . ." It does not communicate specific information about what the student will do or learn.

7. Write objectives for what the students will do, not what the teacher will do. Objectives may be written for one student or a group of students.

Examples of Measurable Objectives

- Given 10 incomplete sentences, students will *rewrite* each as a complete sentence that includes a subject and a predicate.
- In a role-play situation, students will *demonstrate* all five steps of the "accepting *no* for an answer" social skill.

Conditions

It is important to describe the conditions—circumstances, situation, or setting in which the student will perform the behavior. These conditions provide additional specificity about what the student will learn. It is the conditions that will apply when the student is being evaluated, rather than the learning condition, which must be described. In the example objective on p. 15, the students must write answers to 20 subtraction problems, with the condition "on a worksheet," not in a real-world context such as "in a check register."

Notice that the *italicized* conditions in the following objectives result in three different learning outcomes. They affect the level of difficulty of the objective, and thus the lesson and practice activities that you need to plan for your students.

- Students will write the capitals of each of the 17 western states *given a list of the states and a list of the capitals.* (They will be asked to recognize state capitals. This is really a matching task.)

- Students will write the capitals of each of the 17 western states *given a list of the states.* (They will be asked to recall the state capitals rather than simply recognize them.)

- Students will write the capitals of each of the 17 western states *on a blank outline map.* (They must recall the names and locations of the states and the names of the capitals in order to write the capitals in the correct places.)

Types of Conditions

Various types of conditions may be included in objectives. A very important condition is whether we are asking students to perform a skill in isolation or in context, or in artificial or real-world circumstances. This is important to think about when sequencing objectives and when planning for generalization or transfer of the skill. The information or materials provided—often called the "givens"—may be important to specify. Visualize the evaluation or testing situation and what the students will have available. A third type of condition—a description of the setting or situation—may help clarify the objective as well, especially social skill and learning strategy objectives. Obviously, all conditions need not be mentioned (for example, the lights will be on in the room). However, be sure to include those that communicate important information about the learning outcome.

Examples of Conditions

In isolation or in context

- Compute measurement equivalents *on a worksheet* or *while following a recipe*
- Respond to teasing *in a role play* or *on the playground*

- Correct punctuation errors *in given sentences* or *while proofreading an essay*
- Pronounce words *when shown flash cards* or *in a story*

You may want to specify whether the student is going to solve mixed math problems or correct mixed grammar errors. Otherwise, you may only be evaluating whether students can figure out the pattern (for example, all problems require regrouping or all sentences are missing a question mark).

Information or materials provided

- On a diagram
- Given a list of 10 nouns
- Given a description of symptoms
- Given an incomplete proof
- Given population figures for each country
- With a calculator, ruler, scale
- Using notes, dictionary, word processor
- From memory, with nothing provided

Setting or situation

- In front of class
- During seatwork; on homework
- In familiar situations; with strangers
- When given directions
- When corrected
- During class discussions
- During teacher presentations
- When working with a small group of peers
- During free time
- When given a choice
- On an in-class test
- In a textbook
- When teased; when angry; when refused

A combination of conditions

- Given 10 problems and a calculator
- Given eight map terms (key) and a dictionary

Independently or with assistance

- With or without reminders
- With or without physical assistance
- With or without verbal cues

In some cases, for example, when writing objectives for students with severe disabilities or for very young students, it may be important to specify whether students will be performing the behavior independently. Note that typically the "default" condition is without assistance.

Nonexamples of Conditions

- *Describing the learning condition rather than the evaluation condition.* It doesn't matter where or when the students learned the knowledge or skill. Remember that objectives focus on outcomes. Avoid using the following conditions: "As a result of my instruction . . . ," "After a lesson on . . . ," "After completing the weather unit . . . ," "After studying . . . ," and so on.
- *Adding unimportant information.* Avoid using conditions such as, "When asked by the teacher . . ." or "Given a blank piece of paper. . . ." Some conditions are obvious and do not need to be written.
- *Selecting conditions at random from lists of examples.* Incorporate conditions that reflect important decisions about how learning will be measured.

Examples of Measurable Objectives

- *Before turning in seatwork assignments,* students will write a heading on their paper that includes name, subject, period, and date, on eight consecutive assignments.
- *Given six topics receiving attention during the presidential campaign,* (such as medical care for the elderly), students will explain in writing how each presidential candidate would likely vote on the issue (explanation must include a rationale supported by facts).

Criterion

The criterion specifies the level of acceptable performance, the standard of mastery, or the proficiency level expected. This component describes how well the students should perform in order to say that they have met the objective. In the example objective, students will write answers to 20 subtraction problems (two-digit numbers from three-digit numbers with regrouping) on a worksheet, the criterion is "with no errors."

Examples of Criterion

As a total number or proportion

- Comparing or contrasting four key issues
- Using two types of figurative language
- At every opportunity
- In three out of three trials
- At least five times daily
- With no errors
- With 10 out of 10 correct
- With 90 percent accuracy
- At least three of the steps
- Five paragraphs in length

In terms of time

- Within 10 minutes; per minute
- For one hour each day
- The first time
- For five consecutive days
- By September 6

As a variation

- Within plus or minus 1 inch
- To the nearest mile
- Within 1 percent
- To the closest hundredth

As a description or result

- Light bulb turns on
- Liquid disappears
- Until consensus is reached
- Story includes a conflict and resolution
- The strategy selected solves the problem in the fewest steps

Often a combination of criteria is used

- 50 per minute with 100 percent accuracy by March 10
- Backing up opinion with data from three relevant research studies
- Paragraphs include topic sentences and at least three supporting details

Nonexamples of Criterion

Does not pass the "stranger test"

- As judged by teacher
- To teacher's satisfaction

These obviously do not pass the "stranger test" (Kaplan 1995), that is, they are open to interpretation. A stranger may not interpret them the same way as you do. Remember that one of the purposes of writing objectives is to communicate clearly with students, families, and other teachers and professionals.

Common Errors When Writing the Criterion

1. *The criterion is too low.* Keep high performance standards, especially for basic skills in reading, writing, and arithmetic. Do not confuse setting criteria in objectives with assigning grades. It will take some students longer to reach an objective. You may want to set gradually increasing criteria—50 percent accuracy by October 1; 75 percent accuracy by November 1; 100 percent accuracy by December 1. However, be sure that the final outcome is high enough. If a student is only 80 percent accurate on number recognition, he is doomed to failure in arithmetic.

2. *The criterion is set arbitrarily.* Do not make the error of automatically writing 85 percent accuracy for every objective. Set realistic standards and time limits. Establish criteria either by doing the task yourself or by having a successful peer do the task. Do *not* write: ". . . will say the multiples of 10 from 10 to 100 in 3 minutes" or ". . . locate a word in the dictionary in 5 minutes." Try it! If it took you 5 minutes to find a word, you would never choose to use the dictionary.

3. *"Percent accuracy" is misused.*
    - When there are many possible divergent or complex responses, percent accuracy as the criterion does not make sense. One cannot write a story with 100 percent accuracy nor manage anger with 80 percent accuracy.
    - There needs to be a number of responses for percent accuracy to be sensible—not simply correct or incorrect. For example, choose

"name the state you live in" or "correctly name the state you live in," rather than "name the state you live in with 100 percent accuracy." Write "turn off the computer correctly" or "without damaging anything," rather than "turn off the computer with 100 percent accuracy."
- Sometimes percent accuracy works, but it would be too much work to compute. To decide if someone reached 85 percent accuracy in punctuating a story, you would first have to count all of the opportunities for punctuation within the story.

4. *There is no end in sight.* If the objective is for the student to spell words correctly in all written work, when would you be able to say that a student had met this objective? At the end of his life?

Suggestions When Writing the Criterion

1. Think about how many times you want the students to demonstrate the skill during evaluation to be confident that they have met the objective. For example, do they need to write their addresses five times to prove they can do it? If Jorge responds to teasing appropriately during one recess, are you sure he has learned that skill?

2. Be specific enough so that any evaluator would reach the same conclusion as to whether the student meets the objective. Avoid writing, "Student will write *descriptive* sentences." This criterion is not specific enough to determine if the objective of the lesson has been met. The following two sentences cannot be evaluated reliably using this criterion: "The bike is big," and "Perched on the seat of the bike, I felt like Hillary on the peak of Everest."

3. Make sure the criterion addresses the skill you want. For example, if the skill you are looking for is writing descriptively, do not write your criterion as, "all words need to be spelled correctly." Do not write a criterion solely because it is easy to think of. In attempting to make the objective specific and measurable, don't end up making it trivial!

Examples of Measurable Objectives:

- Given addition problems with sums no greater than 18, students will write *40 correct sums* in no more than *one minute*.
- In a debate, the student will argue for one side of a controversial issue (for example, capital punishment) and provide *three reasons supported with facts* for their position.

Bloom's Taxonomy of the Cognitive Domain

Benjamin Bloom (1956) and colleagues designed a hierarchy of intellectual skills, called Bloom's Taxonomy of the Cognitive Domain. Bloom developed this hierarchy in response to the observation that teaching in schools focused heavily on having students recall facts (low-level thinking) rather than developing their higher-level thinking skills. The six categories in the taxonomy of the cognitive domain are organized in a hierarchy from basic understanding of information to high-level information processing. The taxonomy was originally developed to help teachers recognize the varying degrees of complexity involved in various classroom activities so they could construct objectives that included higher-level learning outcomes.

Bloom's taxonomy has been used in classrooms in a variety of ways since it was developed, and we will discuss two of those applications. The first application helps teachers plan questions that promote various kinds of thinking. You will read about these questions in Chapter 4. The other application helps teachers write objectives. Heacox (2002) writes that one of the most important applications of Bloom's taxonomy is in the design of learning activities. "Looking at instruction through the lens of *challenge* means considering the rigor, relevance, and complexity of what you're teaching" (ibid., 67). By thinking about the instructional challenges of various outcomes included in objectives, teachers can plan for variation that can better meet the needs of a diverse classroom of students.

A group of Bloom's students recently revised the taxonomy that Bloom and colleagues designed. Lorin Anderson and others (Anderson and Krathwohl 2001) updated the taxonomy so it would better mesh with current theories about how children learn. The taxonomy has been renamed "taxonomy for learning, teaching and assessing" (Arends 2004). When we present each level of Bloom's taxonomy, we will include the label used in the revised version (in parenthesis) as well as in the original one. We will also include references and resources about both taxonomies at the end of this chapter.

Knowledge (Remembering): This is the lowest level of the cognitive domain. The learning outcome here is the simple recall of facts and information. The information to be recalled can be quite complicated, but nonetheless, all that is required is for one to remember and recall it.

- General types of outcomes: knows specific facts, concepts, methods, and procedures
- Behavior stem examples: define, tell, name, label, recite, match
- Sample objective: Teacher education students will recite the names of the levels of Bloom's Taxonomy in order from simple to complex, from memory without error.

Comprehension (Understanding): The learning outcome at the comprehension level of the cognitive domain is understanding. Here students go beyond mere recall and show that they understand.

- General types of outcomes: interprets charts and graphs, estimates future consequences implied in data, understands facts and principles
- Behavior stem examples: restate/rewrite, give an example of, recognize examples, summarize, describe, paraphrase, conclude
- Sample objective: When given a list of the levels of the cognitive domain, teacher education students will define the learning task for each, in their own words, with no more than one error.

Application (Applying): The application level refers to an outcome where students use the new information they have learned. This requires a higher level of understanding than does comprehension.

- General types of outcomes: constructs charts and graphs, applies concepts and principles to new situations, demonstrates correct usage of a method or procedure
- Behavior stem examples: predict, solve, demonstrate, operate, illustrate, solve, construct
- Sample objective: When given a list of 12 objectives, teacher education students will select those that are at the application level with 100 percent accuracy.

Analysis (Analyzing): When students analyze information, they break it down so they can understand the parts as well as the whole. This outcome requires that students understand both the content and the structural form of the material.

- General types of outcomes: distinguishes between facts and inferences, analyzes the organizational structure of a work (art, music), evaluates the relevancy of data
- Behavior stem examples: compare, contrast, categorize, diagram, outline, subdivide, distinguish
- Sample objective: When shown a list of objectives from a social studies unit, teacher education students can support their conclusion that the writer did or did not include objectives from all levels of the cognitive domain, citing specific examples of each.

Synthesis (Creating): This learning outcome of the cognitive domain is where students take the information they know and put it together into something new. The main idea is the creation of something new.

- General types of outcomes: writes a clearly organized research paper, creates a plan for an experiment to test a hypothesis, designs a new system for organizing information
- Behavior stem examples: produce, design, develop, reorganize, combine, compose, devise
- Sample objective: Given a topic, teacher education students will accurately write objectives that represent each level of the cognitive domain.

Evaluation (Evaluating): The learning outcome for evaluation is the highest level of all, because in order to evaluate, one must use information from the other levels. Evaluation is not random, but rather occurs against a set of criteria.

- General types of outcomes: judges the adequacy of a rationale, rates how well a written product meets established criteria, selects the most appropriate example
- Objective stem examples: select, predict, rate, explain, justify, interpret, support

- Sample objective: When given three lesson plans, teacher education students can judge the quality of each and decide which best encourages higher-level thinking skills, giving at least three reasons for this judgment.

Bloom's taxonomy can be used to help you write effective, relevant objectives. As you plan, make sure that you write objectives that encourage higher-level thinking as well as those that provide students with basic information. This does not mean that your goal should be to include an objective for higher-level thinking in every lesson or activity you teach as this is probably not reasonable. Rather, strive to emphasize higher-level thinking as often as possible. Objectives written to reflect a variety in outcomes better meet the needs of a diverse group of students.

Responding to Diversity When Planning the Objective

Consider the following when writing objectives for the diverse classroom:

- Be sure that your objective represents important learning and is connected to generalizations and big ideas, state standards, or IEP goals.
- Pretest to make sure the objective is necessary for students.
- Examine the criterion. Is it at the right level? Basic skills that are prerequisites for higher-level skills need high criterion levels. For example, 100 percent accuracy is necessary for letter recognition because that is an important basic skill needed for acquiring later skills. On the other hand, 100 percent accuracy in distinguishing reptiles from amphibians may not be necessary.
- Examine the condition. Is it realistic? Students may be more motivated to reach objectives when they can see the real-world applications.
- After analyzing prerequisite skills, the objective for individual students may need to be altered. For example, could students who have poor writing skills demonstrate that they can recognize the key conflict in a short story by saying it rather than writing it? Could students who are inaccurate on multiplication facts demonstrate that they know how to find the area of a rectangle using a calculator? In other words, the purpose of altering the objective is to allow the student to go on learning, not to be held back by those writing or multiplication difficulties. On the other hand, in most cases the student continues to need instruction and practice on writing and multiplication.
- Don't rush to make changes in the curriculum for students with learning problems. Changes may affect success in upper grades, options for employment, or further schooling in the long term. Having a student draw a picture or sing a song rather than write a paragraph may provide momentary success, but it is unlikely to be an option offered by future employers.

Summary

1. Write objectives that describe learning *outcomes,* not activities or assignments (TenBrink 1999).

   NOT: Wally will write spelling words missed on the pretest five times each.

   NOT: Students in pairs will take turns throwing dice, adding the numbers together, and stating the total.

   NOT: Students will play a quiz show game in which they divide into two teams, and ask and answer questions from Chapter 4 in the social studies book.

   NOT: Ben will write letters to the main character in the story.

2. Keep objectives clean and simple. Save creativity for instruction.

   NOT: Students will demonstrate their understanding of the reasons that pandas were endangered by graphing the average number of panda babies born and the number of pandas who died per year for the last 10 years.

   NOT: Students will create a poster that demonstrates their knowledge of modern Mexican culture.

3. Be sure to write objectives that represent *important* learning outcomes!

   NOT: Michelle will write the names of the counties in each state in the United States from memory without error.

Examples of Measurable Objectives

- Given 10 sets of five pictures, four of which are related—belong to the same category, such as vegetables or tools—students will point to the one in each set that does not belong, without error (lesson objective).
- Students will correctly state temperatures, with an accuracy of plus or minus 1 degree, shown on pictures of five thermometers depicting temperatures between −20 degrees Fahrenheit and 95 degrees Fahrenheit (lesson objective).
- Randi will write correct answers to five of five inference questions on a grade-level reading passage (IEP objective).
- Students will return the change from $1.00, using the fewest possible coins, for four purchases, with no errors (long-term unit objective).
- When the fire alarm sounds for a fire drill, students will form a line within 30 seconds and leave the building following the correct route, without teacher prompting (lesson objective).
- Kathi and Chuck will correctly compute the amount of wallpaper needed to cover a wall of given dimensions (lesson objective).
- When teased by peers, Fadia will respond by ignoring, walking away, or quietly asking the person to stop in eight out of eight observed opportunities by May 1 (IEP objective).
- Richard Michael will complete all of his independent seatwork assignments during class with at least 90 percent accuracy for two consecutive weeks (IEP objective).

A Final Thought

We wish to restate the importance of beginning your lesson or activity planning with a clear idea of what you want your students to learn. Writing a specific, measurable objective will cause you to think this through. It has been our observation that when teachers experience frustration with a particular lesson or activity, it is often the case that they are unable to clearly state what students were to learn. Using the process of backward planning will prevent this problem. First, decide where you want them to be. Then decide on the steps along the way. Next, decide how you'll know they got there and last how to get them there.

Practicing Writing Objectives: Study Suggestions

Once you have mastered the skill of writing measurable objectives, planning useful activities and lessons will be easier and less time-consuming. Following are strategies to help you become accurate and fluent at writing objectives. As with other writing tasks, editing and rewriting will always be important.

1. Study the component names and definitions. Paraphrase them.
2. Review the lists of component examples. Explain why each example fits the definition. Create your own examples.
3. Practice writing your own objectives.
   a. Think of a general instructional goal, such as the following:
      - Know how to use an index
      - Learn baseball skills
      - Understand cell division
      - Distinguish between fact and fiction
      - Resolve conflicts nonviolently
      - Do homework
   b. Specify the content ("index" becomes "subject index" in textbook, for example).
   c. Specify the behavior ("know how to use" becomes "locate page numbers for topics").
   d. Add necessary conditions (for example, "given a textbook and a list of topics").
   e. Add criteria (no errors, within 30 seconds).

Notice that there are many possibilities for each component. You may wish to practice writing a variety of objectives on one topic.

   f. Put the components together into a one- or two-sentence objective. For example, given a textbook and a list of topics, the student will locate page numbers for topics in the textbook's subject index with no errors, within 30 seconds.

g. Examine for clarity and conciseness and rewrite as necessary. For example, given a textbook, the student will write the correct page number from the index for four out of four listed topics within 2 minutes.

4. After you have written an objective, critique it following these self-evaluation steps:
   a. Are all four components present? (Label them.)
   b. Is each component correct?
      - Content specific? Generic? Materials-free?
      - Behavior observable?
      - Evaluation condition described?
      - Criterion specific? Measurable? Realistic?
   c. Does the objective need editing? Is it wordy? Is it awkward?
   d. Does it pass the stranger test?
   e. Does it represent an important learning outcome?

References

Alberto, P., and A. Troutman. 2006. *Applied behavior analysis for teachers.* 7th ed. Upper Saddle River, NJ: Pearson.

Anderson, L. W., and D. R. Krathwohl, eds. 2001. *A taxonomy for learning, teaching, and assessing: A revision of Bloom's taxonomy of educational objectives.* New York: Longman.

Arends, R. I. 2004. *Learning to teach.* 6th ed. Boston: McGraw Hill.

Bloom, B. S., M. D. Englehart, E. J. Furst, W. H. Hill, and D. R. Krathwoh. 1956. *Taxonomy of educational objectives, handbook I: The cognitive domain.* New York: David McKay Co. Inc.

Gronlund, N. 2004. *Writing instructional objectives for teaching and assessment.* 7th ed. Upper Saddle River, N.J.: Pearson.

Heacox, D. 2002. *Differentiating instruction in the regular classroom: How to reach and teach all learners, grades 3–12.* Minneapolis, MN: Free Spirit Publishing.

Howell, K. W., M. Hosp, and J. Hosp. n.d. *Curriculum-based evaluation: Teaching and decision making.* 4th ed. Belmont, CA: Wadsworth/ Thomson Learning. Forthcoming

Kaplan, J. S. 1995. *Beyond behavior modification.* 3rd ed. Austin, TX: Pro-Ed.

King-Sears, M. E. 2001. Three steps for gaining access to the general education curriculum for learners with disabilities. *Intervention in School and Clinic 37* (2): 67–76.

Lignugaris/Kraft, B., N. Marchand-Martella, and R. Martella. 2001. Writing better goals and short-term objectives or benchmarks. *Teaching Exceptional Children 34* (1): 52–58.

Matlock, L., K. Fielder, and D. Walsh. 2001. Building the foundation for standards-based instruction for all students. *Teaching Exceptional Children 33* (5): 68–73.

TenBrink, T. D. 1999. Instructional objectives. In *Classroom teaching skills,* 6th ed., ed. J. M. Cooper. Boston: Houghton Mifflin.

Walsh, J. M. 2001. Getting the "big picture" of IEP goals and state standards. *Teaching Exceptional Children 33* (5): 18–26.

Wiggins, G., and J. McTighe. 2005. *Understanding by design.* 2nd ed. Alexandria, VA: ASCD.

Bloom's Taxonomy

Kauchak, D. P., and P. D. Eggen. 2003. *Learning and teaching: Research-based methods.* 4th ed. Boston: Allyn and Bacon.

Krumme, G. *Major categories in the taxonomy of educational objectives—Bloom 1956.* http://faculty.washington.edu/krumme/guides/bloom.html (accessed April 2005).

Moore, K. D. 2005. *Effective instructional strategies: From theory to practice.* Thousand Oaks: SAGE Publications.

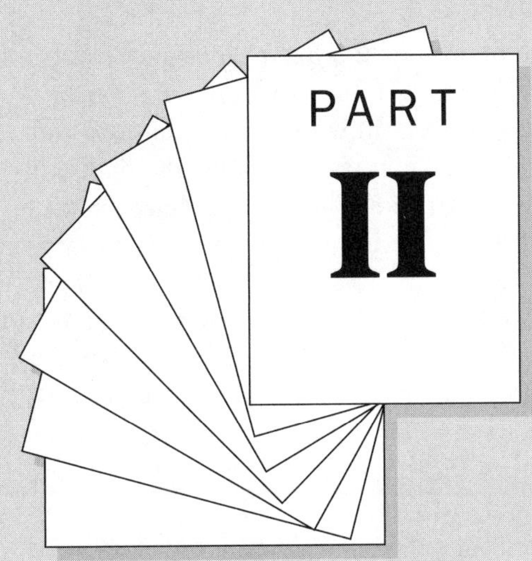

Planning How to Teach

A Framework for Diversity Responsive Teaching

PLANNING *WHAT* TO TEACH	PLANNING *HOW* TO TEACH	PLANNING THE *CONTEXT* FOR TEACHING AND LEARNING
<u>Content</u> About diversity For a diverse world Carrier content <u>Completeness</u> Thorough coverage All contributors Varied perspectives Similarities & differences <u>Connections</u> To student experiences Importance to students' lives Build on student ideas	<u>Universal instructional interventions</u> Universal design for learning Differentiated instruction Critical teaching skills <u>Selected instructional interventions</u> Accommodations for: Acquisition of information Processing and memorizing Expressing information	<u>Environment</u> Physical Social Emotional <u>Universal behavioral interventions</u> Rules, routines, & social skills Critical management skills <u>Selected behavioral interventions</u> ABC

Because we are moving on to Part 2 of our book, it would be a good time to review the Diversity Responsive Teaching framework that was first shown in the Introduction. It provides the "big picture" of the content and organization of this book. In the first part of our book, you learned about *what* to teach, that is, the content to be used for lessons and activities. You learned where to go for content ideas, how to decide what to teach, and how to best organize the content for teaching. You also learned about writing instructional objectives, which provide focus for planning what and how you will teach. Once you have made decisions about what you will teach, you are ready to move to the next planning step.

Deciding *how* to teach is what Part 2 of this book is all about. Once teachers know what they will teach, they must determine how to best teach it. Fortunately, teachers today have access to many ideas and strategies that have been proven to be effective through research. This means that even beginning and preservice teachers can develop a repertoire of many effective strategies to use when they teach. Educational journals are just one good source of effective techniques considered to be best practice. Additional sources of specific instructional ideas for use in lessons and activities include teachers' guides that accompany student texts, Internet sites that are designed for teachers, books, and workshops. A teacher's creativity can flourish in designing specific activities to include in instruction.

We will present three general categories of universal instructional interventions in this section of our book: universal design for learning, differentiated instruction, and critical teaching skills. Universal interventions are strategies, techniques, or methods that will benefit most if not all of the students in your class. They are built in right from the start—as part of your initial planning. We present many ideas for universal interventions in Chapters 3 through 8. Selected instructional interventions are designed for one or a few students and are accommodations or modifications that are added on. Ideas for selected interventions are presented in Chapter 9. The easiest way to meet the needs of a diverse student group is to build in many options for success in the first place to lessen the need for selected interventions.

General Approaches to Universal Instructional Interventions

Introduction

This chapter includes two approaches to universal instructional interventions. One is *universal design for learning* and the other is *differentiated instruction*. Both approaches are designed to address the diversity found in today's classroom by becoming part of up-front planning. In this chapter, we will also discuss planning for English language learners. These students have specific learning needs, many of which can be addressed through universal instructional interventions, and by strategies that are built in rather than added on later.

Universal Design for Learning

The term *universal design* was first used in the field of architecture. The concept of universal design emerged from the need to construct buildings in a way that provided access to persons with disabilities, for example, individuals who used wheelchairs. As buildings were being retrofitted with options for accessibility, it was noted that many of the modifications benefited people without disabilities. For example, ramps, which are essential for people in wheelchairs, also work well for parents pushing strollers, and are handy for people carrying things. Ron Mace developed the idea of designing buildings from the outset to be accessible to everyone (without the need for adaptation or specialized design) and named it *universal design* (Rose and Meyer 2002).

The principles of universal design were next applied to the field of education. Individuals at the Center for Applied Special Technology (CAST) were instrumental in developing educational curriculum materials that provided access to a wider audience. The idea was to build options into classroom materials so that more students would have access to the information and related activities (Rose and Meyer 2002). Orkwis and McLane explained it well when they said, "In terms of learning, universal design means the design of instructional materials and activities that allows the learning goals to be achievable by individuals with wide differences in their abilities to see, hear, speak, move, read, write, understand English, attend, organize, engage, and remember" (1998). The development of instructional technology (voice-activated programs), and the design of curricular materials (digital textbooks, for example) are examples of applications that provide built-in options to curriculum and learning activities for all students. The educators at CAST created the term *universal design for learning* to describe these and similar applications. The key idea is that necessary supports are available to provide all students opportunities to learn.

Applications

You can use the principles of universal design in developing your lessons and activities. When you do so, you build in, rather than add on, alternatives that provide support and choice for all students in your class. For example, building video captions into a lesson may benefit everyone in a noisy classroom—not only individuals with hearing impairments or English language learners. Providing a handout with varying print sizes for a seatwork assignment can be beneficial to both a student with a visual impairment and provides a choice for other students. You can build universal design alternatives into your lesson and activity plans in several ways. Orkwis and

McLane (1998) suggest incorporating multiple methods of presenting information and multiple methods of student response and engagement:

1. *Presenting Information* When presenting information in a lesson, plan to say, demonstrate, and write the information. This redundancy allows all students—those with visual and auditory impairments, learning disabilities, and those learning the English language—to access and benefit from the information. When you use visual supports in your lessons or activities, provide verbal descriptions to go with them. Provide written captions for audio materials. Whenever possible, use digital text so that it can be enlarged and changed in other ways to make it more accessible. The following are examples in presenting information:
   - When teaching the steps for dividing fractions, *state the rule*, "When dividing fractions, invert the divisor and multiply." *Write the steps* on the board. *Show a diagram* of a completed problem. Then *demonstrate* by solving problems on an overhead transparency while *stating the steps again* and *pointing to them* on the diagram.
   - When conducting a lesson about the Vietnam War, the teacher *says* the information, *shows* a written outline on the overhead projector, and passes out a partially filled out copy of her outline for the students to *write* on as they listen. The teacher also *shows* visual supports (pictures from an Internet site about the war) to illustrate key concepts.

2. *Student Responses* When asking students to express their learning, include every student by providing alternatives, such as saying or recording, writing, typing, drawing, or demonstrating the response. Word-processing programs provide students with many supports, such as grammar and spelling checks. Students who are unable to make oral presentations may create multimedia presentations, or supply computer graphics as an alternative to hand drawing. Decide whether you will select the response type for individuals or allow students to freely choose. The following are suggestions for providing alternatives for student responses:
   - When responding to a math fact question—"What is 4 times 3?"—consider variety in student responses, for example, writing the answer, saying the answer, or pointing to the answer on a number chart.
   - At the conclusion of a series of lessons on Native American history, provide flexibility in how students will demonstrate their knowledge. Taking a written test or putting together a portfolio of assignments that meet unit objectives are examples.

3. *Student Engagement* Keep students engaged in learning by providing variety in supports or scaffolds. This variation will help challenge individuals appropriately. Techniques for maintaining student engagement include planning various student groupings (for example, partner groups, skill groups, peer tutoring), using a variety of lesson models, incorporating students' interests into lessons and activities, and helping students understand the value of what they are learning and how it applies to life outside of school. The following are examples for engaging students:
   - Give students opportunities to follow their individual interests by providing choices, such as copying popular music lyrics to practice handwriting.
   - Allow flexibility in practice activities (working independently or with peers, for example), as it can be helpful in drawing in some students.

Six Principles for Designing Instruction for Diverse Learners

Kame'enui et al. (2002) discuss six universal design principles that help students gain cognitive access to the curriculum. These principles were developed to guide the design of curricular materials, but many of the ideas can be applied as you develop lessons and activities. When these principles are built into lessons and activities, they provide support for students with a wide variety of learning needs. The principles are as follows:

1. *Big Ideas* are the fundamental concepts and principles in an academic area that help connect or "anchor" the smaller ideas. Big ideas help teachers decide what to teach, to select and sequence objectives and to focus on important

learning outcomes (see Chapter 1). Big ideas also help students make connections and focus on the most important ideas. Consider big ideas as you design the opening to lessons. When presenting information, summarize and emphasize key points by referring to big ideas. The following are examples of big ideas:

- The interactions of humans with their environments shape the characteristics of both people and the environment.
- People read to be informed and to be entertained.
- Writing is a process.

2. *Conspicuous Strategies* are the steps for solving a problem or accomplishing a task. When you teach strategies explicitly, they become clear and usable for students. When preparing a task analysis, list the steps of the strategy. During the lesson state, list, explain, and model the strategy by using "think-alouds." In extended practice, provide opportunities to use the strategy in varied applications. The following are examples of using conspicuous strategies:
   - During a lesson on how to write a capital letter *M*, the teacher says the steps out loud: "I start by putting my pencil on the headline. I draw a line straight down to the foot line," and so on.
   - After learning about how to develop and use mnemonics for memorizing information, give students chances to develop mnemonics in geography (the names of the great lakes), in science (the steps in the scientific method), and other content areas.

3. *Mediated Scaffolding* is the temporary support and assistance provided by the teacher, the materials, or the task during instruction. Provide varying levels of supports and gradually withdraw them. This allows each student to be successful during instruction and eventually become independent. Mediated scaffolding can include sequencing examples and tasks from easy to more complex; moving from the whole group, to partner, to individual practice; and providing varied materials (such as note-taking guides) to help students learn. The following are examples for using mediated scaffolding:
   - In the math unit where students are learning about adding up to three digits and three digits with regrouping in the ones and tens columns, students are first taught how to regroup in the ones column and then how to regroup in both the ones and tens columns.
   - During a lesson where students are learning how to summarize, the teacher provides them with opportunities to practice first as a whole group, then with a partner, and then alone.

4. *Primed Background Knowledge* is the recalled prerequisite skills and knowledge needed for the new task. Having the necessary background knowledge and applying it to the new task is required for success in learning. List prerequisites in the content analysis. Assess the students' prior knowledge and then remind, review, and develop background knowledge as needed. The following are examples of using recalled background knowledge:
   - Suppose that a teacher intends to teach her students how to write a persuasive essay, five paragraphs in length. She plans to concentrate on the persuasive elements of the essay, so she first checks to see that her students remember the main components of a paragraph and the specifics of writing a five-paragraph essay.
   - To identify examples of racial stereotyping in their social studies text and chapter books, students are first taught to define racial stereotyping and identify examples in controlled examples.

5. *Strategic Integration* involves putting together essential information and skills, which leads to higher-level thinking skills. As part of your long-term planning, be sure to plan lessons and activities in combinations that will lead to integration. The following are examples of such integrating:
   - As a culminating activity for a unit on nutrition, students designed an informational brochure for teen parents. The brochure includes the following information: specific types and amounts of nutrients that infants and toddlers need, foods that are high in particular nutrients, simple recipes that are packed with nutrients, and why nutrients are important (impact on development).

- The civics class students put together events and activities designed to ease tensions between different "groups" at school. The planning of these events causes students to draw on a wide variety of concepts that are taught in their class. Some of the key ideas that are incorporated into their planning include learning about and appreciating cultural variation, anti-bullying, and ally-building. These ideas were all woven throughout a series of events that helped students accept each other.

6. *Judicious Review* provides opportunities for students to review important learning. Carefully planned review will help students remember and apply what they have learned. Include review in the openings and closings of lessons and activities, and build in extended practice and activities. The following are examples of reviewing:
   - After teaching a lesson on how to put a heading on a paper, the teacher follows up by reviewing the essential elements for the heading. Then he instructs his students to write a heading on their papers in math, social studies, and science.
   - In the opening of a lesson on proper nouns, the teacher reviews what students already know about nouns in general as well as common nouns.

In summary, as you design lessons and activities, ask yourself if you are building in multiple methods for presenting, keeping students engaged, and allowing for multiple means for students to respond. Also ask yourself if you are incorporating big ideas, explicit strategies, scaffolding, primed background knowledge, integration, and review in such a way that all students can achieve the objectives.

Differentiated Instruction

Differentiated instruction is another approach or philosophy of teaching with the goal that all students will learn. This type of instruction begins with the assumption that students in a class will vary in their readiness for a particular learning task, and in their personal interests and preferences. "At the most basic level, differentiating instruction means 'shaking up' what goes on in the classroom so that students have multiple options for taking in information, making sense of ideas, and expressing what they learn. In other words, a differentiated classroom provides different avenues to acquiring content, to processing or making sense of ideas, and to developing products so that each student can learn effectively" (Tomlinson 2005, 1). This approach also emphasizes the importance of teaching toward important learning outcomes (that is, crucial concepts and principles, big ideas), assessing each student's prior knowledge and progress, determining student interest, maintaining high standards, and challenging each student.

Providing Options

Differentiated instruction is possible by providing options in content, process, and product:

- *Content* is *what* is taught. Differentiating content means flexibility in choosing curriculum topics, for example, selecting content that is personally meaningful to students (Heacox 2002) and incorporating big ideas (OSPI 2005). It also means flexibility in providing access to what we want students to learn (Tomlinson 2005). The three guiding themes in differentiating content are student readiness, student interest, and student learning preferences. This means that teachers must routinely assess what students already know and what interests students have, and they must provide multiple ways of presenting information. The following are examples of providing differentiated content:
  - As part of a unit on famous non-Caucasian U.S. inventors, students are given an assignment to write a report on an inventor. They are given their choice of which inventor to write about rather than being assigned a particular one.
  - When the teacher writes the story problems for math, she includes problems that address occupations of the parents of the students in her classroom. For example, if a teacher has students from dairy farms in her class, she could write problems such as "If the average

milk production of a Guernsey cow is about 5 gallons a day, how many gallons of milk will be produced in a week on a farm where 86 cows are milked each day?" She writes different problems for students who come from logging families. It is hoped these types of problems will grab student interest.

- *Process* means sense-making or, just as it sounds, an opportunity for learners to process the content or ideas and skills to which they have been introduced (Tomlinson 2005, 79). Flexible groupings, cooperative learning activities, and hands-on activities are all examples of techniques that teachers can use to provide options for processing the information that has come to students. The following are specific examples:
  - Some students construct models of the heart to increase their understanding of heart anatomy. Others read about and examine diagrams of heart anatomy. Some students verbally explain heart anatomy to a peer.
  - Students explore the concept of fractions and work with fraction manipulatives individually, in pairs, or in heterogeneous groups.

- *Product* means the end result of learning, that is, what students will do to show you that they know. A key idea here is that students are given options when it comes to demonstrating what they know. Models, presentations, portfolios, tests, and demonstrations are all examples of products. The following are specific examples:
  - When students are learning about the impact of the stock market crash in 1929, they are given the choice to do an oral presentation with charts, a written report, or a PowerPoint presentation.
  - To test students' knowledge of term definitions in science, students are given the choice to say the answers into a tape recorder or write them on the test booklet.

When a teacher uses differentiated instruction, she uses flexibility in her teaching. Teachers can use differentiation in various subject areas, units, or tasks for individuals or small groups by varying materials, pacing, activities, grouping, scaffolding, products, and so on (Tomlinson 1999; Pettig 2000). These choices and options increase the probability that all students will learn.

Similarities between Universal Design and Differentiated Instruction

You have undoubtedly noticed that the concepts of universal design for learning and differentiated instruction have numerous elements in common. The idea behind both philosophies is the same: students in classrooms are all different and therefore, a single approach to teaching and learning is neither appropriate nor effective. Neither approach is the same as individualized instruction, but both approaches are meant to make learning possible for all students.

The concepts of universal design and differentiated instruction had their roots in two different areas of education. Universal design was originally thought of as something specific to special education, because it began as a way to provide access in the physical environment for persons with disabilities. When these principles were applied to curriculum, it was clear that many students could profit from specific universal design strategies. "The attention of general education has been captured by a compatible philosophy known as differentiated instruction," writes Edyburn, (2004). It is apparent that although these philosophies started in different areas of education, there is a great deal of overlap. The Council for Exceptional Children for example, refers to differentiated instruction as one of a number of effective instructional practices that help make universal design work (CEC 2005). The following, adapted from Hall, Strangeman, and Meyer (2003) illustrates how the main elements of one approach line up with the main elements of the other:

Universal Design for Learning	**Differentiated Instruction**
Flexible Means of Presentation	Content
Flexible Means of Student Engagement	Process
Flexible Methods of Student Responses	Product

Both approaches provide for built-in options and flexibility with the intent that students will be successful. Obviously, as teachers plan how to incorporate these ideas into their classrooms, they are thinking about their specific students and what they know about them. The difference between these general approaches and selected interventions is that, these options are almost always built in for all students, whereas selected interventions are often added on for one or a few students. Universal design and differentiated instruction are complementary approaches and both emphasize options. Providing choices for students has a positive impact on student learning (Jolivett, Stichter, and McCormick 2002).

Planning for English Language Learners

We will discuss English language learners in various places throughout this book, but we talk about them here in more detail because of the complexity and importance of this topic. First, we know these students encounter special challenges in the typical classroom that most other students do not. They are expected to learn content (like other students) but are trying to learn it in a language they do not know well (unlike other students) and they do this with varying amounts of success. They often have difficulty in school when program design, instructional goals, and student needs are mismatched (Echevarria, Vogt, and Short 2004).

Secondly, many teachers have English language learners in their classrooms and the numbers of such students are increasing; for example, the number increased 84 percent between 1992 and 2003 (NCELA 2004). Traditionally, these students received instruction from specially trained teachers outside of the main classroom. Echevarria, Vogt, and Short (2004) write that increasing numbers of students and a shortage of qualified English as a Second Language (ESL) and bilingual teachers has quickly extended the need to teach content to these students outside of the ESL classroom. This means that general and special education teachers both have an opportunity to greatly impact the success of English language learners. Obviously, the numbers of students and the challenges they have in school makes meeting their needs a high priority for all teachers.

Finally, teachers can impact the success of these students often without much additional planning. You might think that when working with English language learners, you would need to add on numerous selected interventions because of the specialized needs of these students. Interestingly, many strategies and techniques that are used to address general diversity in a classroom are also very effective for students who are learning English. In other words, many of the instructional strategies and techniques that you will learn in Part 2 of this book will apply to English language learners as well. We talk about these students here because we want you to be thinking about them as you peruse the ideas in the chapters that follow.

Stages of Language Acquisition

Although you do not need to become an expert on second language acquisition, it is helpful to have a basic understanding of the stages students go through as they learn English. To begin with, teachers need to understand the distinction between social language proficiency and academic language proficiency. Jim Cummins (1986) called these basic interpersonal communication skills (BICS) and cognitive academic language proficiency (CALP). A student may communicate quite well in social situations, such as chatting with peers at lunch. The same student may need extensive language support during academic instruction. Don't be fooled by oral fluency in conversational English. Cummins (1986) suggests that academic language proficiency may take five to seven years to acquire. A teacher should also understand that the process of acquiring a second language spans predictable and sequential stages. These stages of language development begin with no knowledge of English and end with a command of English much like a native speaker (Reed and Railsback 2003). Planning various types of classroom events, such as questions, is most effective when matched to the students' levels of language development. The following explanations, adapted from Reed and Railsback (2003) and Herrell and Jordan (2004), summarize the stages of language acquisition:

- *Preproduction Stage* Students in this stage understand more words than they can speak or feel comfortable speaking. Sometimes students respond through techniques such as gestures, pointing, or nodding. This stage can last anywhere from hours to months, and teachers need to be careful to wait until students are ready to speak, rather than forcing them. These students can understand somewhere around 500 words.

- *Early Production Stage* During this stage, which can last six months or so, the English language learner acquires a receptive vocabulary close to 1,000 words. Answering in one- or two-word phrases is common at this stage, and students can often provide short answers to questions such as those beginning with who, what, and where.

- *Speech Emergence Stage* When in the speech emergence stage, students develop a vocabulary of around 3,000 words. They can use short phrases and simple sentences and can also ask simple questions. This stage lasts about a year.

- *Intermediate/Advanced Language Proficiency Stage* This stage can take up to a year to go through but it is one of great growth. Those in this stage have vocabularies that grow to about 6,000 words. They are able to speak in much longer sentences and can, for example, make complex statements and express opinions. It may take between five and seven years for students to become academic language proficient. At this time, they know specialized content vocabulary and can actively participate in classroom and school activities. These students may need support at times, but when advanced proficiency is obtained, they are quite independent.

Throughout this section and in other parts of this book, we will focus on providing you with strategies and ideas to include in lessons or activities with the primary objective of content learning rather than learning English. Note, however, that sometimes strategies serve a dual purpose—they help with content knowledge and with learning English. A good place to start when thinking about language acquisition is to recognize whether a student's academic language proficiency may need support, even if the student's social or conversational English is quite fluent.

In the section that follows, two general areas can give direction when planning. The first is what you can do to help students understand what you say or present. The second is what you can do to provide opportunities for language use. (Many of these ideas are adapted from Gersten, Baker, and Marks (1998).) These two categories of strategies are especially applicable when planning activities and lessons.

Make What You Present Understandable

Many authors call this "comprehensible input." Comprehensible input means that students are able to understand the sense or substance of what teachers present, although they may not necessarily understand every word. The following strategies help promote comprehensible input:

1. *Teach vocabulary.* Selecting and defining key terms and vocabulary is an important part of content analysis (see Chapter 1). When teaching English language learners, it is absolutely essential to consider the following suggestions:
   - Select a small number of words to introduce at a time. Gersten and Baker (2000) suggest seven or less.
   - Select important and useful words.
   - Pre-teach the vocabulary words at the beginning of lessons or activities or before reading.
   - Directly teach the words and meanings by saying them, writing them, and using visual supports and active participation strategies.
   - Help the students connect the words with prior knowledge and personal experience through discussions and semantic webs.
   - Provide various practice opportunities, such as acting out meanings, creating word banks, writing journal entries, or defining with partners.

2. *Use visual supports.* Visual supports are a very important method of scaffolding to help English language learners understand vocabulary, concepts, principles, and procedures. The four types of visual supports described in Chapter 5 are helpful in various ways during instruction. For example, real objects, models, and pictures are very helpful in teaching vocabulary. Demonstrations and role plays make directions and procedures much more understandable. Writings are helpful for reinforcing verbal information in many parts of activities or lessons. Finally,

graphic organizers can improve comprehension, clarify abstractions, organize concepts, or demonstrate connections.

3. *Provide context and activate background knowledge.* New information is more easily understood when teachers present it in a context rather than as stand-alone material. At the beginning of a lesson, use the following methods to build background knowledge and provide a context:
   - Provide a familiar example (introduce fractions by saying, "Three friends have only one cookie and they want to share it . . .").
   - Ask questions (introduce a history unit on migrations by asking, "How many of you have moved to a new place? What did you take? How did you get there?").
   - Use group or individual brainstorming for creating webs or maps of what students already know about a topic.
   - Have the class, small groups, or individuals complete "KWL" charts (what I already **K**now about a topic, what I **W**ant to learn, and later, what I did **L**earn).
   - Connect an introduction of new concepts with the students' native languages.
   - Build background knowledge for the students by providing experiences, such as brief activities at the beginning of lessons ("I'm going to give one cookie to each group of three, and you need to share it fairly . . ."); activities that come before lessons (an activity involving experimenting with magnets before a lesson on how magnets work); or field trips, guest speakers, multimedia presentations, or stories that are relevant to the new learning.
   - Provide a context as you present by gesturing and demonstrating, showing examples of completed products, using graphic organizers, thinking aloud, or showing objects, pictures, videos, or audio recordings (see Chapter 5).

4. *Use consistent language.* Decide on the important words and phrases to be used in a lesson or activity, teach them, and then use those terms consistently. Avoid using synonyms at random. Name the steps consistently when teaching procedures and strategies. Remember that idioms, metaphors, and other figures of speech can be difficult to understand. Use them carefully and check for understanding frequently.

5. *Give explanations or directions in a variety of ways.* As you speak, use gestures and demonstrations; put information in writing; be explicit and explain step by step; give many examples; use "think-alouds"; show completed products; and check for understanding (see Chapters 5 and 7).

Provide Opportunities for Language Use

In addition to providing comprehensible input, teachers need to help students process that input, and express and practice that learning. Gersten and Baker argue "that both extended discourse about academic topics and briefer responses to specific questions about content are cornerstones of academic growth for English-language learners" (2000, 465). The following are some strategies for providing opportunities for language use in lessons and activities:

1. *Use active participation strategies.* These strategies (discussed extensively in Chapter 6) are designed to keep all students actively engaged in learning. Ask students to actively respond during lessons by talking, writing, or signaling rather than passively listening. As you select those strategies likely to be most valuable for English language learners, look for strategies that require oral responses from students; provide opportunities for long, complex responses, as well as brief, one- or two-word responses; encourage discussions with peers (Think-Pair-Share, for example); and create nonthreatening opportunities to respond (unison responses).

2. *Use partner and small-group work.* Having students work with partners or in small groups during lessons and activities provides many opportunities for language use. (Formal peer tutoring and cooperative learning programs are highly recommended as well.) Peers act as language models and can provide feedback. Their support can create a safe environment for using language. Chances to discuss new concepts or solve problems with other students, including

those who speak the same native language, can be very beneficial. Teachers need to carefully structure and monitor partner and small-group work to be most effective (see Chapter 8 for more on this approach).

You can have a very positive influence on helping English language learners in your classroom learn, even if you are not an expert in second language acquisition of these students. You can begin by carefully analyzing the progress of your English language learners in both content and language acquisition and planning accordingly. Gertsen and Baker point out that, "effective instruction for English-language learners is more than just 'good teaching.' It is teaching that is tempered, tuned, and otherwise adjusted, as a musical score is adjusted, to the correct 'pitch' at which English-language learners will best 'hear' the content (i.e., find it most meaningful) (2000, 461). This idea implies the importance of trying out techniques and strategies and monitoring their effectiveness (see Chapter 7).

Summary

The students you work with will be successful with a variety of instructional methods and activities in varying degrees. The suggestions presented in this chapter that are designed to help students be successful are only a beginning assortment of ideas. It is important to continue to add to your repertoire of ideas. When you plan, incorporate the principles of universal design for learning and ideas about differentiated instruction. By applying these principles in your classroom, you will increase the chances that all of your students will learn.

References and Suggested Reading for Universal Design and Differentiated Instruction

Baca, L., and H. Cervantes. 2004. *The bilingual special education interface.* 4th ed. Upper Saddle River, NJ: Pearson Education, Inc.

The Center for Universal Design. http://www.design.ncsu.edu/cud/index.html.

Cawley, J., T. Foley, and J. Miller. 2003. Science and students with mild disabilities: Principles of universal design. *Intervention in School and Clinic* 38 (3): 160–171.

Council for Exceptional Children. 2005. *Universal design for learning: A guide for teachers and education professionals,* ed. and rev. J. Castellani. Upper Saddle River, NJ: Merrill Prentice Hall.

Edyburn, D. 2004. Research & practice associate editor column. *JSET E Journal* 19 (2). www.cast.org/teachingeverystudent/ideas/tes/chapter1_4.cfm (accessed July 14, 2005).

Hall, T., N. Strangmean, and A. Meyer. 2003. *Differentiated instruction and implications for UDL implementation.* Wakefield, MA: National Center on Accessing the General Curriculum. http://www/cast.org/publications/ncac/ncac_diffinstructudl.html.

Heacox, D. 2002. *Differentiating instruction in the regular classroom: How to reach and teach all learners, grades 3–12.* Minneapolis, MN: Free Spirit Publishing.

Hitchcock, C., A. Meyer, D. Rose, and R. Jackson. 2002. Providing new access to the general curriculum: Universal design for learning. *Teaching Exceptional Children* 35 (2): 8–17.

Howard, J. B. 2003. Universal design for learning: An essential concept for teacher education. *Journal of Computing in Teacher Education* 19 (4): 113–118.

Jolivette, K., J. P. Stichter, and K. M. McCormick. 2002. Making choices—improving behavior—engaging in learning. *Teaching Exceptional Children* (Jan/Feb): 24–29. Arlington, VA: The Council for Exceptional Children.

Kame'enui, E. J., D. W. Carnine, R. C. Dixon, D. C. Simmons, and M. D. Coyne. 2002. *Effective teaching strategies that accommodate diverse learners.* 2nd ed. Upper Saddle River, NJ: Prentice-Hall.

Law, B., and Eckes, M. 2000. *The more-than-just-surviving handbook: ESL for every classroom teacher.* 2nd ed. Winnipeg, Manitoba, Canada: Portage & Main Press.

Orkwis, R., and K. McLane. 1998. A curriculum every student can use: Design principles for student access. *ERIC/OSEP Topical Brief.* Reston, VA: Council for Exceptional Children.

Washington Office of Superintendent of Public Instruction (OSPI). 2005. Grade Level Expectations Guidance Task Force. *Connecting Systems: A standards-referenced approach to accessing the curriculum for each student.* Olympia, WA Office of Superintendent of Public Instruction.

Pettig, K. L. 2000. On the road to differentiated practice. *Educational Leadership, 58* (1): 14–18.

Rose, David H., and Anne Meyer. 2002. Education in the digital age. In *Teaching every student in the digital age: Universal design for learning.* Baltimore, MD: Association for Supervision & Curriculum Development. www.cast.org/teachingeverystudent/ideas/tes/chapter1_4.cfm (accessed July 31, 2005).

Tomlinson, C. A. 1999. *The differentiated classroom: Responding to the needs of all learners.* Alexandria, VA: ASCD.

Tomlinson, C.A. 2005. *How to differentiate instruction in mixed-ability classrooms.* 2nd ed. Upper Saddle River, NJ: Merrill Prentice Hall.

Watson, S., and L. Houtz. 2002. Teaching science: Meeting the academic needs of culturally and linguistically diverse students. *Intervention in School and Clinic* 37 (5): 267–278.

References and Suggested Reading for Linguistic Diversity

Chamot, A. U., and J. M. O'Malley. 1994. *The CALLA handbook: Implementing the cognitive academic language learning approach.* Reading, MA: Longman.

Cummins, J. 1986. Empowering minority students: A framework for intervention. *Harvard Educational Review* 56 (1): 18–36.

Echevarria, J., M. Vogt, and D. J. Short. 2004. *Making content comprehensible for English learner: The SIOP model.* 2nd ed. Boston: Pearson.

Gersten, R., and S. Baker. 2000. What we know about effective instructional practices for English language learners. *Exceptional Children, 66* (4): 454–470.

Gersten, R., S. K. Baker, and S. U. Marks. 1998. *Teaching English-language learners with learning difficulties.* Reston, VA: Council for Exceptional Children.

Herrell, A., and M. Jordan. 2004. *Fifty strategies for teaching English-language learners.* 2nd ed. Upper Saddle River, NJ: Prentice-Hall.

National Clearinghouse for English Language Acquisition. 2004. *The growing numbers of limited English proficient students.* http://www.ncela.gwu.edu/policy/states/reports/statedata/2002LEP/Growing_LEP0203.pdf (accessed May 22, 2005).

Reed, B., and J. Railsback. 2003. *Strategies and resources for teachers of English language learners.* Portland, OR: NW Regional Educational Lab.

Critical Teaching Skills for Focusing Attention

Introduction

One of the biggest challenges that teachers encounter is keeping students involved, interested, and learning. Many effective teaching practices can be incorporated into your plans that can help you meet this challenge. The critical teaching skills presented in this chapter are designed to help teachers focus the attention of their students on the important elements of any lesson or activity. Effective questioning skills and strong openings and closings are all techniques that teachers can use to help keep students focused and engaged during instruction.

Openings

A lesson or activity opening is the component in which the actual lesson or activity begins and is designed to help students focus attention and make connections. The most important function of openings is to help prepare the students for learning. Openings can include specific strategies designed to motivate and focus students, and strategies that help students see the relationship between the new knowledge or skill and other learning. Generally, openings include both kinds of strategies.

Strategies for Openings

You can select ideas for openings from the following two categories.

1. *Strategies to motivate or focus the students:*
   a. Tell or show the objective (write the lesson objective on the board); describe the evaluation (tell students that they will write two complete sentences in which adverbs are included and used correctly at the end of the lesson).
   b. Tell students the purpose, rationale, importance, and application of the lesson or activity objective (for instance, the current math lesson will help them double-check the change they receive after a purchase).
   c. Use an attention-getting "set" that relates directly to the lesson to capture student interest (jokes, stories, riddles, songs, poems, demonstrations, video clips, and so on).
   d. Preview the sequence of activities in the lesson (tell students they will read and take notes from their texts and then work in cooperative groups to construct a study guide for their upcoming test).
   e. Provide a key idea or generalization as an advance organizer (explain that all foods fit into five basic food groups and that each group is a primary source of specific nutrients prior to providing information about specific foods or food groups).
   f. Preview lesson content through a graphic organizer (show students a concept map of the parts of a paragraph).
   g. Provide initial examples that are humorous or personalized (include the names and interests of students in the classroom in initial story problem examples).
2. *Strategies to help students see relationships between the new knowledge or skill and other learning:*
   a. Connect the learning to personal experience and prior knowledge (have students

brainstorm examples of rhyming words as a way of beginning a lesson on poetry).

b. Build background knowledge (show a video clip of the Grand Canyon before reading a story set there).

c. Review earlier lessons or activities (conduct a quick review of regrouping in the ones column prior to teaching regrouping in the tens column).

d. Create a context for learning (provide one set of materials for two students to open a lesson on sharing).

e. Preview upcoming lessons or activities (explain that the vocabulary words the students will learn in the current lesson will help them understand the story they will read tomorrow).

f. Show students an outline of the whole unit (for example, the table of contents that will be used for the packet of information they will assemble during the respiratory system unit).

g. State the relationship of the objective to a more long-term goal (explain how learning conversational skills will help students gain and maintain friendships).

h. Connect to other subject areas (explain that students will write a letter to a local city council member as part of the social studies lesson, using the same format learned in language arts).

i. Present a graphic organizer (show a concept map for the unit on test-taking skills, highlighting multiple choice tests, the topic of this lesson).

State the Objective and Objective Purpose

One of the most effective strategies to use in the opening of a lesson or activity is to tell students directly what they will learn and why. Generally, students respond more positively when they understand what is expected of them and why the learning is valuable.

When students are told directly what they will be expected to know or to do by the end of the lesson, the teacher is *stating the objective*. For example, "You are going to know the difference between reptiles and amphibians," or "At the end of the lesson, I will ask you to circle the amphibians from a list of animals." Make the statement of objective using words that are appropriate to the age and grade level of the students. It may also be appropriate to show the students the objective in writing and have them write it in their notes.

The *objective purpose* is what teachers tell students about the value or rationale of the lesson. Also state the objective purpose in student terms and let them know why the knowledge or skill they are learning is important to them, that is, how it will help them in their daily lives or in school.

Responding to Diversity When Planning the Opening

Openings may be simple or highly elaborate. When deciding what to include or exclude in the opening, consider (1) variables such as student background, experience, and prior knowledge of the content; (2) prerequisite skills or knowledge; (3) the abstractness or concreteness of the content; (4) whether this is the first lesson or activity in a series; (5) probable student interest and motivation; and (6) the amount of time available for teaching.

The following suggestions will help you plan an opening intended to engage ALL students:

- Add drama, humor, novelty, or excitement to gain attention (for example, use skits, puppets, music, video clips, jokes, riddles, or demonstrations).

- Personalize by using the students' names and experiences. For example, open a writing lesson with a sentence, or a math lesson with a word problem, about the students ("If Mrs. Donahue's champion third graders win 16 games of four square . . .").

- In the opening, involve those students who are the most difficult to motivate or focus.

- Increase time spent on the review of earlier lessons or prerequisite skills and knowledge. Carefully plan ongoing daily, weekly, and monthly reviews.

- Involve everyone in active responses (for example, have all students write the definition of a term from yesterday's lesson rather than asking "Who remembers what ratio means?").
- Invite students to write or say everything they already know about a topic in three minutes.
- Carefully consider each student's background knowledge. Don't make assumptions. Students from cultural backgrounds different from yours will bring different knowledge and experience to a topic.
- Computer software is available that can help develop graphic organizers to show students connections in learning or to preview lessons.

The opening of a lesson or activity serves a very important role. It can be used to help students make connections between what they already know and what is to come. You can also use openings to develop knowledge and experience or to pique interest in the information that you will present. Openings don't always need to be elaborate, but they should be designed with the needs of your students in mind. A well-planned opening can set the stage for the learning that follows.

Questions

The hundreds of questions the typical American teacher asks on a typical day (Gall 1984), and the various reasons for asking them speaks to their value. Use carefully planned questions to focus students' attention on the key ideas of the content that is being presented. Questions play an important role in all lessons and activities.

Sometimes questions play a major role in lessons. In this case, they are the key instructional component of a lesson or activity. Orlich et al. suggest that, "next to lecturing and small-group work, the single most common teaching method employed

in American schools (and, for that matter, around the world) may well be the asking of questions" (2004, 240). Inquiry lessons, for example, depend heavily on asking questions to facilitate learning, as do discussion lessons.

Sometimes questions play a supporting role. None of the models we present in this book, for example, use questions as the major teaching strategy. Instead, questions support instruction in two ways. First, teachers use questions to provide review, rehearsal, and enrichment of the information being presented (for example, "What might have been another way to solve this problem?"). Secondly, teachers use questions to monitor students' understanding of the information being presented (for example, "What is the second step of the editing process?"). The questions used in the sample lesson and activity plans included in this book are all questions that play a supporting role.

Types of Questions

We can think of questions according to their purposes and also according to the type of response they require. The following four types of questions each elicit a specific type of response from students. Each type of question requires a different type of information processing to answer it. Knowing when and why to use each of the question types will help you construct questions that fit your purpose.

Convergent and Divergent Questions

Teachers use *convergent questions* when looking for one correct answer ("What color is the circle?"). Convergent questions, for the most part, elicit short responses from students and focus on the lower levels of thinking, that is, basic knowing and understanding (Orlich et al. 2004).

Examples of Convergent Questions

- What is the name of the NFL team headquartered in Seattle?
- Where is the Amazon River located?
- Who is the hero in this story?

Questions that prompt convergent responses often begin with the following types of stems: *who, what, when, where, list as many as you can think of,* and *how many.* Convergent questions can be especially effective during recitations commonly used in teacher-led lessons. They promote active participation by providing students with an opportunity to rehearse and review information, and provide teachers a way to check for student understanding.

Teachers use *divergent questions* when they wish to evoke a wide range of student responses. This type of question also typically elicits longer student responses (Mastropieri and Scruggs 2000). Divergent questions can help promote higher-level thinking and problem-solving skills. They can be especially useful when you want students to consider issues in depth, such as during an extended practice discussion activity used to enrich informal presentations. Because this question type elicits numerous correct answers, its use can be appealing.

Examples of Divergent Questions

- How would the world be different if the only color was gray?
- What would be another logical ending for this story?
- You have been given the power to stop racism. What would you do first? Why?
- Which political leader would likely be most successful in equalizing job opportunities for all U.S. citizens?

Question stems that will likely encourage divergent responses include the following: *What could happen if . . . ?, How many ways . . . ?,* or *How else might this have happened?* Note that the divergent question has no single right answer but it can have wrong answers. Borich states that, "this is perhaps the most misunderstood aspect of a divergent question. Not just any answer will be correct, even in the case of divergent questions raised for the purpose of allowing students to express their feelings. If Johnny is asked what he liked about *Of Mice and Men* and says 'Nothing,' or 'The happy ending,' then either Johnny has not read the book or he needs help in better understanding the events that took place. A passive or accepting response on the teacher's part to answers like these is inappropriate, regardless of the intent to allow an open response" (2004, 240).

High-Level and Low-Level Questions—Bloom's Taxonomy Revisited

Bloom's taxonomy was discussed in the chapter on objectives (Chapter 2) because teachers can use it to help vary the degree of complexity of learning tasks as they plan their objectives. We discuss it again in this chapter because it can also be a useful guide when writing questions. The taxonomy provides a way for teachers to write questions that prompt students to think about content in various ways. Providing a variety of questions to use in any given lesson or activity is one way to address various learning needs of a diverse group of students. This section shows how Bloom's taxonomy applies to planning questions. We present and define each level of the taxonomy with examples of question stems and questions (as adapted from Sadker and Sadker 2006, Kauchak and Eggen 2003). As in the chapter on objectives, the original level labels and the revised labels (in parentheses) will be used.

A *low-level question* is one that is usually convergent in form and involves repetition or restatement of previously covered information. It is often used in basic skills instruction, or in early stages of learning (Mastropieri and Scruggs 2004). These questions are important building blocks leading to higher-level or divergent questions. It is unlikely that a student can analyze or evaluate information without an understanding of basic facts and information. The first two (or three) levels of Bloom's taxonomy provide a good resource for developing lower-level questions. The following are examples of question stems and sample questions that use Bloom's taxonomy to help design low-level questions and learning tasks:

Knowledge (Remembering): Questions at the knowledge level prompt factual recall of information.

- Question stem examples: who, what, when, why, where, name, list, define, identify
- Sample questions and tasks:
  - Define punctuation.
  - What is a mutual fund?
  - When was the Brown versus the Board of Education of Topeka case tried in court?

Comprehension (Understanding): Questions at the comprehension level go beyond factual recall and are designed to help determine whether or not students understand the meaning of the content presented.

- Question stems examples: Explain in your own words, restate, describe, interpret
- Sample questions and tasks:
  - Give additional examples of punctuation.

- What are the key features of a traditional individual retirement account (IRA)?
- Explain the ruling of Brown case—separate is not equal.

Application (Applying): Application level questions prompt students to solve problems or situations stated in the question by using the information they have learned.

- Question stem examples: explain how, explain why, demonstrate, operate, illustrate
- Sample questions and tasks:
  - Explain how to punctuate this sentence.
  - What type of an investor typically buys a Roth IRA?
  - Explain why the lawyers who brought forth the Brown case were unsatisfied with the "separate but equal" ruling in Plessy versus Ferguson.

High-level questions ask students to make inferences, to analyze, or to evaluate, and are often divergent in form. They require more in-depth thinking to answer than do low-level questions. In order to answer a high-level question, however, a student must know the basic facts. The upper three (or four) levels of Bloom's taxonomy provide a good resource for developing higher-level questions.

Analysis (Analyzing): Analysis questions prompt students to look carefully at the organizational structure of the information presented to formulate ideas.

- Question stem examples: compare, contrast, how, why, diagram, distinguish, differentiate
- Sample questions and tasks:
  - Compare the use of colons and semicolons.
  - What are three main differences between a Roth IRA and a traditional IRA?
  - How would you describe the impact of the Brown case ruling in its attempt to equalize educational opportunities for all students in the United States?

Synthesis (Creating): Synthesis questions give students an opportunity to come up with something new with the information they have learned.

- Question stem examples: design, construct, create, propose, formulate, catalog, plan
- Sample questions and tasks:
  - Create marks to punctuate sad, quiet, hesitant, anxious, bored and quiet statements (as exclamation points are used to punctuate forceful statements) and argue for their use.
  - Design a portfolio of mutual funds for an individual who is 10 years from retirement.
  - Make a plan that a state could implement that would help decrease the achievement gap between nonwhite and white students.

Evaluation (Evaluating): Students are asked to make a judgment about two ideas or concepts using a predetermined set of criteria.

- Question stem examples: evaluate, appraise, judge, choose, predict, rate, estimate
- Sample questions and tasks:
  - Select the sentence that is best punctuated for clarity of meaning.
  - Which of these stock and mutual fund options is best for a 401K plan for a 25 year old?
  - Which court case (Plessy versus Ferguson or Brown versus the Board of Education) had the most positive impact on equalizing resource allocation between African American and European American children in the public schools?

High- and low-level questions have different purposes and both play an important role in lessons and activities. A student's ability to answer a high-level question about a topic is dependent on having an understanding of the basic facts about that topic; the basic fact knowledge is assessed through the use of low-level questions. In this way, the question types at various levels of Bloom's taxonomy are interconnected, and questions at one level of the taxonomy may serve as a foundation for the next. This taxonomy provides a structured way to plan both high- and low-level questions.

You have undoubtedly noticed the overlap among question types. For example, a convergent question is often also a low-level question whereas a divergent question response may require higher-level thinking skills. It is important to understand that one question type is not necessarily superior to another, that is, high-level questions are not "better" than low-level questions. Kauchak and Eggen point out the importance of having clear goals for questions: "Goals that are appropriate for the topic, the age of the students, and their backgrounds should determine the level of question" (2003, 176). This means that the important thing to remember is that questions should be planned to fit the purpose for which they are designed.

Guidelines for Planning and Delivering Questions

It is always best to plan questions in advance. It can be difficult to come up with questions that meet your goals when you are in front of a group of students. This is especially true for beginners or for experienced teachers who are planning to teach new or difficult content. Think about the following guidelines as you plan your questions (Borich 2004):

- Be clear and concise. For example, "How do the cones of volcanoes vary?" is a clear question, as opposed to "We've studied three kind of volcanoes. They all have different kinds of cones and their cones vary in a number of ways; for example, some are larger than others—what would be the things we would study in the cone of a volcano that would tell us about the volcano type and why?"

- Use vocabulary that is appropriate for the age and ability of the students. For example, ask first graders, "What do you think Harry Potter meant when he said . . . ?" rather than, "What is your interpretation of the verbalizations of Harry Potter when he said . . . ?".

- Plan questions that are short enough for students to remember. Do not ask, "What are some of the ways we can preserve energy, water, and timber resources; why do we need to preserve these resources; and what techniques can we use to communicate the need for resource preservation to others in the community?".

- Follow questions with time for students to think (see wait-time 1 and 2 below). Provide adequate wait-time for more meaningful, thoughtful student responses.

- Follow questions with redirections, prompting and probing as necessary. These cues can help students recall information and formulate more complete, complex answers.

- Follow questions with honest feedback. Correct responses can be acknowledged or praised. Incorrect responses need to be corrected so students do not learn or practice incorrect information (see Chapter 7 for information on feedback).

- When you ask questions of your students, your goal should be to involve as many of them as possible. See ideas for specific response strategies in the chapter on active participation (see Chapter 6).

- Avoid ridiculous questions like asking a group of schoolchildren from Seattle, "Have any of you ever seen a cloud?"

Wait-Time

No discussion about questions would be complete without also talking about the importance of wait-time. Wait-time 1 and wait-time 2 are both variations of the idea that students need time to formulate answers to questions.

Wait-time 1 refers to the time between when a question is asked and when a student answers (Rowe 1986; Orlich 2004). When teachers provide students with 3–5 seconds after asking a question, more students usually respond, more responses are correct, and the responses are generally more complex (Rosenberg, O'Shea, and O'Shea 1998).

Wait-time 2 is the time between when a student apparently finishes a response and when the teacher redirects, prompts, or moves on. Adequate think-time at this point in the questioning sequence generally results in more elaborate answers because students are given a chance to add to or modify their initial responses (ibid.).

Consider some special points when planning wait-time. First, low-level, convergent questions usually do not require much wait-time. Usually, the purpose of these questions is factual recall so the student generally either knows or does not know the answer. Second, higher-level or divergent questions need more time. Also, some individuals seem to need additional thinking time to respond to higher-level questions (Mastropieri and Scruggs 2004). Finally, during fluency-building drills and practice activities when speed and accuracy are being developed, wait-time is not desirable (Rosenberg, O'Shea, and O'Shea 1998).

Responding to Skill Diversity When Planning Questions

There are a variety of ways that you can plan questions in response to the varying skill levels of your students.

- Don't make the mistake of only asking low-level and convergent questions of students who are low achievers.
- Vary wait-time.
- Provide additional prompting and probing as necessary.
- Ask questions that help students connect new learning with prior knowledge or personal experience.
- Ask a sequence of questions that build and lead students to correct or higher-level responses.
- Present important questions in writing as well as asking them orally.

Responding to English Language Learners When Planning Questions

When planning questions for English language learners, it is important to consider several factors. First, where students are in relation to the stages of English language acquisition will help a teacher determine the kinds of questions that are appropriate to ask. Second, the stage of English learning influences the type of response that a student is able to produce (see Chapter 3 for more information about language acquisition stages). This means that diversity responsive teachers must match their questioning strategies to the language levels of their English language learners. Following are the language stages (adapted from Herrell and Jordan 2004), and examples of questions and expected responses that match each language stage:

- Preproduction Stage
  - Sample Questions: Is this a man? Point to the girl. Show me "quickly."
  - Typical Question Responses: pointing, nodding, physically demonstrating
- Early Production Stage
  - Sample Questions: What did Jack do? Is it red or blue?
  - Typical Question Responses: providing one- or two-word responses, making choices
- Speech Emergence Stage
  - Sample Questions: Why did Jerell laugh? What will happen next?
  - Typical Question Responses: providing short phrases or sentences (grammatical errors are not unusual)
- Intermediate/Advanced Fluency Stage
  - Sample Questions: What is your opinion on this issue? How are these two stories similar?
  - Typical Question Responses: providing longer sentences, with fewer grammar errors

The following are additional suggestions for designing questions for English language learners:

- Use consistent language in questions. Be sure the language in the question matches the vocabulary used in the lesson or activity.
- Use simple vocabulary and shorter sentences, and limit the use of idiomatic expressions, slang, and pronouns (Salend and Salinas 2003).
- Provide opportunities for students to work with peer language models when answering questions.
- Encourage students to answer questions by providing visual supports and clues such as pictures, gestures, and words (Salend 2005).

Questions can encourage students to think about and act on the material the teacher has presented (Borich 2004). They can be used to enrich content learning and help students review and rehearse information. Questions can also be crafted to help teachers monitor the learning of their students. Arends states that, "beginning teachers should keep in mind one important truth, that is, that different questions require different types of thinking and that a good lesson should include both lower and higher-level questions" (1997, 214). Questions can play varied and valuable roles in all lessons and activities. (See the resources listed at the end of this chapter for more information about questions.)

Closings

The closing is an ending to a lesson or activity. All lessons and activities should include a closing that gives students one more opportunity to consider the learned material. The closing can help create a smooth transition from one lesson or activity to the next.

Strategies for Closings

Closings can help tie things together for students. They may include one or more of the following:

1. *A review of the key points* of the lesson or activity (for example, after reading a biographical sketch to her students, Mrs. Meurer reviews major accomplishments of the life of Langston Hughes).
2. *Opportunities for students to draw conclusions* (Mrs. Vossbeck helps students examine the relationship between lack of supervision and juvenile crime).
3. *A preview of future learning* (for example, following an activity designed to create interest in an upcoming unit on the solar system, Mr. Maberry gives a brief explanation of unit lessons and activities that will occur in the next few days).
4. *A description of where or when students should use their new skills or knowledge* (for example, Mrs. Weidkamp reminds students to try out their new social skill of "joining in" at recess).
5. *A time for students to show their work* (Mr. Isom has students share the three-dimensional shapes they constructed during the math lesson).
6. *A reference to the lesson opening* (Mrs. Begay restates the lesson objective as she prepares to begin the evaluation portion of her lesson).

Responding to Diversity When Planning the Closing

Consider the following when planning the closing:

- Do not assume that students will automatically apply or generalize the new skill or knowledge. Be very direct about where and when to use it.
- Actively involve students in summarizing at the end of the activity or lesson.
- Use the closing as one more practice opportunity.

A closing is an important component of lessons and activities. You can wrap up your lesson or activity in many different ways. You will want to select strategies that are appropriate to the content being taught and the students you are teaching. Although a closing doesn't need to be long and complex, every lesson and activity should have one.

Summary

This chapter has provided numerous ideas for helping students focus their attention on the important parts of lessons and activities. Planning meaningful openings and closings can help set students up to learn, and then help them review their learning. Important questioning strategies and an overview of question types have been included to provide structure for planning questions that help students process important information. The ideas presented in this chapter can guide you in involving your students and keeping them involved in your instruction.

References and Suggested Reading

Arends, R. I. 1997. *Classroom instruction and management.* New York: McGraw-Hill.

Arends, R. I. 2004. *Learning to teach.* 6th ed. San Francisco: McGraw-Hill. (See Chapter 12 in particular.)

Borich, G. D. 2004. *Effective teaching methods.* 5th ed. Columbus, OH: Merrill. (See Chapter 7 in particular.)

Echevarria, J., M. Vogt, and D. J. Short. 2004. *Making content comprehensible for English learners: The SIOP model.* Boston: Pearson.

Gall, M. 1984. Synthesis of research on teachers' questioning. *Educational Leadership* 42: 40–47.

Guillaume, A. M. 2000. *Classroom teaching: A primer for new professionals.* Columbus, OH: Merrill.

Herrell, A., and M. Jordan. 2004. *Fifty strategies for teaching English-language learners.* 2nd ed. Upper Saddle River, NJ: Prentice-Hall.

Jacobsen, D. A., P. Eggen, and D. Kauchak. 2006. *Methods for teaching: Promoting student learning.* 7th ed. Columbus, OH: Merrill Prentice Hall. (See Chapter 6 in particular.)

Kauchak, D. P., and P. D. Eggen. 2003. *Learning and teaching: Research-based methods.* 4th ed. Boston: Allyn and Bacon.

Kellough, R. D. 2000. *A resource guide for teaching: K–12.* 3rd ed. Columbus, OH: Merrill, an imprint of Prentice Hall. (See Chapter 10 in particular.)

Krumme, G. *Major categories in the taxonomy of educational objectives—Bloom 1956.* http://faculty.washington.edu/krumme/guides/bloom.html (accessed April 2005).

Mastropieri, M. S., and T. E. Scruggs. 2004. *The inclusive classroom: Strategies for effective instruction.* 2nd ed. Columbus, OH: Merrill.

Moore, K. D. 2005. *Effective instructional strategies: From theory to practice.* Thousand Oaks: SAGE Publications.

Orlich, D. C., R. J. Harder, R. C. Callahan, and H. W. Gibson. 2004. *Teaching strategies: A guide to better instruction,* 6th ed. Boston: Houghton Mifflin Company.

Rosenberg, M. S., L. O'Shea, and D. J. O'Shea. 1998. *Student teacher to master teacher: A practical guide for educating students with special needs.* Columbus, OH: Merrill.

Rowe, M. B. 1986. Wait time: Slowing down may be a way of speeding up. *Journal of Teacher Education* 23 (January–February): 43–49.

Sadker, M., and D. Sadker. 2006. Questioning skills. In *Classroom Teaching Skills.* 8th ed., ed. J. Cooper. Boston: Houghton Mifflin.

Salend, S. J. 2005. *Creating inclusive classrooms: Effective and reflective practices for all students.* 5th ed. Upper Saddle River, N.J.: Pearson.

Salend, S. J., and A. Salinas. 2003. Language differences or learning difficulties: The work of the multidisciplinary team. *Teaching Exceptional Children* 35 (4): 36–43.

Vallecorsa, A. L., L. U. de Bettencourt, and N. Zigmond. 2000. *Students with mild disabilities in general education settings: A guide for special educators.* Columbus, OH: Merrill, an imprint of Prentice Hall.

Critical Teaching Skills for Presenting Information

Introduction

This chapter is about planning your presentations so that your students will learn. Some of the critical teaching skills included in this chapter address clarity of presentation, including the way that information is explained and how it is demonstrated for students. Variety helps create interest and can help ensure that teachers present the content to be taught in a way that students can understand. Following the basic information about each critical teaching skill are suggestions for how to respond to diversity.

Presentations

Presenting information means to tell about or explain the information being taught, and is often done in conjunction with a demonstration. Without question, presenting information is one of the most important critical teaching skills. It applies to both lessons and activities and cuts across all lesson models. Whenever you present information to students, make sure it is clear and easy to understand.

Designing Presentations

The following suggestions will help you present information in an engaging and effective manner:

- Provide complete explanations and many examples. Teach, teach, teach!
- Teach the content in a step-by-step, piece-by-piece manner. Teach some information, check for understanding, and then reteach or move on.
- Break up the information. Teach a couple of steps and have the students practice; teach a couple more steps, and so on. Keep reminding the students of the whole task or big picture through demonstrations or by using graphic and advance organizers.
- Use visual supports (diagrams, photographs, concept maps, and so on) to supplement explanations.
- Vary voice tones and inflections to create interest. Sound enthusiastic.
- Be sure to use examples that are familiar to the students.
- Repeat key ideas often, using the same wording.
- Tell students which information is important to remember.
- Write important information down, for example, on a transparency, poster, or PowerPoint slide(s).
- Increase interest by using sound effects and animation in PowerPoint slides.
- Use pauses to allow students time to think and write.
- Ask for frequent, active responses. For example, ask all students to process, verbally or in writing, the information just presented. Decrease the use of strategies that involve calling on a few students who raise their hands or asking several students to come up to the board and do a problem.

Instead, ask all students to solve a problem on their individual whiteboards.

- Cue note-taking (for example, "first," "second," or "This is important") to help students recognize key ideas to add to notes.

Clarifying Key Terms and Vocabulary

When presenting information, make sure that students understand the terms and vocabulary used. The following strategies will help ensure that your students, including English language learners, understand the definitions you provide:

- Provide students with both verbal and written definitions.
- Provide pictures, models, and other visual aids to help illustrate important terms.
- Have students write terms and definitions in their notes or locate them in their text.
- Provide students with a list of terms to learn that can be used as a reference throughout a series of related lessons or a unit.
- Post word banks and semantic webs in the classroom.
- If memorization of terms is necessary, provide memorization strategies and time to practice. Flash cards, computer games, and mnemonic devices can all be used for practice.
- Be consistent in the terms you use with students. For example, if you decide to use the term *subtract,* don't randomly alternate with *minus* or *take away.*

Responding to Skill Diversity When Presenting Information

The following suggestions will provide support for students in learning the information you present:

- Pre-teach the important vocabulary words to be used in the presentation.
- Present information in smaller portions and provide practice after each portion.
- Increase opportunities for all students to respond.
- Use analogies, metaphors, or vivid language.
- Stop more often to summarize, review, and clarify how this information fits into the larger picture.
- Increase the use of visual supports, such as photographs, videos, real objects, and computer multimedia presentations.
- Use classroom amplification (for example, wireless microphone and speakers) when you present information.
- Provide partially filled in note-taking guides or graphic organizers that students can complete (outlines, concept maps, or webs, for example).
- Provide mnemonic devices to help students remember information.
- Adjust pacing; a brisker pace typically helps students attend and allows for more teaching.
- Provide a note-taker for a student who has difficulty taking notes while listening.

Responding to English Language Learners When Presenting Information

Some of the strategies previously mentioned are also helpful for English language learners. For example, using visual supports, stopping frequently and checking for understanding, pre-teaching important vocabulary words, and using culturally relevant examples can also benefit English language learners. Following are more ideas:

- Communicate meanings of new terms and concepts by using gestures, facial expressions, voice changes, pantomimes, demonstrations, rephrasing, visuals, props, manipulatives, and other cues (Salend and Salinas 2003).

- When you present, enunciate clearly, but don't raise your voice (Reed and Railsback 2003).
- Repetition can help students acquire the rhythm, pitch, volume, and tone of the new language (Salend and Salinas 2003).
- Don't speak too quickly and use brief pauses at natural points to allow learners to process what they are hearing.
- It is important to write clearly and legibly. Print rather than use cursive until you are sure your English language learners can read cursive (Reed and Railsback 2003).
- Avoid idioms (backseat driver, cute as a bug's ear) and slang (hangout, deep pockets), as they can be confusing for English language learners (Reed and Railsback 2003).
- Summarize the important points of the presentation frequently, always making sure to emphasize key vocabulary words (Reed and Railsback 2003).

Responding to Cultural Diversity When Presenting Information

- Use culturally relevant examples and explanations.
- Students from various backgrounds may prefer listening quietly or call-and-response approaches.
- Allow for active physical responses to the presentation when students are used to that style.
- Emphasize the big picture; create a context for new information.

You can use many techniques to help you present information in a way that engages students and increases their understanding. Providing options in your presentation, such as saying the information and putting it in writing, will help make your presentations clear and focused. With practice, many of the available options will become second nature.

Demonstration or Modeling

Demonstration or modeling means showing the students what it is they are expected to do. When a teacher shows students how to do a computation skill by first doing it herself, she is offering a demonstration. When a teacher role-plays for his students how to respond to teasing, he is providing a model of how the expected skill should look. Effective demonstrations play a key role in helping students better understand what you are teaching.

Types of Demonstrations

Teachers can use two types of demonstrations. The first is a *demonstration of a product*. This means that the teacher shows the students a finished product or pieces of a finished product. For example, Mrs. Wines plans an activity where students make origami birds. Mrs. Wines prepares a model (product) of the bird at each step of completion (after each new fold). This allows her students to see what the bird should look like as it is being created as well as when finished.

The second type of demonstration is the *demonstration of process*. This is where the teacher shows the students how to do the steps of the task. Here, Mrs. Wines completes each step of creating the origami bird while her students watch. She carefully explains what she is doing as she does it, for example, "Now I fold the paper across the diagonal and line up the edges of the paper so that they match exactly." Role plays and skits can also be used as demonstrations of a process. For example, Mrs. Howell acts out how students are to get under their desks during an earthquake drill. Often, teachers will use both a demonstration of process and a demonstration of product. This of course, will depend on the content of the lesson.

It is very important that the teacher or other expert do the demonstration in the initial phases of learning. This will help ensure that students get an accurate picture of the learning task. Demonstrations can be made even more effective by adding clear verbal explanations as you do the demonstration. The following ideas may help when planning demonstrations:

- Actually act out the skill you are teaching, rather than just explaining and asking students to imagine what you want them to do. For example, when demonstrating the routine for entering class, you should walk to the coat hooks and hang up a real coat rather than saying "Next I would put my coat away" and pantomiming hanging up a coat.

- Use a "think-aloud" to explain what you are doing as you do it. For example, when teaching the steps of a proofreading strategy, say "I'm looking at the sentences in my paragraph one sentence at a time to see if each has an end mark. Oh . . . my third sentence is missing an end mark. . . ." Be explicit.

- Supplement the demonstration with visual supports. For example, when demonstrating how to preview a chapter in a content area textbook, post the steps to follow.

- Demonstrating the new skill or knowledge only once is generally not enough. For example, if you are teaching students to find the common denominator of fractions, let them watch you find the common denominator of several different pairs of fractions.

- Actively involve students in the demonstration as appropriate, being careful about not asking them to do the demonstration for you. For example, when teaching how to add two-digit numbers to two-digit numbers without regrouping, ask students to say the answers together.

- When teaching a complicated skill, demonstrate each individual step of the skill, but also demonstrate all steps together. For example, when teaching the routine for doing the Daily Oral Language activity each morning, show students how to do each part followed by showing students how to do the whole routine together.

Responding to Diversity When Planning a Demonstration

- Increase the number of demonstrations.

- Emphasize or highlight important parts or steps in demonstrations with words ("Look carefully at what I do next. . . .") or with visual supports (highlighting key words in the list of steps written on the poster).

- Be sure to use consistent terms and phrasing when demonstrating self-talk and self-questioning.

- Point to steps on a written list as they are demonstrated.

- Show videotaped demonstrations of real applications.

A demonstration is an integral part of teaching information clearly and effectively. Teachers can use demonstrations before, during, or after explaining the information they teach. Remember that it is important to actually do the demonstration rather than to simply tell how to do it. You can increase student understanding about the information being taught by giving effective demonstrations, along with clear explanations.

Visual Supports

Using visual supports effectively is another critical teaching skill. Visual supports can increase the effectiveness of instruction by making information, explanations, and directions more comprehensible to learners. They are very helpful in teaching vocabulary, giving directions, building background knowledge, clarifying difficult concepts and strategies, and in providing scaffolds for new learning. Although visual supports are important in all lessons and are helpful to everyone, they are absolutely essential for students who have difficulty learning or who are learning English as a second language.

Categories of Visual Supports

The following four categories provide some idea of the broad range of visual supports from which to choose:

1. *Real objects, animals, people, working models, models, multimedia presentations, video or audio recordings, computer graphics, photographs, drawings, or maps.* Incorporating these as props in your instruction will help make new information more real and clear to students, especially

when they can see, hear, and touch what they are learning about.

2. *Gestures, demonstrations, or role plays.* These are especially helpful in teaching actions and procedures.

3. *Writings.* Providing information in writing so students can read it as well as hear the teacher speak it is very helpful to many learners. The teacher can use posters, a whiteboard, overhead transparencies, handouts, labels, books, magazines, newspapers, and computer text.

4. *Graphic organizers.* These are used to depict connections and relationships among ideas. Show graphics during instruction, or ask students to fill them in as part of brainstorming, during presentations, while reading, with peer partners or in groups, and as practice or evaluation activities. Examples of graphic organizers include outlines, concept maps, diagrams, webs, T-charts, story maps, word banks, Venn diagrams, compare and contrast charts, problem–solution–effect charts, note-taking guides, and so on.

Various visual supports can be combined during instruction. For example, when teaching students how to put together a completed circuit, the teacher can demonstrate using real objects and provide written directions with diagrams, as well as giving directions verbally.

Responding to Diversity When Planning Visual Supports

- Increase the number of visual supports used.
- Be sure that all students, including those who are English language learners, can understand wording on visual supports (for example, a list of steps for using the reading comprehension strategy).
- Use visual prompts (for example, color-code) to highlight essential information.
- Provide individual copies of the visual support (such as checklists of steps to follow for getting help) for students to have at their desks.
- Use pictures to supplement written words on a visual support. For example, include picture cues for behavior expectations written on a poster so that students can read and see what is expected.

Many sources for visual supports are available. They can be ordered from catalogs or borrowed from libraries, museums, and universities. Teachers can make files of photographs and drawings, and collect objects from garage sales. They can bookmark Internet sites and put photos, drawings, and diagrams on transparencies and slides. Computer software and the Internet have greatly expanded what is available to teachers. A visual support library can be a very valuable asset for teachers in any content area.

The importance of visual supports cannot be stressed enough. Visual supports can help teachers increase interest in the content they are teaching, and can help students "see the big picture" and organize information for learning. They can also make the difference between a lesson or activity that is understood and one that is not. Think carefully about appropriate visual supports as you plan lessons and activities.

Giving Directions for Tasks and Assignments

Teachers use directions to communicate to students the details regarding the assignment or task they are to complete or procedures they are to follow. Teachers give many directions to students throughout the school day and school year. They may need to give directions for how to complete seatwork assignments, projects, games, homework, and so on. They may give directions for routine tasks such as cleaning up or putting away the microscopes, or for procedures regarding earthquake drills.

Making Directions Clear

- Make wording clear and concise. For example, do not use more words than necessary and be sure to use words your students will understand.
- Make directions as short as possible. Avoid long, drawn-out explanations that students cannot follow.

- Present directions orally and in writing, use picture directions, and provide demonstrations of what students are to do.
- Emphasize key words in directions in oral directions ("Notice . . ." or "This is VERY important") and highlight them in written directions.
- Use numbers to emphasize the sequence of directions.
- Follow the directions with questions to check for understanding. Plan responses that require students to explain or demonstrate the directions. Do not simply ask, "Does everyone understand?"

Responding to Diversity When Giving Directions

The following suggestions may help English language learners or students with learning problems understand directions:

- Shorten and simplify directions.
- Give fewer directions at a time and have students repeat or paraphrase what they are to do (check for understanding).
- Cue directions with numbers (for example, "first" or "second") and gestures (showing one finger, then two).
- Emphasize key words with intonations in your voice and with gestures.
- Make the directions into a list of steps that students can check off as they complete each step.
- Check for understanding by asking specific questions to prevent cultural misunderstandings. Some students will say they understand the teacher's directions (even when they don't) to be respectful. Avoid asking, "Do you understand the directions?" Instead, ask a question like, "What is the first thing you should do?" (Zirpoli 2005).

Clear directions make an important contribution to the smooth running of a classroom. When students understand the directions they are given, teachers can avoid the confusion that leads to wasted time as students try to figure out what they are to do next. Careful advance planning of directions for lessons and activities will help ensure that they are clear and effective.

Summary

This chapter has been about critical teaching skills that impact the effectiveness of presenting information to students. These skills influence how information is actually explained and shown to students. Demonstrations and visual supports can have a major impact on the clarity of the information, vocabulary, and directions teachers present.

References and Suggested Reading

Boudah, D. J., B. K. Lenz, J. A. Bulgren, J. B. Schumaker, and D. D. Deshler. 2000. Don't water down! Enhance content learning through the unit organizer routine. *Teaching Exceptional Children* 32 (3): 48–56.

Boyle, J. R., and N. Yeager. 1997. Blueprints for learning: Using cognitive frameworks for understanding. *Teaching Exceptional Children* 29: 26–31.

Bromley, K., L. Irwin-DeVitis, and M. Modio. 1995. *Graphic organizers: Visual strategies for active learning.* New York: Scholastic Professional Books.

Colvin, G., and M. Lazar. 1997. *The effective elementary classroom.* Longmont, CO: Sopris West.

Cruickshank, D. R., D. B. Jenkins, and K. K. Metcalf. 2003. *The act of teaching,* 3rd ed. Boston: McGraw Hill.

DiSarno, N.J., M. Schowalter, and P. Grassa. 2002. Classroom amplification to enhance student performance. *Teaching Exceptional Children* 34 (6): 20–26.

Dye, G. A. 2000. Graphic organizers to the rescue! Help students link—and remember—information. *Teaching Exceptional Children* 32 (2): 72–76.

Echevarria, J., M. Vogt, and D. J. Short. 2004. *Making content comprehensible for English learners: The SIOP model.* Boston: Pearson.

Forte, I., and S. Schurr. 1996. *Graphic organizers & planning outlines for authentic instruction and assessment.* Nashville, TN: Incentive Publications.

Guillaume, A. M. 2004. K–12 *classroom teaching: A primer for new professionals,* 2nd ed. Columbus, OH: Merrill.

Kame'enui, E. J., D. W. Carnine, R. C. Dixon, D. C. Simmons, and M. D. Coyne. 2002. *Effective teaching strategies that accommodate diverse learners,* 2nd ed. Upper Saddle River: Merrill Prentice Hall.

Lewis, R. B., and D. H. Doorlag. 2006. *Teaching special students in general education classrooms.* Upper Saddle River: Pearson.

Luckner, J., S. Bowen, and K. Carter. 2001. Visual teaching strategies for students who are deaf or hard of hearing. *Teaching Exceptional Children* 33 (3): 38–44.

Mastropieri, M. S., and T. E. Scruggs. 2004. *The inclusive classroom: Strategies for effective instruction,* 2nd ed. Columbus, OH: Merrill.

Reed, B., and J. Railsback. 2003. *Strategies and resources for teachers of English language learners.* Portland, OR: NW Regional Educational Lab.

Salend, S. J., and A. Salinas. 2003. Language differences or learning difficulties: The work of the multidisciplinary team. *Teaching Exceptional Children* 35 (4): 36–43.

Zirpoli, T. J. 2005. *Behavior management: Applications for teachers,* 4th ed. Upper Saddle Rive, NJ: Pearson.

Critical Teaching Skills for Promoting Active Participation

Introduction

Active participation, also called active student responding (Salend 2005), and active student engagement (Cohen and Spenciner 2005), involves students in lessons or activities by talking, writing, or doing something—usually overt—that is directly related to the content of the lesson or activity. Any technique that a teacher uses to bring about the involvement of all students is an active participation strategy. Most lessons and activities eventually involve all students in active practice or processing of some sort. However, it is very important that teachers provide students with opportunities to actively respond right from the start.

Importance of Active Participation

Strategies for active participation provide students with opportunities to respond, and are valuable for several reasons. First, using these strategies keeps students engaged, making them more likely to learn, retain, and process the information presented. Next, various active participation strategies allow the teacher to check for understanding early and often during instruction. When students are involved in lessons or activities made interactive through the use of active participation strategies, they are also more likely to be attentive, less likely to be off task, and more likely to feel good about their competence (Lewis and Doorlag 2006). The use of these strategies is likely to make lessons and activities more fun and interesting for students and teachers.

Types of Strategies

Many kinds of active participation strategies can be incorporated into lessons or activities. Recognizing the variation of strategies in terms of their response type and purpose can help teachers select which strategies to use at various points throughout lessons and activities.

One way to think about active participation strategies is by the type of response they require. First, *written responses* involve writing answers on a chalkboard or "paper think pad" for example. Calling out answers or discussing main ideas with partners are examples of *oral responses.* Finally, *signal responses* include actions such as pointing or holding up cards.

Another way to think about active participation strategies is by their purpose. Most strategies can be loosely organized into three main categories. First, *involvement strategies* are designed to keep students alert and attentive. Second, *rehearsal strategies* are used to provide students with opportunities to practice or rehearse the information presented. Finally, *processing strategies* help increase comprehension by providing opportunities to think about, mull over, or discuss content to develop a deeper understanding of the material.

Many strategies serve several purposes. As you read through the following specific strategies, notice how various strategies easily fit into more than one category. For example, unison response can be both an involvement strategy and a rehearsal strategy. Notice also that some active participation strategies allow the teacher to check each student's understanding. The organization of strategies by response type and purpose is simply a general guideline to consider when selecting strategies. It is far more important to select an appropriate variety of strategies to use in your plans than it is to spend time trying to figure out in which category a strategy fits.

Note that teachers can use numerous strategies designed to elicit responses to teacher questions. Considering that teachers ask a large number of questions each day, it is very important to carefully consider how students will participate during question-asking situations. Be sure to select response strategies that will involve as many students as possible during these sessions. An important point must be made here: The act of asking a question is not an active participation strategy, whereas the strategy used for getting a response from students can be.

Involvement Strategies

A major goal of involvement strategies is to keep students alert and attentive during instruction. The following are some examples of how to achieve this goal:

1. Ask for *unison responses* from the whole class or from rows or groups. Say, "The name of this river is . . . Everyone?" Make sure that everyone is, in fact, responding.

2. Ask students to *use response cards.* Say, "When you hear one of the new words in the story, hold up that card."

3. Ask students to *write a response.* Say, "On your list, check off the steps for resolving conflicts as I model them."

Strategies 1, 2, and 3 work well as response strategies when questions or requests require brief responses.

4. Have students *stand to share answers* (Kagan 1992). When students have an answer, have them stand up. Call on one student to share the answer. Have everyone with the same or similar answer sit down. Students continue to answer until everyone is sitting down.

5. Have students do *choral reading* of content text as an alternative to "round-robin" reading. Students can read whole sentences or paragraphs as a group. Teachers can stop at various places and have students fill in words or phrases when they are reading.

6. Have students *take notes* during teacher presentations, speeches, films, or readings. Skilled note-takers can write their own notes; provide others with partially completed notes.

7. Use covert strategies such as a *"think-about"* or *visual imagery.* For example, say to the students, "Imagine for a minute what it would feel like to be teased about the color of your skin," or "Think about a time when you helped a friend." Use visual imagery by asking students to "picture" something in their minds (for example, "Try to imagine how the ferocious lion looked.").

8. Use a *"think-to-write preview"* to get students thinking about today's topic. Give students three minutes to write down everything they know about the topic.

9. *Brainstorming,* followed by the teacher calling on individuals randomly, gives students an opportunity to participate.

Rehearsal Strategies

The goal of rehearsal strategies is to give students a chance to practice or rehearse new information. The following are some examples of how to achieve this goal:

10. Ask a question, and then ask students to *say the answer to their neighbor.*

11. Ask partners to *take turns* summarizing, defining terms, or giving examples.

Strategies 10 and 11 work well when you ask questions that require somewhat longer answers. They are also effective when many students are eager to speak but there is not enough time to call on each student individually.

12. Ask everyone to *write down an answer* on paper, on a small blackboard, or on a dry-erase board. Then have them hold it up so you can see it. For example, tell everyone to write an adjective that describes your chair.

13. Ask students to respond using student *response cards* or other objects. Say, "Hold up the green card if the word is a noun," or "Hold up the isosceles triangle" (Heward et al. 1996).

14. Ask for *finger signals* from everyone. Guillaume suggests, for instance, that "Students hold up numbers of fingers to respond to mastery questions (e.g., 'How many sides on a triangle?'). Other gestures can also be used. For instance, 'I will watch while you draw a triangle in the air'" (2004, 51), "As I point to each number, put thumbs up if you would round upward."

Strategies 12–14 work well when questions require brief answers. Notice that in addition to promoting active participation, they allow you to check the understanding of all students.

15. Use the *pausing technique* (Guerin and Male 1988; Salend 1998). Stop for two minutes after every five to seven minutes of lecturing. Have students discuss and review their notes and the content presented (they can rehearse important points or discuss how the information relates to their own experiences, for example).

16. Use *drill partners* to work on facts students need to know until they are certain both partners know and remember them all (Johnson, Johnson, and Holubec 1991).

17. Have *board workers* work together to answer questions. Have each student play a role: one student is the Answer Suggester; one acts as Checker to see if everyone agrees; and one is the Writer (Johnson, Johnson, and Holubec 1991).

Processing Strategies

The goal of processing strategies is to allow students the opportunity to think about new information. The following are some examples of how to achieve this goal:

18. Ask students to think about the answer to a question. Have them then discuss the answer with their neighbor. Call on pairs to share their answers, such as in *Think-Pair-Share* (Lyman 1992).

19. Two students become *Worksheet Checkers* and complete a worksheet together. One student is the reader (reads the question and suggests an answer) and the other is the writer (agrees with the answer or comes up with a new one). When both students agree, the answer is written in on the worksheet (Johnson, Johnson, and Holubec 1991).

20. Ask a question, and then ask students to share and discuss their answers in small groups, such as in *Buzz Groups* (Arends 2004).

21. Ask a question, and then call on individual team members to answer, such as in *Numbered Heads Together.* After you ask a question, the students in each team (who have numbered off) put their heads together and make sure everyone knows the answer. Then, call out a number and students with that number provide answers to the whole group (Kagan 1992).

Strategies 18–21 are especially effective when the content you are teaching is complicated or difficult. They also work well when you want long and varied responses. Keep groups accountable for involving all members by asking the students to record all answers, to defend their method of reaching consensus, or tell them that you may pick one student at random to speak for the group or pair.

22. "*Bookends* is a cooperative learning strategy whereby students meet in small groups before listening to an oral presentation to share their existing knowledge about the topic to be presented. The groups also generate questions related to the topic, and these questions are discussed during or after the oral presentations" (Salend 1998, 231). This technique could also be used with a group discussion or a videotape presentation.

23. Have students complete a *think-to-write review* in which they write what they learned. Give students three to five minutes to write down everything they learned in the lesson or activity just taught.

In summary, many strategies are designed to get all students in the class to respond at once, to have *everyone* actively participating. You may ask students to say, write, or signal their responses. These active participation strategies encourage attentiveness, provide immediate practice, and encourage students to think about new ideas. Some of these strategies also help you monitor progress by checking the understanding of each student (see Chapter 7). Set a goal to use a variety of active participation strategies and to use them frequently in all lessons and activities.

Responding to Diversity When Planning for Active Participation

As with all teaching and management practices, you need to consider the diversity in your classroom as you design active participation strategies. Think about skill diversity, cultural diversity, and linguistic diversity.

Responding to Skill Diversity When Planning for Active Participation

Consider the following ideas addressing classroom diversity when planning opportunities to respond:

- Increase the number of involvement strategies for students who have difficulty sitting and listening. For example, use frequent choral responses during fast-paced instruction.

- Look around to make sure everyone really is participating during unison and signaled responses. Use proximity or prompts with students who aren't responding.

- Use a variety of response strategies to increase interest and motivation. For example, students can answer questions using choral responses, writing on a whiteboard, or telling a partner.

- Allow students to help plan various physical gestures or signals to be used in lessons or activities. This can be motivating (Salend 2005).

- Provide opportunities to respond in nonverbal ways for students who may be uncomfortable or unable to respond verbally.

- When using strategies that require written responses, match the length of the responses to students' writing skills.

- Use preprinted response cards for students who have difficulty writing.

- Vary the amount of wait-time given. Don't mistake a hesitation to respond as a sign that a student does not know that answer. Students may need extended wait-time, particularly for questions with complicated answers. Response time may also vary with cultural experience.

- Plan how to regain attention, or how to have students show they are ready to go on (for example, they will look at you or put their pencils down).

Responding to Cultural Diversity When Planning for Active Participation

As you plan active participation strategies (and discussions, brainstorming sessions, and questioning techniques) consider the following student variables:

- Students' comfort levels with stating opinions, stating opinions passionately, and disagreeing with others, including the teacher

- Students' comfort level with volunteering to answer questions or initiating their own questions or comments

- Experience with divergent or open-ended questions

- Beliefs as to what constitutes polite responses to questions or statements, and methods of interrupting

- Beliefs about how much talking is polite

- Students' comfort with same-gender partners

Responding to English Language Learners When Planning for Active Participation

The following strategies can benefit your students as they learn English:

1. Encourage the participation of English language learners by asking *yes* and *no* questions at first. As language acquisition increases, intersperse

more difficult questions such as *who, what, when, why, where,* and *how* (Gersten, Baker, and Marks 1998).

2. Provide students who are English language learners with opportunities to practice their English skills as they answer questions. When appropriate, ask questions that require long, complex sentences rather than one or two words. Remember that English language learners can use complex thinking skills even when they are not fluent in English (Gersten, Baker, and Marks 1998).

3. Pair English language learners with positive peer language models. Both English speakers and students who speak the same native language can be excellent models. This support can provide a safe environment for discussing new learning. Students who are uncomfortable speaking to the entire class may readily speak to a neighbor or small group.

Number of Strategies to Include

When planning lessons and activities, strive to frequently use active participation strategies. Cegalka and Berdine (1995) suggest that teachers plan for students to respond in some way, several times during each minute of a lesson. The three-statement rule—the teacher will make no more than three statements without having students make a response—typifies the importance of student participation during lecture presentations (Christenson, Ysseldyke, and Thurlow 1989).

It may be impossible, impractical, or unnecessary to try to specify an exact number of responding opportunities to include in any lesson or activity. Instead, consider (1) using strategies during all parts of the lesson or activity (the opening, closing, and all parts in between); (2) using numerous strategies that focus on the key ideas you are trying to emphasize (have students say the main points to a partner, for example); and (3) adjusting the number of strategies based on student learning and behavior (if you notice that many students are confused, increase their opportunities to rehearse or process information). In summary, remember that having students actively rehearse information will help ensure the transfer of that information into long-term memory.

Active Participation and Hands-On Activities

We want to make a distinction between active participation strategies and hands-on activities. Both provide students an opportunity to be involved during lessons and activities, but they do so at different times. By nature, hands-on activities promote active participation, but active participation strategies do not usually include a hands-on activity.

Having students paint a picture of a story's main character or create a color wheel for subsequent lessons are examples of hands-on activities. Having students choral respond, say answers to a partner, or discuss main ideas with a small group are examples of active participation strategies. Students are involved in all of the activities and strategies mentioned; however, notice the difference between the hands-on activities and active participation strategies themselves. The hands-on activity is the end in itself, whereas active participation strategies are part of the means to the end.

Calling on Individuals

Calling on individuals is not, of course, an active participation strategy because all students are involved at once in active participation strategies. Teachers sometimes choose to call on individuals, however. They may occasionally use a repetitive question-and-response pattern: the teacher asks the question and calls on a student to answer, the teacher asks another question and calls on another student to answer, and so on. When this technique is used only one student participates at a time. It is common practice for teachers to call on individuals to answer questions, but it is not appropriate to use this method extensively or exclusively given all of the reasons discussed previously.

When using the calling-on-individuals technique, however, some things can be done to make it more effective. The goal is to keep the rest of the class engaged and accountable. The following ideas will help you achieve this goal:

1. Ask a question, pause, then call on a student by name, rather than saying, "Ben, what is the definition of . . . ?" This encourages all students to think of the definition, not just Ben.

2. Call on nonvolunteers randomly. If a student knows he could be called on at anytime, he is more likely to be attentive. Here are some ideas to make your selection random:
   - Draw cards or sticks (tongue depressors or ice-cream bar sticks) with student names on them.
   - Use a seating chart or class list.
   - Assign each student a number and draw numbers.
   - Using a spinner board, call on the student whose name the spinner lands on.
   - Tell the class in advance that you will be calling on nonvolunteers and allow them to pass if they choose. The purpose is to keep all students attentive and to send the message that you want to hear from everyone—even those in the back row.
   - Because you may want to select certain students to answer certain questions, do not hesitate to intersperse nonrandom with random selection of students. Sometimes a student is very excited about a topic and bursting to respond. By all means, call on him (Delpit and White-Bradley 2003).
   - Calling on an individual only allows you to check her understanding. If you are trying to assess the understanding of the group, this won't work. You'll need to use other strategies. When those strategies (asking students to signal a response or holding up a written response, for example) don't fit, then you can sample the group's understanding by calling on several selected students. Don't call on volunteers. Instead, call on students who represent a range of knowledge and skill in the topic you are teaching.

3. Develop a system that allows you to keep track of students who have been called on so you don't inadvertently leave students out. Here are some suggestions:
   - If you use a class list or seating chart, put a check by students' names as they answer.
   - Imagine the class divided into quadrants and call on a student from the first quadrant, then the second, and so on.
   - Develop a system to replace name sticks in the can or name cards in the deck so you remember who you've called on (replace them upside down, for example).
   - Don't lay drawn name sticks or cards aside after you have called on a student. It does not take long for students to realize that once they have been called on, they are off the hook until everyone has been called on to answer.
   - Remember that the purpose of calling on students at random is to keep everyone involved and on their toes. Keeping track of who has answered is another way that you can help students be accountable. It also keeps *you* accountable for equitable participation of all students. If students are permitted to call out answers rather than required to raise hands, keep track of (or ask someone else to keep track of) who is responding. If some students are consistently left out, rethink the use of this method.
   - It is never appropriate to call on nonattending students with the intent of embarrassing them. If you call on a nonattending student as a management technique, then prompt the student by repeating the question.
   - When you call on volunteers, avoid calling only on the same few students who raise their hands quickly. Increase the wait-time between when you ask the question and when you call on someone to answer.

A variety of strategies will help keep the rest of the class engaged and attentive when you choose to call on individuals rather than use active participation strategies.

Summary

Students should be given opportunities to respond early and often in lessons and activities. This is a very important critical teaching skill. The kind of strategies that you select for any given part of your plan depends on the needs of the students. For example, if your students need opportunities to process information presented, then use a strategy such as Numbered Heads Together. Select a strategy such as written responses so that you can monitor individual student understanding. In all cases, your goal should be to select a meaningful variety of strategies to use as you provide students with frequent opportunities to respond.

References and Suggested Readings

Arends, R. I. 2004. *Learning to teach.* 6th ed. San Francisco: McGraw-Hill.

Cegalka, P. T., and W. H. Berdine. 1995. *Effective instruction for students with learning difficulties.* Boston: Allyn and Bacon.

Christenson, S. L., J. E. Ysseldyke, and M. L. Thurlow. 1989. Critical instructional factors for students with mild handicaps: An integrative review. *Remedial and Special Education* 10 (5): 21–29.

Cohen, L., and L. J. Spenciner. 2005. *Teaching students with mild and moderate disabilities: Research-based practices.* Upper Saddle River: Pearson.

Delpit, L., and P. White-Bradley. 2003. Educating or imprisoning the spirit: Lessons from ancient Egypt. *Theory into Practice* 42 (4): 283–288.

Gersten, R., S. K. Baker, and S. U. Marks. 1998. *Teaching English-language learners with learning difficulties: Guiding principles and examples from research-based practice.* U.S. Department of Education: ERIC/OSEP Special Project.

Guerin, G. R., and M. Male. 1988. *Models of best teaching practices.* Paper presented at the meeting of the Council for Exceptional Children, Washington, DC.

Guillaume, A. M. 2004. *Classroom teaching: A primer for new professionals.* 2nd ed. Upper Saddle River: Merrill.

Heward, W. L., R. Gardner, R. A. Cavanaugh, F. H. Courson, T. A. Grossi, and P. M. Barbetta. 1996. Everyone participates in this class. *Teaching Exceptional Children* 28 (2): 4–10.

Johnson, D. W., R. T. Johnson, and E. J. Holubec. 1991. *Cooperation in the classroom.* Edina, MN: Interaction Book.

Kagan, S. 1992. *Cooperative learning.* San Juan Capistrano, CA: Kagan Cooperative Learning.

Kern, L., and G. Sacks. 2003. *How to deal effectively with inappropriate talking and noisemaking.* Austin, TX: Pro-Ed.

Lewis, R. B., and D. H. Doorlag. 2006. *Teaching special students in general education classrooms.* 7th ed. Upper Saddle River, N.J.: Pearson/Merrill Prentice Hall.

Lewis, T. J., S. I. Hudson, M. Richter, and N. Johnson. 2004. Scientifically supported practices in emotional and behavioral disorders: A proposed approach and brief review of current practices. *Behavioral Disorders* 29 (3): 247–259.

Lyman, F. T., Jr. 1992. Think-pair-share, thinktrix, thinklinks, and weird facts: An interactive system for cooperative thinking. In *Enhancing thinking through cooperative learning,* eds. N. Davidson and T. Worsham, 169–181. New York: Teachers College Press.

Mastropieri, M. S., and T. E. Scruggs. 2004. *The inclusive classroom: Strategies for effective instruction.* Upper Saddle River, New Jersey: Merrill.

Salend, S. J. 1998. *Effective mainstreaming.* Columbus, Ohio: Merrill.

Salend, S. J. 2005. *Creating inclusive classrooms: Effective and reflective practices for all students.* 5th ed. Upper Saddle River, New Jersey: Pearson/Merrill Prentice Hall.

Critical Teaching Skills for Planning Practice and Monitoring Student Progress

Introduction

This chapter is about planning practice and monitoring student progress. We are presenting these topics together because they are related in several ways. First, student practice activities provide opportunities for teachers to monitor practice progress. In this chapter, you will learn about different types of practice, their purposes, and how to set them up so they are effective. You will also learn about various types of monitoring activities, some of which occur during the lesson and some of which occur at the end of the lesson.

Practice and monitoring also both provide teachers with necessary information to determine what to do next. For example, if teachers notice that many students are making mistakes when they monitor student practice, they will most likely go back and teach some more. Or, they could decide that more practice is needed. On the other hand, if they notice that nearly all students are being successful with the practice, they will likely decide to go on to the next lesson and provide some additional assistance to any students who need it.

Planning Practice

One key to student success in learning new information and skills is having the opportunity for adequate practice. When students first learn, teachers look for them to be accurate with the new information. Once students are accurate, additional practice helps develop fluency that is necessary for easier generalization to new settings and situations. Fluency is also a major factor in whether or not students will use the new information. Some practice opportunities help students become accurate; others help students become fluent; still others are designed to promote application of the knowledge or skill. In this way, practice serves different purposes.

Practice activities are designed based on feedback the teacher receives from the students as they work through the new material. For example, when students are first learning, it is important that the teacher carefully checks progress to make sure that students are not practicing errors. Once students are accurate in their work, the teacher can provide additional practice without such close supervision, such as seatwork or homework. In all cases, teachers use feedback from student progress to determine whether they need more instruction or more or less practice.

Student Practice

Students are generally asked to engage in many different types of practice activities throughout the course of a day or week. Sometimes these activities occur in class as *seatwork*. For example, if students are practicing a computation skill such as how to multiply fractions, they will most likely practice computing problems on a worksheet. If students are learning how to interrupt politely, then role plays are appropriate. A presentation in front of the class would be an authentic appropriate practice activity for students who are learning group presentation skills. Working with a partner on some kind of a project would be appropriate for students who are practicing how to work together. Sometimes practice activities occur out of class as *homework;* for example, a student may play the first 25 measures of the newly learned musical piece on her flute or conduct a diet survey with members of her family. In summary, teachers provide many different types of specific activities for student practice; the variety of activities relates to the variety in learning outcomes.

Teacher Support

Teacher supervision and feedback regarding student performance in practice activities are key to making practice sessions effective. The amount of supervision needed varies with student learning. When students are first learning a new skill or information, teachers should monitor their practice closely to make sure they are not practicing errors. Once students are accurate with the new information, they can practice with less teacher supervision. When students practice out of class, they don't have immediate teacher support. Feedback will be delayed, that is, the teacher will check the homework assignment and give feedback later. The following are two common types of practice that vary in their level of teacher support.

Supervised Practice

Supervised practice is an essential type of in-class practice in many lessons and activities. Students practice with direct, fairly continuous supervision from the teacher after he has presented necessary information about the skill or knowledge to be learned. Teachers use supervised practice when students are first learning new information. The practice activities that teachers use for supervised practice are varied, but all involve direct supervision and immediate feedback (for example, the teacher checks the problems students are completing on a worksheet and gives feedback). Effective supervised practice activities allow the teacher to see if the students are learning.

Teachers can use various levels of supervised practice and each has a different purpose. The following are three levels of supervised practice:

1. *Whole-group supervised practice* After the teacher has demonstrated the new skill numerous times and has checked to see that students understand the various parts of the new skill, she now involves the whole class in practicing the whole skill, that is, all parts together. For example, she may say, "Let's all do a problem together; what should I do first? Second?" or "Say the whole formula. . . everyone?". Notice that the teacher is checking student knowledge of the learning as it is described in the objective. This helps her determine if the students are learning the whole skill. Whole-group practice offers support for the rehearsal of new learning when students are not yet accurate or confident alone.

Note that whole-group supervised practice may not always be possible. For example, let's say that you are teaching a social skill lesson where the objective is to perform a social skill. The performance would need to occur in a role play or authentic situation and it would not be feasible for the teacher to monitor and provide feedback to everyone at once.

2. *Small-group or partner supervised practice* The second level of supervised practice involves asking students to practice with the support of peers while the teacher monitors and provides feedback. Students must be told exactly how to work together (for example, "Partner 1 will circle the errors, and Partner 2 will correct the errors; then switch roles for the second sentence").

The first two levels of supervised practice provide a bridge between teacher presentations and demonstrations and individual practice. This means that initial attempts to perform or express the learned information have peer, as well as teacher, support. This is a form of scaffolding.

3. *Individual supervised practice* The final and essential level involves asking each student to practice alone while the teacher monitors and corrects. The key here is that the teacher monitors and provides feedback. He does not wait until a student raises her hand, but rather checks everyone. Note: If the skill being learned is something like "how to share," then individual supervised practice will involve working with a partner. This is, of course, because one cannot share alone—this type of skill has to occur in interaction with others.

The third level provides the teacher with an opportunity to see what students can do individually (not independently). This is the only required type of supervised practice and it is an extremely important one. It provides the teacher with information needed to determine what to do next. If students perform accurately during the individual practice phase, then the teacher knows that she may move ahead. If students have difficulty at this stage, the teacher knows to go back and reteach.

The three levels of supervised practice allow for flexibility in planning the rehearsal of new information. The essential individual supervised practice portion gives all students an opportunity to receive feedback on their own progress. When the new knowledge or skill is especially difficult or complex, or if prior checks for understanding show that students are struggling, the teacher will probably want to use whole-class, small-group, or partner practice prior to individual practice.

Note that individual supervised practice is *not* the formal evaluation, although it is like the formal evaluation in that the skill practiced is congruent with the objective (and the instruction). This practice is designed as an opportunity for each student to receive performance feedback from the teacher and is a step toward the objective. It is also an opportunity to build high levels of accuracy and fluency before moving to extended practice. During the evaluation portion of the lesson, however, students must perform the objective individually and independently, without the help of peers or the teacher. The evaluation follows the instruction and practice.

Responding to Skill Diversity When Planning Supervised Practice

- Provide more structure and cues at first (such as an outline of a letter showing where to write the date, the greeting, and the other parts).
- Use similar examples for initial practice. Gradually change to more difficult or less similar examples.
- Provide error drills. When you notice that students are making a specific error repeatedly, provide feedback and then additional practice on the correct way.
- Increase the amount of initial practice with teacher support (for example, "Say it with me," or "Do it with me."). Some students will need more practice than others.
- Check on students you think might have difficulty, but do not spend too much time with any one student.
- Increase the amount of initial practice with peer support by using more partner or small-group situations. Remember that although individual supervised practice is the only required type of supervised practice, partner and small-group practice can provide very necessary scaffolding for some students.
- Structure small-group and partner practice by teaching students how to work together (see Chapter 8 for more information).
- Increase the amount of immediate feedback.

Responding to English Language Learners When Planning Supervised Practice

- Decide if it would be advantageous or possible to partner same-language speakers for practice.
- Consider providing longer periods of group- and partner-supported practice.
- Let students practice without being corrected for speaking errors that do not impact the new learning.
- Try to build in as much listening, speaking, reading, and writing practice as possible.

Supervised practice is one of the most important steps in helping students learn. It mirrors the instruction it follows, and provides students with an excellent way to practice. The individual supervised practice piece allows each student a way to receive feedback from the teacher. The teacher is able to see which students are accurate and which students are not. It also provides the teacher with the information needed about whether or not to move ahead or go back and reteach. Supervised practice is an essential step toward evaluation.

Extended Practice

Extended practice is another part of the lesson where the teacher plans opportunities for students to practice what they are learning. The purpose of this practice is to help students deepen their understanding, develop high levels of accuracy and fluency, and/or help students generalize the new information. Extended practice provides less direct support for students than does supervised practice. Whereas during supervised practice, the teacher monitors the practice directly and continuously, the teacher support in extended practice is less direct and less continuous. It is important that it be used only when students have shown that they are accurate and somewhat fluent with the new information. Generally, the teacher moves to extended practice only when it is obvious that the students will be successful with less support.

Teachers can provide extended practice for students in a variety of ways. First, students may be given an additional in-class practice activity, such as additional paragraphs to read and then summarize, or role plays to practice "taking no for an answer." Secondly, students can be given out-of-class activities (homework), such as additional algebra problems to compute. Extended practice activities vary in what students will actually be doing, but they are all designed to provide additional practice on the information presented.

One purpose of extended practice is to help prepare students for the evaluation portion of the lesson. Teacher feedback is an essential part of any activities used for practice (see more information about monitoring and feedback later on in this chapter). When students turn in their homework assignment, for example, the teacher must look carefully at the assignment to see whether or not students were successful. When students do role plays, the teacher will observe them carefully, make suggestions, and give positive performance compliments. In all cases, teachers should communicate the results of their examinations to students so they know how they are progressing. This careful examination of student performance helps teachers decide whether the students need more extended practice or more instruction. Once a teacher is satisfied that students have been successful in extended practice, she will move the lesson to evaluation.

A Special Note about In-Class Practice Activities

Cegelka and Berdine (1995) state that students spend anywhere from 50 percent to 70 percent of the school day in independent activities. When you consider the importance of opportunities to respond in student learning, then it follows that students need to be provided with opportunities for active engagement in practice. The following suggestions can help you plan effective in-class practice activities:

- Explain the purpose of the seatwork practice so that students will know why they are doing it.
- Be sure directions are clearly stated and written, and carefully check for understanding.
- Move around quickly at the beginning to make sure each student gets started quickly.
- Don't just wander; look carefully at each student's work, not just those who raise their hands.
- It may be best to have students complete just a few items before correcting their work.
- Use peers to help monitor ("Compare your answers to questions 1 and 2 with your partner and let me know if they are different.").
- Once students begin working on seatwork, stop and reteach or reexplain when you notice that many students are asking the same questions. Getting the whole group together again will save you time.

Providing Effective Practice Using Role Plays

When practicing communication skills, social and emotional skills, or classroom routines and rules, role plays can provide performance practice. The following suggestions can help you plan effective practice (see Chapter 18 for additional ideas).

- In role plays, be sure each student has the opportunity to take the lead role. If students are practicing making apologies, then each student must *make* an apology.

- Use a variety of scenarios for role plays so students see the various applications of the skill.

- Get ideas for scenarios from students to make sure they are relevant to students' lives.

- Provide support for success in role playing the skill correctly. Coaching, opportunities for rehearsing with peers, and steps written on posters can help.

- If a student makes an error during a role play, stop him immediately, correct the error, and let him do the role play again.

A Special Note about Out-of-Class Practice Activities

Remember that in extended practice, as we are using the term here, students are doing additional practice of the new skill or knowledge rather than acquiring new information, such as reading a chapter of a social studies text. Consider the following when planning out-of-class activities:

- Consider the resources that are available to students at home. Be sure that students are accurate enough with the new information that they can do the homework without help.

- Homework assignments should be work that students can complete successfully. They should be considered practice, not a continuation of instruction (Arends 2004).

- Vary the amount of practice assigned based on student need. Some students need a lot of practice, whereas others need very little.

- Provide incentives for homework completion.

- Go over homework directions and begin the assignment during class. Be sure the task is the same or similar to supervised practice (Salend and Gajria 1995).

- When assigning homework, tell students the purpose of the assignment, directions for completion, due date, required format, needed materials, and source of help (Wood 2006).

- Devise a system to let parents know what their students are to do at home.

- Start a homework club. Regardless of where the club meets (school, library, community agency) or who supervises the students (teacher, social worker, college students), make its main purpose to support a school's efforts to help struggling learners succeed (Sanacore 2002).

- Don't just check off that the homework was turned in. Be sure it was complete and accurate.

Responding to Diversity When Planning Extended Practice

Some of the most challenging times in the classroom can be when students are expected to work independently. You can help students be successful by building in meaningful adjustments to extended practice activities. The following are some examples:

- Reduce the length of each practice session, but provide more sessions.

- Provide varying amounts of homework based on a realistic idea of what each student can finish. Some students can complete more than others (Wood 2006).

- Change the task without changing the content to avoid boredom during a practice session. For example, have students select an answer versus writing an answer; have them write the answer on paper, the blackboard, or a transparency; or have them use computer practice programs.

- Make the practice interesting and fun (for example, use a game format). This applies to both seatwork and homework.

- Increase the amount of support during practice (study guides, peer tutors, and visual supports such as posters and desktop number lines, for example).

- Set up a homework Web site (Salend et al. 2004). This can be of benefit to both students and their parents. Students can double-check assignments and parents can know what their students are being asked to do.

- When possible, provide authentic practice in context as part of real tasks. For example, when students are practicing lining up, let them practice when they must line up to transition to another room.
- Recruit parents to serve as "homework coaches" to their children. The coach can look over assignments, monitor homework completion, and review finished work for accuracy and neatness (Wright 2004).
- Encourage students to submit assignments online (Salend et al. 2004). This eliminates having to keep track of papers.
- Teach a strategy for homework completion, such as the PROJECT Strategy (Hughes et al. 2002).
- Give directions for homework assignments at a reading level appropriate for your students. Use picture cues when possible. This is especially beneficial for students who are English language learners and students who have difficulty reading.

Teachers can use varying types of activities to help students practice the material they are learning. Examples of practice activities include setting up an experiment to test the effect of gravitational pull, playing and replaying one section of a piano sonata, role-playing how to ask for help, drawing various types of angles with a protractor, and writing answers to addition problems on a whiteboard. Prepare some practice activities to be completed in class and others out of class. More direct supervision is provided during in-class activities than for homework. All practice activities should help students work toward the learning outcome that is planned in the lesson or activity objective.

Monitoring Student Progress

When teachers begin to prepare lessons and activities, they start by selecting important content in a particular content area from state standards, national content standards, individual education program (IEP) objectives, and district curriculum guides (see Chapter 1 for more information). The teachers then try to determine what their students already know about the topic through the use of varying assessment methods. Sometimes this assessment is informal. For example, teachers could try to get a general idea of what their students already know about intersecting angles by examining the curriculum that students have moved through. Teachers might also use a more formal test, such as a survey-level test that gives them a general overview of students' skills or knowledge (Howell, Hosp, and Hosp, forthcoming). Teachers generally follow this survey-level test with a specific-level test that gives them very specific information about prior knowledge. The important thing to remember about assessment is that it helps teachers prepare relevant, appropriate objectives and related lessons and activities. This is why assessment is such an important place to start in instructional planning.

Once the objective and the lesson or activity plan has been written, you are ready to teach and monitor student progress. Monitoring allows both you and your students to know how they are progressing. It is imperative that you set up opportunities during lessons and activities to help you determine whether or not the students are grasping the desired learning. After all, that is the purpose of your planning. You need to know whether or not your students are progressing toward the objective and when they have met it. It is equally important that you let your students know how they are progressing by giving them useful feedback.

Terminology Used in Monitoring Progress

Various terms and concepts are key to better understanding the monitoring process. Because there is variation in the usage of these terms, we are going to define terms the way they will be used in this book. Also, we list resources at the end of this chapter that provide more in-depth reading on these topics.

The first terms are *assessment* and *evaluation*. Sometimes the term *assessment* is used to describe the process of trying to determine what students already know about a topic before instruction, whereas the term *evaluation* refers to the process of monitoring progress during and after instruction. These two terms are often used interchangeably and that is how we will use them too. For example, one can evaluate or assess progress before and during lessons and activities. Both terms mean that the teacher is trying to determine what students already know, what they are learning, and what they learned.

The terms *formative evaluation* and *summative evaluation* refer to when the evaluation occurs. Teachers conduct formative evaluation (or assessment) once the lesson or activity is started to see if students are learning. A teacher moving about the room looking at her students' performance on a seatwork assignment is an example of formative evaluation. Teachers conduct summative evaluation after instruction or at the end of the lesson or activity to determine whether or not the students have learned. When teachers observe the final role plays in a social skill lesson, they are performing summative evaluation, because the role plays were part of the lesson objective. Both types of evaluation play an important role in helping teachers know if students are learning or have learned.

Alternative assessment or *authentic assessment* are terms used to describe methods that are unlike traditional testing done through paper and pencil tests. This type of assessment is one where a student is asked to demonstrate new learning in a real-life setting. *Performance assessments* are a type of alternative assessment in which a student shows what she knows by carrying out an activity or producing a product (Kauchak and Eggen 2003). Examples of alternative assessment activities include (1) a teacher observing a student's use of the newly learned reading strategy during a content reading time; and (2) students writing short stories to be made into books that will be given to younger students.

Formative Evaluation

Formative evaluation happens prior to the evaluation of the objective (summative evaluation). Formative evaluation allows teachers to see whether or not students are progressing successfully toward the objective. It also allows teachers to determine what to do next, whether or not to go back and teach more. Students benefit from formative evaluation because they receive important feedback on their performances. When teachers use effective formative evaluation techniques, they preserve valuable instructional time by preventing students from practicing errors.

Teachers can monitor student progress during the lesson or activity in several ways. Monitoring during initial instruction (checking for understanding) and careful monitoring of practice activities where students work with varying amounts of teacher support (supervised and extended practice), can be used to determine whether or not students are learning.

Checks for Understanding

Checks for understanding (CFU) are monitoring opportunities that, when done correctly, provide teachers with excellent ways to evaluate whether students are learning. Teachers should conduct checks for understanding early in both lessons and activities and continue them at appropriate times throughout (when content needs to be rehearsed or when directions are given, for example). Because of their importance, these strategies should be noted directly in the written plan.

Checks for understanding are most reliable when students respond overtly in some way. This response allows teachers to actually see or hear whether students are on the right track. Teachers can effectively use many types of active participation strategies as checks for understanding. Answering questions verbally, showing thumbs up or thumbs down in response to questions, writing information on pieces of scratch paper, and holding up response cards are examples of overt responses that could help teachers monitor for student understanding and progress during a lesson or activity.

The following are examples of using checks for understanding:

- In a lesson where students are learning how to do double-digit addition with regrouping in the ones column, the teacher has all students work each step of the problem on a whiteboard and hold it up for teacher viewing.
- When students follow a series of directions for setting up the science experiment, the teacher moves around the room and looks at the work of all groups of students after they do each step.
- After being shown how to find a line of symmetry, the teacher quickly moves around the room checking to see that students are accurate in completing each step of the task analysis for drawing a line of symmetry of a variety of shapes.
- A transition from one part of the lesson to another requires that students follow a series of directions. Before students begin the transition,

the teacher calls on selected students (nonvolunteers) to check that students know what to do. She is hoping that those students are representative of the entire class.

The most effective CFUs are those that monitor the understanding of every student at once, for example, having each student write an answer on a whiteboard. When you call on a student to answer a question, you can only know the understanding of that one student (see Chapter 6 for many ideas about how to provide opportunities to respond to many or all of your students at once). When you prepare the questions you want to use for your checks for understanding, also carefully plan the response strategies that will provide you with information about every student's progress.

Note that whole-group supervised practice is much like whole-group checks for understanding but with one main difference. A whole-group check for understanding is used to determine whether or not students understand the various pieces of the skill being learned (for example, "Work the first step of the problem on your whiteboard and I'll check it."). Whole-group supervised practice is used when students practice all of the steps together (for example, "Work the first problem on your whiteboard and I'll check it."). Both monitoring activities serve different purposes, but play an equally important role in monitoring student learning.

Supervised and Extended Practice

A second way to conduct formative evaluation is through careful monitoring of practice opportunities that teachers provide for students. Specific activities (worksheets, role plays) within the supervised and extended practice portions of a lesson are examples of these opportunities. Remember that these practice opportunities occur both in and out of the classroom. The following are some examples of monitoring practice activities:

- Students complete a five-paragraph essay as an extended practice homework assignment. The teacher reads each essay and provides written feedback about how each student's work matches up with the essay rubric.

- Following a supervised practice activity where groups of students wrote topic sentences for sets of supporting detail sentences, individual students are given a handout that contains five more sets of supporting detail sentences. The teacher moves around the room and checks each student's work, giving feedback as necessary.

- Students work with a partner on a math game for supervised practice writing number sentences. The teacher checks in with students as they work.

- Students demonstrate speaking up when a peer is being bullied. The teacher observes carefully and provides feedback.

Summative Evaluation

Teachers use summative evaluation to compare student performance to the standard of performance outlined in the lesson or activity objective; the evaluation should match the objective exactly. Summative evaluation for a lesson may occur at the end of a single lesson; summative evaluation for an activity will generally take place after a longer period of time, that is, a week or month, or six months. Whereas formative evaluation helps the teacher determine whether or not students are moving toward the objective, summative evaluation tells the teacher whether or not the students have mastered the objective. The information gained from summative evaluation procedures provides the teacher with important information with which to make future instructional decisions.

In the evaluation section of a lesson plan, which describes the plan for summative evaluation, the teacher writes a clear description of the method that will accurately determine whether or not the students have mastered the lesson objective. The importance of this section seems obvious, yet it is frequently overlooked or addressed as an afterthought. The information gathered through evaluation helps to make sensible planning decisions for the future. It allows teachers to determine whether they should build on the current lesson, or whether they need to reteach some or all of the information again.

When teachers write the lesson objective, they also plan the summative evaluation. A well-written objective contains a clear description of what students will do to provide evidence that they have learned. Consider the following objective: "When shown a blank diagram of a volcano, students will label all five parts correctly." It is easy to "picture" what will be happening during the evaluation of this objective. At the end of the lesson, the teacher will pass out an unlabeled diagram of a volcano, and students will label the various parts. The students will label without help from anyone (no "hints" from the teacher, no help from a partner). Remember that teachers use evaluation to determine an individual student's independent performance in relation to an objective.

Summative evaluation is often much more complex than that described in the volcano example. The evaluation may occur in steps or at various times or locations. This additional information should be explained in the evaluation section of the plan. For example, imagine that you want to teach students to use a reading comprehension strategy. The lesson objective is "Students will use all steps in the XYZ strategy when reading for information in content area texts." You decide to teach the lesson over two days. The steps of the strategy will be taught on the first day and the application of the steps on Day 2. The following is an example of how you might consider the evaluation:

> "I will not be able to test the objective at the end of the first day because all of the necessary content will not have been taught. I will, however, test to see that my students have learned the strategy steps because, if there is confusion, I will need to reteach rather than go on to the application step. The evaluation completed after instruction on Day 1 will be the strategy steps written from memory."
>
> "I can evaluate the objective following Day 2 because students should have the information and practice needed to successfully meet the objective. The evaluation will consist of my observing individual students performing the overt strategy actions during short content area reading assignments throughout the day."

At times it may also be desirable to include a description of a long-term objective and evaluation that relates to the short-term objective for the day. The long-term objective for the reading comprehension strategy might be, "Students will use all steps in the XYZ strategy whenever reading for information in content area texts." Obviously, students could not be evaluated on their use of this strategy when the teacher no longer has contact with them on a regular basis. However, teachers should still include plans to provide ample generalization and review opportunities for the remainder of the school year. This will increase the likelihood that students will use the strategy following that year. Plans are needed to monitor the use of the strategy during these times. The teacher may wish to note this plan in the evaluation section of the lesson plan.

Students need to be monitored carefully during the lesson—especially during individual supervised and extended practice—so the teacher can determine when they are ready to be formally evaluated. Teachers should evaluate only when students are ready, which may or may not be when the teacher had planned for evaluation to occur. This definitely speaks to the importance of having a backup plan for when students progress more or less quickly than expected.

As objectives are planned, it should be remembered that evaluation is not necessarily a paper and pencil test. In fact, that type of evaluation would not be appropriate in many instances, such as when teaching social skills or learning strategies. An alternate assessment should be used. This can take many forms: learning may be evaluated by asking students to complete worksheets, make oral presentations, answer questions verbally, make products, perform, or participate. Strive for relevance and authenticity in evaluation methods and routinely use a combination of techniques. In all cases however, be sure that you have taught what you are testing.

As a note of caution, try not to affect the evaluation by using unrelated skills. For example, an evaluation technique, such as asking students to create a bulletin board to show their understanding of the life cycle of the salmon, may actually be an evaluation of their artistic or organizational skills. Keep the form of evaluation as direct and simple as possible so that you are not inadvertently testing skills irrelevant to the objective (testing reading skills in math word problems, for example).

Responding to Diversity When Planning Evaluation

The following suggestions will help you plan your evaluation:

- Keep evaluating for retention and for improvement.

- Adjust the amount of time given to students to complete evaluation tasks.

- Consider options for responding. For example, if a student has difficulty writing, allow him to explain orally. Include alternatives in the objective.

The Role of Performance Feedback

Throughout this chapter, the use of feedback has been mentioned numerous times. Teachers assist students as they learn new information and skills by giving feedback on their performance; it is a way of communicating progress. Feedback refers to statements teachers make to students about the accuracy or inaccuracy or quality of their responses. During the initial phases of learning, feedback helps ensure that students do not practice errors. Continued monitoring of student work provides additional opportunities for the teacher to let students know how they are progressing toward important learning outcomes. Without feedback, students may not have an accurate idea regarding their progress. Effective performance feedback is one of the most important tools teachers can use as they monitor student practice activities, completed either in or out of the classroom.

Feedback is sometimes used in combination with praise for correct responses ("That's correct! Great!"). Negative feedback for incorrect responses is most effective when it is combined with a statement, an example, or a demonstration of the correct response. Such feedback is often called corrective feedback. Corrective feedback is academic and should be delivered respectfully. It focuses on the lesson content rather than the personality of the student. All feedback should be specific rather than general ("Your definition of photosynthesis includes all key points!," rather than "Nice job!").

Note that sometimes practicum students and student teachers feel reluctant to give corrective feedback because they are afraid telling students their answers are wrong will hurt their feelings. Consider this example: Ms. Rogers is teaching a lesson on nouns. After some initial instruction, she has students brainstorm new examples of nouns. Cindy calls out "sit." Ms. Rogers says, "Well . . . yes . . . , that could be a noun," and then calls on Jerome. Ms. Rogers did not want Cindy to feel badly because her answer was wrong, so she gave Cindy and the rest of the students inaccurate information about what she was teaching. Ms. Rogers could have said, "Cindy, that's a great example of a verb. Remember that a noun names a person, place, or thing. Can you think of an example of a thing that someone would sit on?" This response would have given Cindy, and the other students, an additional reminder of the definition of a noun (and Cindy an easy opportunity to come up with a correct answer).

The Teaching/Learning Cycle

Teacher monitoring plays a key role in the teaching/learning process and informs us about two important instructional outcomes. One of the main pieces of information that teachers learn through monitoring, during and after actual instruction, is whether or not students have learned. Moore writes, "The ultimate question in the instructional process is whether or not you have taught what you intended to teach and whether students have learned what they were supposed to learn" (2005, 161). This means that when teachers monitor progress during instruction as well as when testing the objective, they are able to determine whether or not students are learning the information being taught. This information helps teachers decide what to do next. For example, if a teacher notices through formative evaluation that students are making numerous errors, he can decide to stop, regroup, backtrack, and teach some more. If he sees that students know the new information, he may proceed with the next objective.

The second valuable bit of information that teachers can gain through monitoring student progress is whether or not the instructional methods being used are working. Stanford and Reeves address this issue: ". . . a fundamental truth in effective teaching is that assessment strategies, both formal and informal, must help the teacher determine the most appropriate instruction, in addition to assessing progress" (2005, 18). They imply that the information that teachers gather can inform decisions about which methods are effective with which students. Because it is commonly understood that not all methods are equally effective with all students, then the data teachers collect through monitoring can help them decide appropriate methods. For example, let's say that you notice that a large number of your students are having difficulty accomplishing the objective for the inquiry math lesson. Decide whether this particular group of students needs a more direct approach and try a direct instruction lesson on the same material.

Teachers have various sources from which they can and should gather information about student progress. Cruickshank, Jenkins, and Metcalf write that effective classroom assessment is more than just paper and pencil tests or projects that are completed at the end of instruction. They state that good classroom assessment "requires teachers to continually gather information about their students from a variety of sources, to synthesize that information, and then to make a judgment or evaluation about how well or how much each student has learned" (2003, 271). Gathering this information allows teachers to make informed decisions about student progress.

Summary

This chapter has addressed how to provide students with opportunities to practice what they are learning. It has discussed how to determine whether or not they are learning. Both play a very important role in the teaching/learning cycle. When planning monitoring opportunities and activities, consider the following:

- Projects such as informational posters or brochures and demonstrations are all examples of how students can show what they know (Tomlinson 2001; Castellani 2005) rather than using just paper and pencil tests.
- Rubrics, T-charts, rating scales, checklists, systematic observations of student performance, and portfolio assessments are examples of techniques that can be used to score performance (Kleinert, et al. 2002; Kauchak and Eggen 2003; Cruickshank, Jenkins, and Metcalf 2003). It is important to remember that in all cases, performance is compared to a preset standard.
- Assessment results are an important communication tool for talking with students and parents about progress (Pemberton 2003).
- Self-charting of progress can be an important motivational strategy (Gunter et al. 2002).
- Learning is facilitated when teachers regularly integrate assessment into instruction and involve students in assessment, such as having a student help assemble her own portfolio of products (Kleinert et al. 2002).
- Assessments differ based on the setting in which they take place. Authentic assessments take place in real-life settings whereas other performance assessments take place in testing situations (Arends 2004).

References and Suggested Readings

Arends, R. I. 2004. *Learning to teach.* 6th ed. Boston: McGraw-Hill.

Castellani, J., ed. (2005). *Universal design for learning: A guide for teachers and education professionals.* Arlington, VA: The Council for Exceptional Children.

Cegelka, P., and W. Berdine. 1995. *Effective instruction for students with learning problems.* Needham Heights, MA: Allyn and Bacon.

Cruickshank, D. R., D. B. Jenkins, and K. K. Metcalf. 2003. *The Act of Teaching.* Boston: McGraw-Hill.

Demmert, W. G. 2005. The influences of culture on learning and assessment among Native American students. *Learning Disabilities Research and Practice* 20 (1): 16–23.

Gunter, P. L., K. A. Miller, M. L. Venn, K. Thomas, and S. House. 2002. Self-graphing to success: computerized data management. *Teaching Exceptional Children* 35 (2): 30–34.

Hosp, M. K., J. L. Hosp, and K. W. Howell. n.d. *The ABCs of CBM: An easy guide for implementing curriculum-based measurement.* New York: Guilford. Forthcoming.

Howell, K. W., M. Hosp, and J. Hosp. n.d. *Curriculum-based evaluation: Teaching and decision making.* 4th ed. Belmont, CA: Wadsworth/Thomson Learning. Forthcoming.

Hughes, C. A., K. L. Ruhl, J. B. Schumaker, and D. D. Deshler. 2002. Effects of instruction in an assignment completion strategy on the homework performance of students with learning disabilities in general education classes. *Learning Disabilities Research & Practice* 17 (1): 1–18.

Kauchak, D. P., and P. D. Eggen. 2003. *Learning and teaching: Research-based methods.* 4th ed. Boston: Allyn and Bacon.

Kleinert, H., P. Green, M. Hurte, J. Clayton, and C. Oetinger. 2002. Creating and using meaningful alternate assessments. *Teaching Exceptional Children* 34 (4): 40–47.

Konold, K. E., S. P. Miller, and K. B. Konold. 2004. Using teacher feedback to enhance student learning. *Teaching Exceptional Children* 36 (6): 64–69.

Marzano, R. J., D. J. Pickering, and J. E. Pollock. 2001. *Classroom instruction that works: Research-based strategies for increasing student achievement.* Upper Saddle River: Pearson/Merrill Prentice Hall.

Mastropieri, M. S., and T. E. Scruggs. 2004. *The inclusive classroom: Strategies for effective instruction.* 2nd ed. Columbus, OH: Merrill.

Moore, K. D. 2005. *Effective instructional strategies: From theory to practice.* Thousand Oaks: Sage Publications.

Pemberton, J. B. 2003. Communicating academic progress as an integral part of assessment. *Teaching Exceptional Children* 35 (4): 16–20.

Salend, S. J., D. Duhaney, D. J. Anderson, and C. Gottschalk. 2004. Using the Internet to improve homework communication and completion. *Teaching Exceptional Children* 36 (3): 64–73.

Salend, S. J., and M. Gajiria. 1995. Increasing the homework completion rates of students with mild disabilities. *Remedial and Special Education* 16: 271–278.

Sanacore, J. 2002. Needed: Homework clubs for young adolescents who struggle with learning. *The Clearing House,* (November/December). Washington DC: The Clearing House.

Stanford, P., and S. Reeves. 2005. Assessment that drives instruction. *Teaching Exceptional Children* 37 (4): 18–22.

Tomlinson, C. A. 2001. *How to differentiate instruction in mixed-ability classrooms.* 2nd ed. Upper Saddle River, NJ: Merrill Prentice Hall.

Wood, J. W. 2006. *Teaching students in inclusive settings—adapting and accommodating instruction.* 5th ed. Upper Saddle River, New Jersey: Pearson/Merrill Prentice Hall.

Wright, J. 2004. *Classwork and homework: Troubleshooting student problems from start to finish.* Tips for Study and Organization. http://www.interventioncentral.org (accessed May 23, 2005).

Critical Teaching Skills for Planning Partner and Small-Group Work

Introduction

This chapter is about another important aspect of preparing activities and lessons for a diverse classroom, planning how students will work and learn together.

Reasons for Using Peers in Instruction

Throughout various chapters of this book, we emphasize the importance of active student participation in the diverse classroom. Teachers must carefully and imaginatively plan and work hard to ensure that all students are involved and can obtain success. Because teachers cannot be everywhere at the same time, an abundant source of help can come from students. Having students work with their peers can increase opportunities for active responses and practice with immediate feedback. Using peers may also be motivating, provide practice in social skills, increase social integration, and offer more variety in methods. All of this helps satisfy individual differences and preferences, and increases engaged time. Carefully planned partner and small-group activities can provide English language learners with many opportunities for language use. Peers can serve as language models and can provide feedback within a safe setting. Opportunities to discuss new learning with other students, including those who speak the same native language, can facilitate learning.

Examples of Using Peers in Instruction

Teachers can have peers work together in any of the following ways:

- *Active participation strategies* During informal presentation and direct instruction lessons, students may be encouraged to process new information with peers through techniques such as "tell your neighbor."
- *Support strategies* Peer helpers may provide assistance with paying attention, reading directions, homework, and so on, to students with learning or behavior problems.
- *Activities* An activity plan may incorporate the use of groups or teams of students for working on projects, solving problems, engaging in discussions, playing games, and so on.
- *Supervised practice in lessons* Include partner or small-group practice as a bridge between teacher demonstrations and individual practice.
- *Extended practice* Plan ongoing partner practice, using flash cards for building accuracy and fluency on math facts, for enhancing vocabulary, and so on.
- *Structured discovery* Pairs of students or groups may work together to discuss the examples and nonexamples and to discover the concept or rule.
- *Informal presentation* As extended practice, students may form debate teams and prepare arguments based on the information presented.
- *Behavior management* Teams may earn points for quick transitions with students helping and reminding each other of the rules.

Notice that, in all of these examples, partner or group work builds on teacher instruction but does not replace it.

Many formal cooperative learning and peer-tutoring programs can also be very effective in a diverse classroom. Individual teachers may implement some of these programs, and some are school-wide programs. See the suggested readings at the end of this chapter for information on cooperative learning and peer-tutoring programs.

Potential Problems

Although there are many benefits to using peers in instruction, there are potential hazards as well. Simply telling students to work together is rarely enough. Most people have had experience working with others at school or at work when much time was wasted, when one person did all of the work, or when nothing was accomplished. Using peers, like all other teaching techniques, requires careful planning to avoid time spent chatting, fighting, exchanging misinformation, or chaos as students are forming groups or moving furniture. Students will not necessarily know how to work together, cooperate, share, listen, encourage, or challenge each other. It is important to establish and communicate rules or routines and to assess and teach necessary cooperative social skills.

Planning for Using Peers in Instruction

Many variables must be considered as you plan for using peers in instruction.

When to Plan

The time and effort that teachers spend planning for using peers depends on how they are going to be used. If teachers intend to use peer partners or groups often (as an active participation strategy, part of supervised practice, or a regular part of the reading or math or spelling program), then it is most efficient to plan and teach direct instruction lessons on the procedures or routines in advance. That time will be well spent because it will help avoid more planning and teaching time later. For example, in plans for reading lessons, you may simply write, "Find your reading partner and follow the oral reading routine." That will be sufficient if students have previously been taught the routine and have established partners. If you teach and provide practice on using the "Numbered Heads Together" procedure, then, in activity and lesson plans, you only need to write "Form your Heads Together groups, count off, and discuss . . ." (Kagan 1992).

In some cases, teachers will plan for the use of peers as a one-time event. For example, suppose you are planning an inquiry activity in science. For that particular activity, you must plan the membership, the meeting places, and the procedures for the groups to follow. You would write detailed directions into the "activity middle" component of the activity plan.

Planning Decisions

Regardless of when you plan for using peers in instruction, it is always necessary to make decisions about why, how, who, and where. Consider the reason for using peers, the size of the groups, how tasks will be shared, the prerequisites, who will work together, and the context for partner and small-group work. Some of the following suggestions are adapted from various authors (Arends 2004; Johnson, Johnson, and Holubec 1991; Slavin 1995).

Reasons to Use Peers in a Lesson or Activity

Don't assume that using peers is always superior to individual work. It is necessary to consider the reason for using partners or small groups. For example, in an activity, the benefits of having students work on group projects rather than on individual projects might be to generate more ideas, provide the opportunity for individuals to study one narrow topic in depth, and provide practice on cooperative social skills. To bring about a higher success rate, you may use peers as part of supervised practice to provide additional support as students are attempting new skills. Be sure that all students involved in peer practice will benefit from it.

Determining the Size of Groups

Decide whether it is preferable to use pairs of students or small groups. Small group size typically ranges from three to six members. Consider the following factors when trying to determine the most appropriate group size:

1. *More cooperative social skills are needed in larger groups.* It is easier to share materials,

take turns, or reach consensus with one other person than it is with five other people. Also, in larger groups, equal participation is more difficult to achieve. The decision about group size, therefore, should be partly based on the level of cooperative skills the students have.

2. *All groups do not necessarily have to be the same size.* You can accommodate diversity by having some smaller and some larger groups. This may need to be done anyway, depending on the total number of students in the class. For example, if you have 23 students, you can form five groups with three members and two groups with four members.

3. *The type of task may influence the group size.* If students are to take turns reading aloud, they will get more practice in groups of two than in groups of three or more. Larger groups may be appropriate if the task is a project where each student has something different to do, such as researching a different topic, and all tasks can be done at once.

4. *The task may logically divide itself.* Group size may be determined by needed roles, such as a reader and a writer, or according to the content, such as reporting on the three branches of government.

5. *Time is a factor.* Typically, the larger the group, the more time will be needed. For example, if the students are to discuss or solve problems together, more time will be needed for larger groups so that each member gets a chance to contribute.

6. *Sometimes more mundane elements must be considered.* The number of materials or available equipment, the size of tables, and so on, may all affect group size.

Determining How Students Will Share Tasks

It is important to consider what each student will do during the partner or group work and to communicate this to the students. It is usually not enough to simply tell students to work together, cooperate, help each other, teach each other, or discuss. It is essential to be much more specific. For example, for partner practice on vocabulary, you might say, "Partner 1 will define the first word, and Partner 2 will use it in a sentence. Then switch for the second word."

Teachers may think about the typical roles needed in partner or group work, such as reader, recorder, checker, encourager, and timer. Then they may decide which roles are needed in a particular task. It is most efficient to directly teach those roles that they will commonly use, so all students know how to carry them out. It is also necessary to decide whether the teacher or the group will assign the roles.

If it is difficult to figure out what each student will do, ask yourself whether this is a task that can be shared or whether the size of the group is appropriate. Remember that not all learning is best done in group situations.

Determining Prerequisite Skills and Knowledge

In addition to analyzing whether students have the necessary content knowledge and skills, it is essential to analyze whether they have the interaction skills required to be successful at the task. The following examples illustrate how you may consider required academic and social skills as you plan:

1. Provide instruction on summarizing paragraphs before partner work. This way, you would know that all students have the necessary preliminary content knowledge on how to summarize. However, you would also need to decide whether students have the skills to listen to each other, to accept criticism, to take turns, and so on.

2. Before planning to have students discuss a particular topic in small groups, decide whether they have the necessary information or knowledge about the topic to make a discussion productive. You also need to analyze the students' discussion skills, such as making relevant comments, criticizing ideas rather than the person, and asking for clarification.

3. To form groups and pick a subject to investigate, students have to possess not only the necessary research skills, but also skills in offering ideas, reaching consensus, and so on.

Several options are available for teaching students who do not have the prerequisite cooperative social skills to be successful at the task. First, avoid the problem by changing the lesson or activity to eliminate the use of peers or structure the task carefully to help students be successful, that is, provide clear and specific directions, change the group size, assign specific roles, and so on. Finally, you may wish to pre-teach the necessary social skills, using the direct instruction model (see Chapter 18 for more detail).

Deciding Who Will Work Together

Teachers may sometimes choose to form groups at random or to allow students to decide. More typically, they will want to plan the membership of pairs and groups carefully. When students will be working together for more than brief periods of time (for a one-hour science experiment or a month-long reading partnership), consider the following factors when planning who will work together:

1. *Skills* Consider the task and purpose when choosing whether to pair or group homogeneously or heterogeneously. For example, if you intend to individualize the content of the tasks, with some students needing to practice addition facts, some working on multiple-digit addition, and some working on multiplication, then choose homogeneous pairs so both students are getting practice on the skills they need. On the other hand, if all students are practicing the same skills, it makes sense to pair a higher achiever with a lower achiever. In that way, students who are skilled at the task can help the lower achievers, while reinforcing their own learning by giving those explanations. When forming pairs and groups, it is important to consider the study and interaction skills of the students, in addition to academic skills.

2. *Compatibility* It is also necessary to consider how students get along together when forming pairs and groups. Students who actively dislike each other or who distract each other should not be put together, unless the purpose is to provide practice on conflict resolution or on ignoring distractions. Also, consider cultural diversity in cooperation and communication skills. For example, discuss with students variations in what is considered acceptable in expressing opinions and disagreements. Some students may be uncomfortable with raised voices and table pounding. This is a good opportunity to broaden perspectives.

3. *Integration* Another consideration in forming pairs and groups is that of promoting social integration. Mixing boys and girls, individuals with and without disabilities, and students from varied cultural backgrounds can increase tolerance and promote friendships in the classroom. However, the teacher must carefully plan for this outcome.

Planning the Context for Partner and Small-Group Work

The teacher needs to support cooperative behaviors by careful planning for management and organization. Following are examples of how you can use critical management skills to plan effective partner and small-group work (see Chapter 11 for a complete discussion of critical management skills):

1. *Arrange the room to facilitate group or partner work.* When students will be working together briefly, as in active participation strategies, it makes sense for students who sit near each other to be grouped together. Teach students who their "neighbor" is (for example, the person to their left), and who is included in their small group so these groupings can be set up quickly during instruction. If desks are in rows, plan for odd numbers and for the person at the end of the row when thinking about partnerships. Show students how to turn or move their chairs to form small groups. (Note that you will not want much furniture moving for brief group work.) If your typical arrangement is to have desks in clusters or if students sit at tables, then you'll need to designate partners. Consider whether peer practice will be used often when making desk arrangements and seating assignments.

Sometimes you will form pairs and groups based on factors other than seating proximity. In that case, decide where in the room they will meet and plan for moving desks or tables. If students are to work together, they will need to be physically close together. No one should be physically excluded from the group, and everyone should be able to see the materials and each other. Situate the pairs and groups far enough apart so that groups do not distract each other and so they can be easily monitored.

2. *Plan how to gain attention.* When students are focused on each other in pairs and small groups, they may not easily see or hear the teacher. Therefore, plan a stronger signal for attention such as ringing a bell or turning off the lights. Also, when students are working and talking together, it can be difficult for them to shift their attention back to the teacher. It may be helpful to provide practice in responding quickly to the signal for attention. It may also be helpful to provide time warnings, such as, "In three minutes I'll ask you to finish your discussions and listen to my directions for the next activity."

3. *Communicate behavior expectations.* Think about the rules and routines that apply and the social skills that students will need for success during the partner or small-group work you have planned and communicate these to them. Consider the following examples of cooperative behaviors. They demonstrate how complex partner and group work can be and how important it is to teach students relevant rules, routines, and social skills.

moving into groups	staying with the group	talking in quiet voices
accepting partners	getting help	sharing materials
taking turns	what to do when finished	listening to each other
doing your share	encouraging participation	disagreeing with ideas
reaching consensus	taking others' perspectives	accepting feedback

In addition, plan how you will communicate the procedures for working together to the students. Be sure that your directions are clear and concise. Also, be sure that students know the task expectations, that is, individual and group objectives, the time lines, and the evaluation procedures. Consider putting all of these in writing rather than simply saying them.

4. *Acknowledge appropriate behavior.* Plan to acknowledge students for following the behavior expectations you've communicated and for using other important cooperative skills. Think about the behaviors that are challenging for individuals. If some students tend to dominate, acknowledge them for letting others participate. If some students are uncomfortable talking in groups, acknowledge them when they make a contribution. Acknowledge the group as well as acknowledging individuals: "Your group managed to reach consensus even though each of you began with very different goals. Well done." These kinds of statements provide students with valuable feedback that is directly related to the skills needed to work with others.

5. *Monitor the students.* Be sure to move around to monitor each group or pair. Your proximity will encourage students to stay on task. If you are sitting with a group, position yourself to see the other groups. Think about which pairs or groups may need more monitoring and more interactions (encouragement, feedback, reminders) with you.

6. *Plan for logistics.* You may want to designate, or have the groups designate, individuals to gather, distribute, and return needed materials and equipment for the group.

7. *Manage transitions.* The transition to and from group or partner work has the potential to be chaotic. Don't let this keep you from using this effective teaching method. Plan carefully to avoid wasted time and behavior problems. Plan how to communicate who will work together, such as listing groups and their members on a transparency for students to read. Plan where groups will meet. You may display a diagram or map, or put signs up to show where groups are to sit. Describe and demonstrate how to move desks and chairs if that's necessary. Communicate behavior expectations for the transition itself. (Proactively teaching the routine of how to move into groups may be time well spent.)

Responding to Skill Diversity When Planning Partner and Small-Group Work

If students are not yet skilled at working with partners or in small groups, don't avoid using these techniques, but do temporarily minimize the cooperative skills needed. You can do this in various ways:

- Use smaller groups because students will find it easier to cooperate with one or two people than with four or five.
- Assign roles rather than having the group make all decisions.
- Provide enough materials for everyone so sharing isn't necessary.
- Be careful in assigning groups; good friends or bad enemies may have difficulty working together.
- Focus on one cooperative skill at a time and review it just before the partner or small-group work. For example, ask students to state what listening to your partner looks like and sounds like.
- Be direct about how to solve problems. For example, say, "If more than one person wants to go first, then use rock-scissors-paper to decide."

Summary

Having students work with partners or in small groups during lessons and activities is a strategy with many potential benefits. However, careful planning is needed to ensure that students work together effectively and efficiently. Planning is necessary to determine the size and membership of groups, how students will share tasks, and how to evaluate the knowledge and skills needed by students.

References and Suggested Readings

Arends, R. I. 2004. *Learning to teach.* 6th ed. Boston: McGraw-Hill.

Arreaga-Mayer, C. 1998. Increasing active student responding and improving academic performance through class-wide peer tutoring. *Intervention in School and Clinic* 34 (2): 89–94.

Cohen, L., and L. J. Spenciner. 2005. *Teaching students with mild and moderate disabilities: Research-based practices.* Upper Saddle River, N.J.: Pearson.

Copeland, S., J. McCall, C. Williams, C. Guth, E. Carter, S. Fowler, J. Presley, and C. Hughes. 2002. High school peer buddies: A win-win situation. *Teaching Exceptional Children* 35 (1): 16–21.

Goodwin, M. 1999. Cooperative learning and social skills: What skills to teach and how to teach them. *Intervention in School and Clinic* 35 (1): 29–33.

Hock, M. F., J. B. Schumaker, and D. D. Deshler. 2001. The case for strategic tutoring. *Educational Leadership* 58 (7): 50–52.

Jenkins, J. R., L. R. Antil, S. K. Wayne, and P. F. Vadasy. 2003. How cooperative learning works for special education and remedial students. *Exceptional Children* 69 (3): 279–292.

Johnson, D. W., R. T. Johnson, and E. J. Holubec. 1991. *Cooperation in the classroom.* Edina, MN: Interaction Book.

Kagan, S. 1992. *Cooperative Learning.* San Juan Capistrano, CA: Resources for Teachers.

Lovitt, T. C. 2000. *Preventing school failure: Tactics for teaching adolescents.* 2nd ed. Austin, TX: Pro-Ed.

Marzano, R. J., D. J. Pickering, and J. E. Pollock. 2005. *Classroom instruction that works: Research-based strategies for increasing student achievement.* Upper Saddle River, N.J.: Pearson.

Mastropheri, M. A., and T. E. Scruggs. 2004. *The inclusive classroom: Strategies for effective instruction.* Upper Saddle River, N.J.: Pearson.

Mastropheri, M. A., T. E. Scruggs, L. J. Mohler, M. L. Beranek, V. Spencer, R. T. Boon, and E. Talbott. 2001. Can middle school students with serious reading difficulties help each other and learn anything? *Learning Disabilities Research and Practice* 16 (1): 18–27.

Mathes, P. G., and A. E. Babyak. 2001. The effects of peer-assisted learning strategies for first-grade readers with and without additional mini-skills lessons. *Learning Disabilities Research and Practice* 16 (1): 28–44.

McMaster, K. N., and D. Fuchs. 2002. Effects of cooperative learning on the academic achievement of students with learning disabilities: An update of Tateyama-Sniezek's review. *Learning Disabilities Research & Practice* 17 (2): 107–117.

Mercer, C. D., and A. R. Mercer. 2005. *Teaching students with learning problems.* 7th ed. Upper Saddle River, N.J.: Pearson.

Olson, J. L., and J. M. Platt. 2003. *Teaching children and adolescents with special needs.* 4th ed. Columbus, Ohio: Merrill, an imprint of Prentice Hall.

Polloway, E. A., J. R. Patton, and L. Serna. 2004. *Strategies for teaching learners with special needs.* 8th ed. Upper Saddle River, N.J.: Pearson.

Salend, S. J. 2005. *Creating inclusive classrooms: Effective and reflective practices for all students.* 5th ed. Upper Saddle River, N.J.: Pearson.

Slavin, R. E. 1994. *A practical guide to cooperative learning.* Needham Heights, MA: Allyn & Bacon.

Slavin, R. E. 1995. *Cooperative learning: Theory, research, and practice.* 2nd ed. Needham Heights, MA: Allyn & Bacon.

Sonnier-York, C., and P. Stanford. 2002. Learning to cooperate: A teacher's perspective. *Teaching Exceptional Children* 34 (6): 40–44.

Utley, C. A., S. L. Mortweet, and C. R. Greenwood. 1997. Peer-mediated instruction and interventions. *Focus on Exceptional Children* 29: 1–23.

Vaughn, S., M. T. Hughes, S. W. Moody, and B. Elbaum. 2001. Instructional grouping for reading for students with L.D.: Implications for practice. *Intervention in School and Clinic* 36 (3): 131–137.

Wolford, P. L., W. L. Heward, and S. R. Alber. 2001. Teaching middle school students with learning disabilities to recruit peer assistance during cooperative learning group activities. *Learning Disabilities Research & Practice* 16 (3): 161–173.

CHAPTER 9

Selected Instructional Interventions

Introduction

When you are planning lessons and activities, you are not only thinking about the various components of your plans and how to make them most effective, you are also thinking about your students. You may be thinking, "There is a long list of steps to follow in this lesson, and my class has trouble with that. What can I do to help them be successful?" Or you may be thinking, "Tim, Andrew, Bridget, and Anne are going to have a hard time sitting down long enough to finish this assignment. How can I help them?" Depending on the makeup of the class, the suggestions presented in this chapter may be built into initial planning for the whole class or added on as individual accommodations (Cohen and Lynch 1991).

Distinguishing between Universal and Selected Interventions

In the preceding chapters in Part 2 of the book, you learned many methods that are generally considered universal interventions—they are built in to help most of the students in your class. For example, when teachers plan to say, show, and write the key ideas of the lesson, every student will benefit. When they consider cultural diversity, everyone benefits. When they use evidence-based critical teaching skills, everyone benefits. In spite of all of the upfront planning that teachers do to address classroom diversity however, at least one, or perhaps a few, students will need more support.

Selected instructional interventions come into play here. Selected interventions are accommodations or modifications that are added for one or a few students. They are not appropriate for all students and, as a matter of fact, any particular selected intervention may be detrimental to some students. For example, it would not be appropriate for a teacher to provide reading material on a content topic at a reduced reading level when only one or two students need such an accommodation. Such a strategy could be detrimental to the grade-level readers in the classroom. So, selected interventions are added only for those who need them.

Accommodations and Modifications

Selected interventions can be accommodations or modifications. Accommodations and modifications impact teaching and learning in different ways, so it is important to understand how they are different. An *accommodation* is a change in the *how* of teaching. All students are expected to meet the same objectives, but the path to the objective varies. Examples of accommodations include giving more instructional time or practice, preparing individual behavior contracts, and providing an interpreter, highlighted textbooks, books in their native language, detailed study guides, peer tutors, or special seating. None of these interventions change the learning outcome; they simply change the route one takes to reach the outcome.

On the other hand, a *modification* is a change a teacher makes to *what* is taught. It may be a change in curriculum or in expectations. For example, a teacher may teach the same subject matter but at a different level of difficulty (he may have one student work on locating named cities on a map while the rest of the class learns to predict the locations of cities based on natural features such as rivers). Other examples include reducing the criterion in an objective (accepting 75 percent rather than 100 percent accuracy on capitalizing), or teaching different content (functional academics or life skills). These strategies change the expected outcome for the students for whom the modification is made. We are going to focus on accommodations, not modifications, throughout this book.

Sometimes a modification is used temporarily, assuming that students will catch up with their peers. Consider the serious implications if students are learning less than their peers in the long run due to the modifications. Changing what you teach students can impact their future success in school and employment. Make these modifications very thoughtfully and involve families in decision making. Teachers should always begin with the assumption that students, including students with disabilities, will learn the same content as their peers. However, if instructional accommodations do not allow the student to progress in the general curriculum and meet state standards, then modifying expected learning outcomes may be in the best interest of the student.

The Challenging Class

The issue of building in versus adding on (or universal versus selected interventions) comes into play as teachers choose interventions to include in their plans. Remember that the needs of a particular class of students dictate whether to build in or add on. Here are some examples that help explain this issue.

- One teacher finds that he can meet the needs of his students as he predicts them, by using techniques that are typically considered effective teaching practices and universal design principles. He builds in these strategies.

- Another teacher decides that, to meet the needs of her two students with significant reading problems, she will need to add on a strategy for them that would not be appropriate for all of her students. In fact, she thinks the strategy may have a negative effect on the learning of most of her students. So, she adds on a selected intervention.

- A third teacher decides that the add-on intervention that he originally thought he would use to meet the needs of four of his students would really be helpful for all the students. So, he decides to build it in for everyone rather than add it on. The intervention, at first considered a selected intervention, becomes a universal intervention instead.

When you begin planning which interventions to include in a lesson or activity, first think about universal interventions and build them in. Next, decide on selected interventions and add them on. Consider that selected interventions can be more time-consuming or take more effort to add on, and incorporate them only when universal interventions are not enough for each student's success.

Specific Areas of Challenge

In the following sections of this chapter, we are going to present strategies that are categorized by fairly common challenges that some students face. We have loosely organized the strategies into general categories of difficulty (acquiring information, processing information, expressing information). We have further organized them by specific challenge, for example, difficulty maintaining attention or beginning tasks.

Some of the ideas in the following sections come from the literature on instructional recommendations for students with attention deficits, but will be helpful for many students (Bender and Mathes 1995; Council for Exceptional Children 1992; Dowdy et al. 1998; Kemp, Fister, and McLaughlin 1995; Lerner, Lowenthal, and Lerner 1995; Rooney 1995; Yehle and Wambold 1998). The suggestions that are included focus on mild to moderate learning and behavioral problems and do not include accommodations necessary for complex, low-incidence disabilities. Notice that these strategies provide positive behavioral support for students as well as increase academic learning.

We will not be referring to selected interventions that involve remedial or specialized instructional programs in reading, writing, math, and so on. Of course, entire books and programs are available for how to teach reading to students who are not learning to read in the regular classroom program, for example. In this chapter, we refer to less-intrusive selected interventions.

Acquisition of Information

The first general area of student challenges has to do with acquiring information. Students who have difficulty reading, attending, and sitting still can have difficulty learning. The following are some strategies to try.

Difficulty Maintaining Attention

Consider the following suggestions for students who have difficulty staying focused:

- Provide preferential seating. Sit the student near the teacher or another adult, near quiet peers, or at an individual desk rather than at a table with other students, and away from high-traffic areas, such as doors or windows.
- Teach the student to ignore distractions in the long run. Reduce distractions in the short run through preferential seating, the use of study carrels, screens, or headphones, or by reducing sounds and visual stimuli.
- Provide more frequent breaks or changes in tasks.
- Use more active participation strategies.
- Regain the student's attention frequently through proximity, touch, eye contact, or private signals.
- Teach students to self-monitor their own behavior.
- Have a peer helper prompt the student to pay attention.

Difficulty Keeping Still

When teaching students who have difficulty remaining still, consider the following strategies:

- Let students stand or move when this doesn't disrupt learning. For example, let them stand at their desks to do independent work or walk around while doing oral practice.
- Allow students to use various desks or work areas.
- Let students use worry beads or doodle when this does not interfere with the task.
- Build in movement for students in the daily schedule (hand out papers, run errands, clean up, or do stretching exercises).
- Build in movement in lessons and activities by using active physical responses. For example, tell students to "stand up if you think this is the topic sentence" or "walk to the blackboard and write the definition".
- Teach students to signal when they need a break.

Difficulty Reading

When teaching reading is not the objective, the following suggestions may help students who experience difficulty in reading:

- Have a peer or other volunteer read to the student.
- Have a peer summarize information orally to the student.
- Provide highlighted text.
- Provide study guides, outlines, or graphic organizers to go with the reading to help with comprehension.
- Provide assistive computer technology that supports reading.
- Provide the necessary information in other forms, such as oral presentations, audiotapes, videotapes, or computer multimedia programs.

Difficulty with Selective Attention

Students who have difficulty with selective attention have trouble attending to the important aspects of a task or information. The following suggestions help with this challenge:

- Use color cues, highlight, or bold important details.

- Provide study guides or advance questions to go with readings or presentations.
- Provide flash cards or cue cards that include key information and examples with no extraneous information.
- Use a consistent format for instruction and on worksheets.

Processing or Memorizing Information

The second general area of challenge for many students involves processing and/or retaining information. Behaviors such as impulsiveness, difficulty starting and finishing tasks, and organizing information can create substantial difficulty.

Difficulty Waiting or Impulsiveness

This may be a problem when students are standing in line, taking turns, responding on assignments or tests, during discussions, and so on. The following suggestions may help students with such difficulties:

- Use a cue that reminds students to remain quiet during the wait-time after questions.
- Tell students to discuss responses with their partners before saying or writing the answers.
- Teach students to highlight important words in test questions or in assignment directions.
- Cue the use of problem-solving steps.
- Teach students to outline essay test answers before writing.
- Teach students to think of the answer on their own before looking at multiple choices on a test.
- Teach students what to do while waiting for help (try another problem or task, ask a partner for help, or reread directions, for example).
- Cue the use of self-talk (for example, "I need to take a deep breath and . . .").
- Provide students with something to do while waiting in line or for a turn (play a game, sing a song, have something in their pockets to play with, for example).
- Teach students how to interrupt politely.

Difficulty Beginning Tasks

When students find it difficult to begin tasks, consider the following suggestions:

- Provide cue cards on their desks, describing how to begin a task. Have students check off steps as completed. For example: (1) write name on paper, (2) read directions, and so on. (This is similar to reminders that appear on billing envelopes, such as "Have you written the account number on your check?") Go to the student right at the beginning of seatwork to help him start. Say that you will be back shortly to check.
- Provide a peer helper to prompt or to do the first step or problem together.

Difficulty Completing Tasks

To ensure that students finish tasks, consider the following methods:

- Assist students in setting goals for task completion within realistic time limits, and help them self-reinforce.
- Clarify what constitutes completion and write this on the board or on cue cards on the student's desk (for example, "Answer all five questions in complete sentences, put name on paper, and place paper in assignment box on teacher's desk.").
- Establish routines for turning in assignments.
- Provide peer help in reminding students to finish and turn in completed tasks.
- Help students list tasks to do and check them off as completed.

Difficulty Organizing

The following suggestions may help students to organize:

- List assignments and materials needed on the board or a transparency.
- Teach students to use an assignment calendar or a checklist.
- Have students use notebooks with pockets or dividers.
- Provide places to put materials in desks or in the room (in boxes or trays).
- Help students to color-code materials needed for various subjects.
- Provide time to gather materials at the beginning or end of each class or day.
- Teach a consistent routine for turning in or picking up assignments.
- Provide peer help.
- Help students divide assignments into steps or parts.

Difficulty with Tasks That Require Memorization

Help students increase their ability to memorize by incorporating (and teaching) memory strategies, such as mnemonics, visualizing, oral practice or rehearsal, and many repetitions. For example, teach students to make a word or sentence using the first letters of words in a list to be learned, or help students memorize new terms using picture clues and known words (Mastropieri and Scruggs 1998).

Expressing Information

The third main area of challenge refers to students expressing what they know. Sometimes students are challenged by the actual writing of the information, sometimes by difficulty with following directions or sticking with the task at hand and other times because of inadequate test-taking skills. In all cases, these challenges can make it difficult for a student to show what they know.

Slow or Poor Handwriting

When students exhibit handwriting difficulties, consider the following suggestions:

- Teach handwriting and provide for increased practice to build fluency. Provide practice that uses content of personal interest (for example, have students copy information about skateboarding).

When the objective of the lesson or activity is not to teach or practice handwriting, consider the following:

- Decrease nonessential writing. For example, don't require students to copy questions before writing the answers.
- Give students a copy of your notes or a copy of a peer's notes.
- Allow the use of other methods, such as using a word processor, giving oral presentations, having someone take dictation, or taping answers.
- Don't worry about handwriting as long as it is readable.

Messiness

Use the following techniques to help students maintain neatness:

- Allow students to use a pencil and eraser, graph paper that helps organize writing on a page, or a word processor.
- Provide time and support for cleaning a desk or work area.
- Provide storage places (boxes, shelves, extra desks, or notebooks) and reminders of where to put things.

Difficulty with Taking Tests

When students find it difficult to take tests, consider the following options:

- Allow alternative forms of testing (oral rather than written, for example).
- Provide help with understanding directions for taking tests.
- Teach test-taking skills (for example, cross out incorrect answers on multiple choice tests or outline answers on essay tests).

Difficulty Sticking with Routine Tasks

The following methods may be effective when teaching students who find it difficult to persevere with tasks:

- Divide tasks into smaller segments, with brief breaks or reinforcement between segments, or spread tasks throughout the day or class.
- Remove anything unnecessary from tasks, such as copying sentences before correcting them.
- Analyze the amount of practice needed and remove unnecessary repetitions. Make sure the difficulty level is appropriate, and the objective is important.
- Alternate preferred tasks with less preferred ones.
- Alternate forms of practice and offer choices (for example, students can practice math problems on paper, the board, with a partner, or using a computer).
- Add novelty and interest with games, materials, personal interests, and so on.
- Teach on-task behaviors, including self-monitoring and self-reinforcement.

Difficulty Following Directions

If students find it difficult to follow oral or written directions, consider the following methods:

- Before giving directions, make sure you have the student's attention (for example, gain eye contact, say a name, or touch).
- Give only one or two directions at a time.
- Teach and follow consistent routines so directions do not have to be given too often.
- Simplify the language and vocabulary.
- Emphasize key words with your voice or with gestures.
- Ask the student to repeat the directions, at first to you and eventually to self.
- Give students their own copy of written directions.
- Teach the meaning of "direction" words.
- Underline key words in written directions.
- Teach the students to circle important words in written directions.
- Have a peer read directions to the student.

Summary

Many more selected interventions are described in the professional literature. See the references and suggested readings for more ideas. Remember that when you select strategies that you think will benefit one or a few of your students, be sure to determine whether the strategy would in fact, benefit many students in the class. If it would, build it in rather than add it on.

References and Suggested Readings

Algozzine, B., J. Ysseldyke, and J. Elliott. 2000. *Strategies and tactics for effective instruction.* 2nd ed. Longmont, CO: Sopris West, 1992.

Banikowski, S. K., and T. A. Mehring. 1999. Strategies to enhance memory based on brain research. *Focus on Exceptional Children* 32 (2): 1–16.

Bender, W. N., and M. Y. Mathes. 1995. Students with ADHD in the inclusive classroom: A hierarchical approach to strategy selection. *Intervention in School and Clinic* 30:226–234.

Bowe, F. 2005. *Making inclusion work*. Upper Saddle River, N.J.: Pearson.

Bullard, H. 2004. 20 ways to ensure the successful inclusion of a child with Asperger's syndrome in the general education classroom. *Intervention in School and Clinic* 39 (3): 176–180.

Cegelka, P. T., and W. H. Berdine. 1995. *Effective instruction for students with learning difficulties.* Needham Heights, MA: Allyn and Bacon.

Cohen, S. B., and D. K. Lynch. 1991. An instructional modification process. *Teaching Exceptional Children* 23: 12–18.

Council for Exceptional Children. 1992. *Children with ADD: A shared responsibility.* Reston, VA: Author.

Cox, P., and M. Dykes. 2001. Effective classroom adaptations for students with visual impairments. *Teaching Exceptional Children* 33 (6): 68–74.

Cruickshank, D. R., D. B. Jenkins, and K. K. Metcalf. 2006. *The act of teaching.* 4th ed. Boston: McGraw-Hill.

Cummings, C. 1990. *Teaching makes a difference.* 2nd ed. Edmonds, WA: Teaching, Inc.

Dowdy, C., J. Patton, T. Smith, and E. Polloway. 1998. *Attention-deficit/hyperactivity disorder in the classroom.* Austin, TX: Pro-Ed.

Evertson, C. M., E. T. Emmer, and M. E. Worsham. 2006. *Classroom management for elementary teachers.* 5th ed. Needham Heights, MA: Allyn and Bacon.

Fisher, J. B., J. B. Schumaker, and D. D. Deshler. 1995. Searching for validated inclusive practices: A review of the literature. *Focus on Exceptional Children* 28: 1–20.

Howell, K. W., J. L. Hosp, and M. K. Hosp. n.d. *Curriculum-based evaluation: Teaching and decision making.* 4th ed. Belmont, CA: Wadsworth/ Thomson Learning. Forthcoming.

Kaplan, J. S. 1995. *Beyond behavior modification.* 3rd ed. Austin, TX: Pro-Ed.

Kemp, K., S. Fister, and P. J. McLaughlin. 1995. Academic strategies for children with ADD. *Intervention in School and Clinic* 30: 203–210.

Larkin, M. 2001. Providing support for student independence through scaffolded instruction. *Teaching Exceptional Children* 34 (1): 30–34.

Lerner, J. W., B. Lowenthal, and S. R. Lerner. 1995. *Attention deficit disorders.* Pacific Grove, CA: Brooks/Cole.

Lovitt, T. C. 1995. *Tactics for teaching.* 2nd ed. Englewood Cliffs, NJ: Prentice Hall.

Mastropieri, M. A., and T. E. Scruggs. 1998. Enhancing school success with mnemonic strategies. *Intervention in School and Clinic* 33: 201–208.

Mastropieri, M. A., and T. E. Scruggs. 2004. *The inclusive classroom: Strategies for effective instruction.* 2nd ed. Upper Saddle River, N.J.: Pearson.

Mathews, R. 2000. Cultural patterns of South Asian and Southeast Asian Americans. *Intervention in School and Clinic* 36 (2): 101–104.

Meltzer, L. J., B. N. Roditi, D. P. Haynes, K. R. Biddle, M. Paster, and S. E. Taber. 1996. *Strategies for success: Classroom teaching techniques for students with learning problems.* Austin, TX: Pro-Ed.

Ormsbee, C., and K. Finson. 2000. Modifying science activities and materials to enhance instruction for students with learning and behavioral problems. *Intervention in School and Clinic* 36 (1): 10–21.

Pakulski, L. A., and J. N. Kaderavek. 2002. Children with minimal hearing loss: Interventions in the classroom. *Intervention in School and Clinic* 38 (2): 96–103.

Prater, M. A. 1992. Increasing time on task in the classroom. *Intervention in School and Clinic* 28: 22–27.

Prestia, K. 2003. Tourette's syndrome: Characteristics and interventions. *Intervention in School and Clinic* 29 (2): 67–71.

Reid, R. 1999. Attention deficit hyperactivity disorder: Effective methods for the classroom. *Focus on Exceptional Children* 32 (4): 1–20.

Rhode, G., W. Jenson, and H. Reavis. 1993. *The tough kid book.* Longmont, CO: Sopris West.

Rooney, K. J. 1995. Teaching students with attention disorders. *Intervention in School and Clinic* 30: 221–225.

Salend, S. J. 2005. *Creating inclusive classrooms: Effective and reflective practices for all students.* 5th ed. Upper Saddle River, N.J.: Pearson.

Salend, S. J., and M. Gajria. 1995. Increasing the homework completion rates of students with mild disabilities. *Remedial and Special Education* 16: 271–278.

Salend, S. J., H. Elhoweris, and D. VanGarderen. 2003. Educational interventions for students with ADD. *Intervention in School and Clinic* 38 (5): 280–288.

Sprick, R., M. Sprick, and M. Garrison. 1993. *Interventions: Collaborative planning for students at risk.* Longmont, CO: Sopris West.

Stormont-Spurgin, M. 1997. I lost my homework: Strategies for improving organization in students with ADHD. *Intervention in School and Clinic* 32 (5): 270–274.

Uberti, H., M. Mastropieri, and T. Scruggs. 2004. Check It Off: Individualizing a math algorithm for students with disabilities via self-monitoring checklists. *Intervention in School and Clinic* 39 (5): 269–275.

Welton, E. N. 1999. How to help inattentive students find success in school: Getting the homework back from the dog. *Teaching Exceptional Children* 31 (6): 12–18.

Williamson, R. D. 1997. Help me organize. *Intervention in School and Clinic* 33 (1): 36–39.

Wood, J. W. 2006. *Teaching students in inclusive settings—adapting and accommodating instruction.* 5th ed. Upper Saddle River, New Jersey: Pearson/Merrill Prentice Hall.

Yehle, A. K., and C. Wambold. 1998. An ADHD success story: Strategies for teachers and students. *Teaching Exceptional Children* 30: 8–13.

The Context for Teaching and Learning

A Framework for Diversity Responsive Teaching

PLANNING *WHAT* TO TEACH	PLANNING *HOW* TO TEACH	PLANNING THE *CONTEXT* FOR TEACHING AND LEARNING
Content About diversity For a diverse world Carrier content	**Universal instructional interventions** Universal design for learning Differentiated instruction Critical teaching skills	**Environment** Physical Social Emotional
Completeness Thorough coverage All contributors Varied perspectives Similarities & differences	**Selected instructional interventions** Accommodations for: Acquisition of information Processing and memorizing Expressing information	**Universal behavioral interventions** Rules, routines, & social skills Critical management skills
Connections To student experiences Importance to students' lives Build on student ideas		**Selected behavioral interventions** ABC

Teaching and learning don't happen in a vacuum. Rather, they happen in a place that has a climate or atmosphere. We call this place the context or the environment for teaching and learning. This context is made up of physical, social, and emotional elements.

A positive context for teaching and learning is welcoming, safe, supportive, engaging, challenging, inclusive, and respectful. This context has the appropriate amount of structure, orderliness, and efficiency. It is responsive to diversity. A positive context for teaching and learning supports appropriate student behavior. A positive context doesn't just happen; it results from careful planning. It's just as important for teachers to plan the context for teaching and learning as it is to plan curriculum and instruction.

Teachers take action to create a positive context at the very beginning of the year. They create this environment by connecting with each student, by being responsive to diversity, and through the use of universal and selected behavioral interventions. Universal interventions are those that are used proactively for all students. Selected interventions are targeted only to those students who need them. In Chapter 10, we will describe these aspects of planning the context for teaching and learning.

Teachers also take action to create a positive context in each lesson and activity they teach throughout the year. They do this by incorporating critical management skills in their lesson and activity plans. Planning these management skills helps support appropriate behavior and prevent behavior problems. We'll focus on each critical management skill in Chapter 11.

This part of the book, of course, is not meant to replace a full text on classroom or behavior management. Many, many variables impact the context for teaching and learning. Our primary focus is to show how to build in preventive management as you plan daily lessons and activities.

Supporting Student Behavior

Introduction

You create a positive context for teaching and learning when you support appropriate student behavior, which is behavior that promotes, or does not interfere with, the learning of the student or his classmates. Supporting appropriate student behavior begins with connecting with each student. Creating a diversity responsive environment that welcomes and includes each student is another fundamental aspect of this support. In addition, teachers must implement proactive universal behavioral interventions such as establishing and teaching classroom rules, routines, and social skills. Finally, teachers must use selected, individualized interventions for those students who need them. Developing a positive context for teaching and learning starts at the beginning of the school year and continues throughout the year. Planning for the support of appropriate student behavior in each lesson and activity can then rest on this foundation.

Connecting with Students

Connecting with students is fundamental to all else in creating a positive context for teaching and learning. This is easier with some students than others. The key is acting like you like your students. Let us repeat that. Act like you like them! ALL of them. Show that you are thrilled to have each of them in your class. Act like it makes your day when they walk in the door. There are many ways to connect with students. The following is a list of ideas to get you started:

- Greet them—know their names and pronounce them correctly.
- Smile and make eye contact.
- Be available to them and listen, *really* listen.
- Have informal conversations with them and spend time with them outside of class, such as at lunch.
- Attend their school and community activities.
- Remember their interests and concerns and share yours.
- Joke with them and laugh at their jokes.
- Do favors for them and let them do favors for you.
- Plan surprises for them.
- Notice when they've been absent and welcome them back.
- Deal with their misbehavior calmly and matter-of-factly and never hold a grudge.

Responding to Diversity When Connecting with Students

You will want to consider diversity as you attempt to connect with students. Students will vary in their expectations or levels of relationships with teachers: some will prefer close, warm, informal relationships, and others, more distant, formal relationships. They will have preferences about touching and being touched. Students' beliefs regarding talking and conversations will vary, such as the amount of talking that's polite, who initiates, sharing personal information, and what is considered private. Don't assume your students are just like you. They may be horrified if you sit on the floor with them or ask them to call you by your first name. They may believe you don't like them if you don't hug them or ask about their families. Take time to learn about your students' cultural backgrounds so you can reach out to them in ways with which they are comfortable, and recognize their attempts to reach out to you.

Make a special effort to connect with students who have emotional or behavioral difficulties and are typically rejected or ignored by their peers and by adults. They may resist your overtures at first, but stick with it. Connecting with you can make a huge difference in their lives.

Creating a Diversity Responsive Environment

As a diversity responsive teacher, you will attempt to make connections between the classroom environment and the students' experiences—at home, in their communities, and perhaps in other countries. You can develop these connections through instructional methods, curriculum, and management. Mismatches between home and school culture can result in misunderstandings and a less than positive context for teaching and learning.

You may find it useful to use the "Planning the Context" component of the Diversity Responsive Teaching framework (in the Introduction to Part 3 of this book) as you develop the context for teaching and learning in your classroom. It is intended to support teachers in creating diversity responsive environments, that is, those that are welcoming, safe, supportive, and respectful to *all* students and families. This doesn't happen by chance. It takes careful planning. Think of the environment as made up of physical objects, social interactions, and emotional climate.

The Physical Environment

When planning a diversity responsive environment, consider making the physical environment welcoming and stimulating for all. When students and families walk in the door, you want them to think, "Hey, I can read that sign," "There's a picture of someone who looks like me," "Whew, the aisles are wide enough for my wheelchair," or "There's a poster about a holiday my family celebrates." A diversity responsive environment is also one that engenders interest in diversity. You want your students, when they enter the classroom, to think, "I wonder what language I'm hearing," "There's a book about someone who is deaf, I wonder what that's like," or "I'd like to know more about the people who make that art." Begin your planning by thinking about all of the things that make up the physical environment in a classroom, such as books, photographs, recordings, signs, artifacts, toys, games, and technology devices, and then work at making these objects and materials fully representative of diversity. The desired outcome is a physical environment where all students and families feel represented and comfortable and where students are stimulated to learn about diversity.

The Social Environment

Also think about creating a diversity responsive social environment in the classroom when planning. The social environment is made up of interactions among students and between adults and students. Your goal is to ensure that all students are part of these interactions, that no one is excluded, and that the interactions are positive. Building a community and fostering friendships among all students is essential in creating a diversity responsive social environment. You want all to feel included, including those who look or speak differently from the majority, have different skills, different family structures, different economic resources, different sexual orientations, different beliefs, and so on. Again, this doesn't happen by chance. You can model respect in your verbal and nonverbal communication through correct pronunciation of names, culturally correct use of touch and gestures, and greetings in student languages, for example. You can model acceptance by making connections with all students. You can encourage inclusion as you form cooperative groups, devise seating arrangements, and develop buddy systems. You can build community as you develop rules about name-calling, help students develop cross-cultural social skills, teach students to be allies, and implement bullying prevention programs. The desired outcome is a social environment where all students are welcomed and supported, where friendly and respectful interactions are the norm, and where there is full social inclusion and integration.

The Emotional Environment

A third area to consider when planning is creating a diversity responsive emotional environment in the classroom. In this area, you will focus on the activities and assignments used. The goal is to ensure that no one is inadvertently made to feel embarrassed or abnormal. If you use holiday activities in the classroom, be sure they reflect diversity in religion, ethnicity, and family structure. For example, think about Mother's Day activities and the fact that your students may be mothered by a variety of people or not at all. That doesn't mean that making Mother's Day cards should be eliminated, but make sure that you are inclusive in how you design this activity. Another area in which to be respectful of varied family structures is in assignments for writing autobiographies or family trees or interviewing grandparents. Consider diversity in family resources if you assign students to bring treats for the class or to pay for field trips. When you give homework assignments, be careful about assumptions you might make about materials available at home and the availability of help. Being sensitive and respectful does not mean lowering expectations. It doesn't mean eliminating homework that's necessary for achievement. Everyone should be challenged. Think about the diversity of families—to whom you address notes sent home, in what language, where and when meetings are scheduled, and so on. The desired outcome is an emotional environment that is sensitive to all students and families, where all are considered and respected, and where feelings are considered as you plan activities and assignments.

Creating a diversity responsive environment is an important part of establishing a positive context for teaching and learning.

Universal Behavioral Interventions

Another important part of developing a positive context for teaching and learning is the use of universal behavioral interventions. Universal behavioral interventions are those interventions that are used proactively for the whole class. They are meant to encourage appropriate behavior by making expectations clear and specific and by teaching students the important behaviors they will need to be successful in learning and in getting along with others. We will discuss the universal behavioral interventions of establishing and teaching rules, routines, and social skills.

It is important to establish classroom rules and routines at the beginning of the school year. Students are more likely to behave appropriately when they know what is expected and when they are involved in setting those expectations. Further, this provides you with a solid frame of reference for communicating expectations for behavior throughout the year.

Developing Classroom Rules

Basic to planning the context for teaching and learning is developing classroom rules. The goal is to provide a physically and emotionally safe environment with the right amount of structure. Ideally, school-wide general rules will be enacted and then made specific for the classroom (and other settings, such as the lunchroom and playground).

- Some examples of general rules include "Respect others," "Be prepared," "Always do your best," and "Be kind." General rules establish standards of behavior. They define "ways to be." They are general enough to apply in a variety of settings and to a variety of situations. General rules by themselves don't tell students what (and what not) to do. They *must* be clarified with specific rules.

- Examples of specific rules include "Be inside the classroom when the bell rings," "Raise your hand and wait to be called on before speaking," "Turn in tasks on time," and "Keep your hands and feet to yourself." Specific rules describe what to do or not do; they specify how to behave. Specific rules help students understand what is expected and translate general rules into visible actions. Well-written specific rules are observable, measurable, stated positively, such as what to do ("walk") rather than what not to do ("don't run"), and are short and simple (Rhode, Jenson, and Reavis 1993).

Notice how the following paired examples of general and specific rules differ and how they connect:

General Rule	Specific Rule
Be safe.	Walk inside the building.
Be responsible.	Bring notebook and pencil to class.
Be respectful.	Touch people only with their permission.
Be a learner.	Ask questions when you don't understand.

As guidelines to follow in establishing rules, (1) develop rules with students, (2) keep them few in number so everyone can remember them, (3) post them, (4) refer to them often, (5) support students in following them, (6) teach the students what each rule means, (7) acknowledge students for following them, and (8) enforce them consistently.

Responding to Diversity When Developing Classroom Rules

General rules such as "Be respectful" or "Be responsible" are open to interpretation. People from different cultural backgrounds will have different ideas on how to show respect, responsibility, and so on. For example, strong teasing and verbal sparring are valued in some cultures but considered disrespectful in others. Some people would see making independent choices (such as leaving class to use the restroom) as responsible behavior, whereas those who value adult permission would see it as irresponsible. Different cultures vary in valuing simultaneous talking, entering conversations at the briefest of openings, or leaving long pauses in discussions. In some cultures silent listening to a speaker is respectful whereas in others, calling out responses and affirmations is polite (Weinstein, Curran, and Tomlinson-Clarke 2003).

These differences are one reason it is important to have specific rules for common understanding. They are also a reason why it is so important to involve students in developing rules and to learn what you can about the cultural backgrounds of your students. Don't automatically impose your cultural view when establishing rules. Make room for varied perspectives and compromises. For example, some of your students may have a strong sense of private property and may have difficulty sharing their school supplies unless specifically asked permission. Others may come from a more communal background and are comfortable with general sharing. Through discussion, the students may compromise on a rule that says items inside student desks and backpacks may only be borrowed with permission, but that materials may be freely taken from the community resource boxes.

The purpose of rules should be to promote comfortable, predictable, orderly environments where people can teach, learn, and feel safe. The purpose should not be obedience for its own sake. Carefully examine rules about being quiet, sitting still, walking in lines, and so on to make sure they are in the students' best interest and are not overcontrolling. Don't automatically require behaviors such as raising hands without thinking about whether they will encourage learning for all students.

Establishing Classroom Routines

Routines are ways of getting things done in the classroom. Many events, such as the beginning or ending of class, turning in assignments, or lining up, need to happen efficiently to avoid wasted time and behavior problems. It is important that teachers establish and teach routines to students, just as it is important to establish and teach rules. Once students are familiar with classroom rules and routines, the teacher can state behavior expectations at the beginning of each lesson or activity by telling the students what specific rules and routines apply. Some examples of events for which you may want to establish classroom routines include the following:

responding to a signal for attention	free time; snack time; centers
correcting assignments in class	finding a partner
using the restroom, pencil sharpener	getting help on tasks
getting assignments when absent	finishing a task early

To establish routines, begin with deciding what classroom events would benefit from clear procedures to avoid wasted time, prevent behavior problems, and foster student independence. For example, perhaps you want to prevent the problem of students spending too much time with their hands in the air, waiting for help. You choose to establish a routine for "Getting Help on In-Class Tasks." Next you (and perhaps your students) will decide on the steps for students to follow. This is called a task analysis (see Chapter 1).

Following is an example of steps for getting help.

How to Get Help

1. If you run into difficulty, help yourself:
   a. look at examples, reread directions, use resources
   b. try again
2. If you still need help:
   a. ask neighbor (if permitted)
   b. use help signal to teacher
3. While waiting for help:
   a. plan the question to ask
   b. skip the problem and go on if possible

Finally, you will decide how to teach the routine to the students. (This is discussed in a following section.)

Responding to Diversity When Establishing Classroom Routines

Established routines are helpful for English language learners because they help these students predict what's expected and to follow what is happening even when they don't understand what is said. They are especially important to students new to this country and unfamiliar with the school system. Routines create stability, reduce anxiety, and allow English language learners to be more fully involved in the classroom. Consider using buddies to teach or model routines (Herrell and Jordan 2004; Law and Eckes 2000; Curran 2003). Established routines are also helpful to students who have difficulty with change and novelty, such as students with autism spectrum disorders.

Planning Social Skills Instruction

An important aspect of the context for teaching and learning is the social environment, the interactions between people. Students need many social skills to negotiate this environment. They need social skills to be successful in lessons and activities, to follow the rules and routines, to make friends, to get along with adults in authority, to solve inter- and intrapersonal problems, and so on. (See Chapter 18 for more information about social skills.)

It makes sense to teach these skills proactively to everyone because they are so important for a positive context. Many students will have picked up these skills without formal instruction, but teaching them universally is important as a way of establishing classroom expectations, demonstrating how important they are, getting everyone on the same page, and preventing the development of antisocial behavior patterns. All students could benefit from more instruction on at least some social skills (such as conflict resolution).

You will need to decide which (of the many) social skills to teach universally in your class. Begin by analyzing the instructional methods you use often in lessons and activities such as partner work, group work, or discussions. These methods will require social skills such as giving and receiving feedback, active listening, and disagreeing politely. Also analyze typical events and activities such as free time, lunch, or show and tell (which require social skills in joining in, starting a conversation, inviting others to do something, and taking turns). In addition, analyze your classroom rules for embedded social skills (showing respect, including others). Finally, think about typical issues for this age group or setting (name-calling, sharing, dealing with teasing, resisting peer pressure, accepting *no* for an answer).

Responding to Diversity When Planning Social Skills Instruction

Remember that social competence is culturally defined. You will need to know whether the social skills you plan to teach are accepted in your students' families, communities, and peer groups. When there are differences, you will want to teach alternatives and help students decide how to choose the skills to use in a given situation. Talking with families, attending community events, observing students with their peers, and facilitating class discussions on this topic will help you understand diverse perspectives on what is socially skilled behavior.

How to Teach Rules, Routines, and Social Skills

Begin by evaluating your students' present levels of understanding and performance of the rule, routine, or social skill. They may require a simple precorrection, an activity, or a formal lesson. Use a precorrection when students know the skill but would benefit from a brief reminder of how and when to use it. Use an activity when students are familiar with the skill but need a more elaborate review, instruction in applying it to different situations, and/or motivation to use it. Use a formal lesson when students need initial, elaborate instruction for understanding and using an important or complex skill. This doesn't mean they have no experience at all with the skill but do need more than a review.

A precorrection includes a quick reminder and practice immediately before the rule, routine, or social skill is needed. For example, you can tell the students in advance that they should use the skill ("We're having an assembly today and you will need to listen politely"), review the skill ("Can someone help me describe polite listening?"), and rehearse the skill with them ("Imagine that I'm the assembly speaker and show me what polite listening looks like and sounds like."). This may be all that's required when the skill has been taught in the past or when it's a simple skill. Colvin (2004) suggests that with older students a reminder of the skill, supervision while they use it, and feedback may be all that is necessary.

Teachers have many possibilities for using activities to teach rules, routines, and social skills. For example, perhaps your students know that they are not supposed to use name-calling with their peers but they are doing it anyway. They know what words and names they should and shouldn't use so they don't need a lesson on that aspect. Instead you create an activity that involves having your students survey others about their feelings when called names and then making posters to put up around the school on how name-calling hurts. Your intention is to develop empathy and motivation to follow the rule (see Chapter 14 for how to plan activities).

Rules, routines, and social skills can also be taught as formal lessons in the same way that academic skills are taught. Teach the skill explicitly by explaining it, demonstrating it, and providing practice in performing the skill. See Chapter 13 for information on how to write lesson plans and an example lesson plan for teaching a routine ("How to Get Help on In-Class Tasks"). See Chapter 18 for how to teach social skills lessons and an example lesson plan for teaching a social skill ("Standing Up for Someone").

Selected Behavioral Interventions

Universal behavioral interventions will likely be sufficient for creating a positive context for teaching and learning and preventing behavior problems with the majority of your students. Some students, however, will need additional individualized interventions. These are called selected or targeted interventions. We will briefly discuss types of selected interventions and describe a few examples. A full treatment of behavior management is beyond the scope of this book.

When to Use Selected Behavioral Interventions

Use selected interventions as small-group or individual accommodations when one or a few of your students are having a difficult time behaving appropriately. Some students might have trouble with self-control, paying attention, following rules, getting along with others, handling frustration, resolving conflicts, complying with adult requests, dealing with change, and staying on task, to mention a few.

You need to begin by evaluating your own behavior and your use of universal interventions and critical management skills to determine whether you are implementing these interventions consistently and correctly. Then observe carefully and interview to gather information about the student behavior (for example, its frequency), what happens before the behavior (its antecedents), and what follows the behavior (its consequences).

If you think the whole class could benefit from a selected intervention, by all means build it into the lesson or activity, that is, make it a universal intervention. For example, perhaps a few students are having a lot of difficulty working with peers. You decide to try having them use goal-setting for improving peer interactions during partner practice. You then decide that everyone could benefit from experience with goal-setting and improvement in getting along with others, so you build this intervention into the opening of the lesson for everyone.

Types of Selected Behavioral Interventions

One way to categorize selected interventions is as **A**ntecedent interventions, replacement **B**ehavior interventions, and **C**onsequence interventions—**ABC.** It can be helpful to use the ABC acronym/organizer to develop a variety of types of selected interventions. Teachers have a tendency to overuse consequence interventions, particularly punishments. Avoid that. We strongly encourage that you use positive behavior support as much as possible and especially avoid negative interventions that exclude students from instruction.

Many resources on behavior management are available to teachers and we encourage you to use them. However, you'll find that you can also generate ideas of your own by using ABC, your common sense, and your belief that everyone can learn and change. Following are a few examples to stimulate your thinking.

A (Antecedents)

Antecedent interventions are those that you implement to make it less likely that the inappropriate behavior will occur. Think of them as scaffolding or support for appropriate behavior. They include advance changes to the setting, the situation, the task, the prompts, and so on. Following are a few examples of antecedent interventions:

- Make adjustments to the curriculum to make content interesting, relevant, and at the correct level of difficulty for individuals. Inappropriate behavior can be a reaction to inappropriate content.
- Instructional accommodations may be needed for the academic success and challenge of individuals. Effective teaching can prevent behavior problems from arising. Chapters 3 through 9 have many suggestions that will help you make accommodations.
- Intensify and individualize universal interventions, such as using individualized precorrections (reminders, reviews, rehearsals) of behavior expectations.
- Arrange peer support such as modeling, buddying, assistance, or encouragement. An assigned buddy for recess, for example, can prevent behavior problems that arise when a student has no one with whom to play.
- Change how you make requests to students who tend to be noncompliant. For example, offering simple choices such as, "Would you rather do your math problems at the back table or at your desk?" or ". . . with this pencil or with that one?" sometimes lets students feel more in control and supports compliance.

So many variables affect behavior that this is an area where careful assessment followed by team brainstorming is particularly useful.

B (Replacement Behaviors)

These interventions involve teaching students alternative behaviors to replace the inappropriate behaviors they display. For example, teach verbal conflict resolution skills to replace fighting, or teach students to ask for help when they are frustrated, as an alternative to swearing or tearing up papers. Think about the function of the inappropriate behavior and an appropriate behavior that would achieve the same purpose.

Explicit one-to-one or small-group teaching, with plenty of practice through role playing, provides initial instruction of the replacement behavior (social skill). It is essential to follow up with precorrection, prompts, corrective feedback, strong reinforcement, and other coaching techniques in the context where the social skill is needed. Look for "teachable moments" to promote generalization. (See Chapter 18 for additional information about teaching social skills.)

C (Consequences)

Consequences means what happens after a behavior. Consequences can be positive or negative. They can be used to strengthen appropriate behavior and to weaken inappropriate behavior. Consequence interventions are important selected interventions.

When a student who struggles with self-control *does* display appropriate behavior, use strong, immediate, and frequent reinforcement consequences. Verbal acknowledgements alone may not be enough. Rewarding the student with preferred activities and privileges or with tangible items may be needed to strengthen the appropriate behavior.

When the student behaves inappropriately, use systematic warnings and negative consequences. Be sure these are planned, fair, and explained to the student ahead of time. They must not be random punishments by an annoyed adult—that doesn't teach the student self-control. Response cost is a commonly used negative consequence. Misbehaviors cost the students lost privileges, points, or time from desired activities. It's very important to use positive interventions along with these.

You can use written behavior contracts to spell out an agreement between the student and teacher. They are negotiated as business contracts. You and the student agree upon a goal (such as being on time) and pinpoint a specific behavior (student will be inside the classroom when the first bell rings). Decide upon the positive consequence for fulfilling the contract (extra computer time). Make the terms explicit (on time for four days equals extra computer time during lunch period). It's important that the contract is very clear, written and signed, fair, and likely to result in success.

Another useful selected intervention is a self-management plan. Teach students to self-evaluate, self-monitor/record, set goals, and self-reinforce. This, of course, is very empowering and promotes independence. The teacher and the student develop a self-management plan and the teacher gradually turns more and more of the responsibility over to the student.

You can put the three types of interventions (ABC) together in individual behavior plans. These plans should be developed as a team effort that includes families. Remember that the purpose is to provide positive behavior support for students who need more help than the universal interventions used in the class provide.

Responding to Diversity

Don't mistake behavior differences for behavior problems. For example, teachers who are from a different cultural background than their students may mistake exuberance, enthusiasm, and liveliness for disrespect, aggression, or hyperactivity. Or they may mistake politeness and respect for lack of interest, lack of motivation, or lack of attention.

Also, don't mistake language learning issues for behavior problems. Curran (2003) points out that when students don't understand the language of instruction, their anxiety may come out as laughter. They may speak to peers in their first language to seek understanding. They may become tired and silent. It can be easy to misinterpret these behaviors.

Summary

The suggestions in this chapter are based on several assumptions or beliefs. One is that teachers need to support appropriate student behavior in positive ways. Another is that it is most helpful to see misbehaviors as behavior errors and to emphasize teaching rather than punishment. A third assumption is that our job is to help students learn self-control and self-management rather than trying to do all the controlling ourselves.

References and Suggested Readings

Alberto, P., and A. Troutman. 2006. *Applied behavior analysis for teachers.* 7th ed. Upper Saddle River, NJ: Pearson.

Bucalos, A., and A. Lingo. 2005. What kind of "managers" do adolescents really need? Helping middle and secondary teachers manage classrooms effectively. *Beyond Behavior* 14 (2): 9–14.

Cartledge, G., and J. Milburn. 1995. *Teaching social skills to children and youth.* Needham Heights, MA: Allyn and Bacon.

Chamberlain, S. 2005. Recognizing and responding to cultural differences in the education of culturally and linguistically diverse learners. *Intervention in School and Clinic* 40 (4): 195–211.

Colvin, G. 2004. *Managing the cycle of acting-out behavior in the classroom.* Eugene, OR: Behavior Associates.

Curran, M. 2003. Linguistic diversity and classroom management. *Theory into Practice* 42 (4): 334–340.

Duhaney, L. 2003. A practical approach to managing the behaviors of students with ADD. *Intervention in School and Clinic* 38 (5): 267–279.

Elksnin, L., and N. Elksnin. 2006. *Teaching social-emotional skills at school and home.* Denver, CO: Love Publishing.

Emmer, E., C. Evertson, and M. Worsham. 2006. *Classroom management for middle and high school teachers.* 7th ed. Needham Heights, MA: Allyn and Bacon.

Evertson, C., E. Emmer, and M. Worsham. 2006. *Classroom management for elementary teachers.* 7th ed. Needham Heights, MA: Allyn and Bacon.

Grossman, H. 1991. Multicultural classroom management. *Contemporary Education* 62: 61–166.

Herrell, A., and M. Jordan. 2004. *Fifty strategies for teaching English-language learners.* 2nd ed. Upper Saddle River, NJ: Prentice-Hall.

Kaplan, J. S. 1995. *Beyond behavior modification.* 3rd ed. Austin, TX: Pro-Ed.

Kern, L., and G. Sacks. 2003. *How to deal effectively with inappropriate talking and noisemaking.* Austin, TX: Pro-ed.

Law, B., and M. Eckes. 2000. *The more-than-just-surviving handbook: ESL for every classroom teacher.* 2nd ed. Winnipeg, Manitoba, Canada: Portage and Main Press.

Maag, J. 2004. *Behavior management: From theoretical implications to practical applications.* 2nd ed. Belmont, CA: Wadsworth/Thomson Learning.

Martella, R., J. Nelson, and N. Marchand-Martella. 2003. *Managing disruptive behaviors in the schools: A schoolwide, classroom, and individualized social learning approach.* Boston, MA: Allyn and Bacon.

Rhode, G., W. Jenson, and H. Reavis. 1993. *The tough kid book.* Longmont, CO: Sopris West.

Rosenberg, M., and L. Jackman. 2003. Development, implementation, and sustainability of comprehensive school-wide behavior management systems, *Intervention in School and Clinic* 39 (1): 10–21.

Smith, S., and D. Gilles. 2003. Using key instructional elements to systematically promote social skill generalization for students with challenging behavior. *Intervention in School and Clinic* 39 (1): 30–37.

Strout, M. 2005. Positive behavioral support at the classroom level: Considerations and strategies. *Beyond Behavior* 14 (2): 3–8.

Sugai, G., R. Horner, and F. Gresham. 2002. Behaviorally effective school environments. In *Interventions for academic and behavior problems II: Preventive and remedial approaches,* eds. M. Shinn, H. Walker, and G. Stoner, 315–350. Bethesda, MD: National Association of School Psychologists.

Walker, H., E. Ramsey, and F. Gresham. 2004. *Antisocial behavior in school: Evidence-based practices.* 2nd ed. Belmont, CA: Wadsworth/Thomson Learning.

Webb-Johnson, G. 2003. Behaving while black: A hazardous reality for African-American learners? *Beyond Behavior* 12 (2): 3–7.

Weinstein, C., M. Curran, and S. Tomlinson-Clarke. 2003. Culturally responsive classroom management: Awareness into action. *Theory into Practice* 42 (4): 269–276.

Zirpoli, T. 2005. *Behavior management: Applications for teachers.* 4th ed. Upper Saddle River, NJ: Pearson Education, Inc.

Critical Management Skills

Introduction

When teachers have established a solid foundation by connecting with each student, creating a diversity responsive environment, and implementing universal and selected behavioral interventions, they are able to focus on management issues as they apply to the lessons and activities they plan throughout the school year.

Teachers must develop certain basic, essential management skills that they employ in each lesson and activity to support appropriate behavior, prevent behavior problems, and promote learning. In other words, they must develop a positive context for teaching and learning in *each* lesson and activity they teach. These critical management skills include arranging the room, gaining attention, communicating behavior expectations, acknowledging appropriate behavior, monitoring student behavior, planning for logistics, and managing transitions. Each is described in this chapter.

Arranging the Room

One critical management skill is using the physical arrangement of the classroom to support appropriate behavior. Set up the room so you can see all of the students and they can see you, each other, the board, and so on. Eliminate major distractions when possible; for example, face desks away from the door and windows, and teach students to ignore distractions in the long run. Arrange the room so you can move around easily and so students can move around without bothering others. All of this will help students pay attention and will help you include everyone and ensure safety (Evertson, Emmer, and Worsham 2006; Sprick, Garrison, and Howard 1998).

The way you arrange desks and tables will depend on the instructional methods you'll be using. Create your basic room design and then adjust for different lessons and activities. Typically, arranging desks in pairs that face the front works well for active participation during teacher presentations. Putting desks in a circle or U-shape works best for discussions because everyone can see each other as they talk, and participation will be more general. Separated desks are best for individual work as students are less likely to distract each other. Clusters of desks or tables are best for group work because they facilitate interacting. Be aware that when the desk arrangement doesn't match the method used (for example if you have students sitting together in groups but want them to work by themselves) more behavioral self-control is required—perhaps more than the students have.

If you are using several methods in the same lesson or activity, then you'll need to select an arrangement that can be easily transformed. You won't want multiple complicated transitions that involve major furniture moving as that wastes time and begs for behavior problems. All arrangements have advantages and disadvantages and you'll have to balance those.

Responding to Diversity When Arranging the Room

When arranging the room, think about seating assignments. Consider the needs of students who have vision or hearing impairments, who use wheelchairs, who have difficulty focusing attention, who often need redirection or encouragement, and who frequently need to stand or move. Don't permanently seat some students away from the rest of the class.

English language learners may benefit from sitting with those who speak the same languages. Be sure they are seated where they can easily see and hear. English language learners (as well as other students) may benefit from having certain parts of the room designated for certain activities, such as group work, silent reading, or playing (Herrell and Jordan 2004). Be sensitive about cultural values regarding having male and female students seated together.

Gaining Attention

It is critical to be able to gain students' attention when you need it. One place you'll need it is at the beginning of lessons and activities. You'll also need to regain attention at various other points in your lessons and activities. A great deal of instructional time can be wasted when teachers have to repeat instructions or directions because they did not have the students' attention. In addition, students may learn that they don't need to listen as everything is repeated.

Teachers can use signals to gain the attention of the class. Signals can be verbal—"Attention, please," or "Eyes up here." They can be visual—raising your arm or making mime movements. Or they can be sounds—clapping your hands or turning on music. The signal you choose will depend on how difficult you believe it will be to gain your students' attention in a given situation. For example, if students are working in labs with partners, it would work better to clap your hands than it would to stand in front of the room with your arm raised.

You'll need to teach the students the signals you'll be using and the routine you want them to follow to respond to the signal (for example, stop, look, and listen). When you give the signal, position yourself so you can see the faces of all your students and ensure that all of the students are looking at you (Colvin and Lazar 1997). Following the signal, you should remain silent. Make the students responsible, giving no reminders, warnings, or nagging. Remember to acknowledge students for responding quickly. Encourage the students to help each other through nudges, whispered reminders, and so on. Of course, be sure *you* are ready to begin as soon as you have their attention.

Responding to Diversity When Gaining Attention

You will need, of course, to consider hearing or visual impairments as you develop signals. Involving students in creating signals may increase buy-in by those who are otherwise not inclined to respond. Using culturally or linguistically significant signals sends an inclusive message. Songs, rhymes, alliterations, and using various languages are possibilities. Consistent signals (especially nonverbal ones) are very helpful to English language learners.

The Challenging Class

Sometimes you have a class that has difficulty behaving appropriately even when you use universal interventions and critical management skills. If your class struggles with responding to the signal for attention, choose a stronger signal such as ringing a bell or turning off the lights. Teach a formal lesson on how to respond to the signal (for example, "Freeze and wait"). Challenge the class to set a goal for a quick response. Reward the class for "beating the clock."

Communicating Behavior Expectations

It is essential to communicate your expectations for behavior to students. Clarifying expectations acts as a precorrection and prevents behavior problems. Remember that you have already established classroom rules and routines and taught social skills to your students at the beginning of the year. Now you are going to identify which rules, routines, and social skills apply during this particular lesson or activity. Consider the following suggestions for determining your behavior expectations.

Think about your *goals for student behavior.* Remember that the purpose of rules and routines in the classroom is to facilitate student learning and positive interactions. Then consider what will be happening during this lesson or activity. Decide what behaviors will help the lesson or activity go smoothly, efficiently, safely, and allow everyone to learn. Determine what previously taught routines students will need to use and whether you should review them at the beginning of the lesson or activity. For example, routines for getting help, finishing tasks early, and clean up may be relevant. Decide what social skills students will need to use and whether you should review them with students. Social skills such as sharing, accepting feedback, or disagreeing politely may apply. Recognize that you will need to be especially clear about those rules that vary by situation (raising hands during presentations versus talking during partner work, being out of seat during tests versus during projects). Identify what students should say or do to participate during a lesson or activity ("Each group member should offer at least one idea for a skit.").

Next you will need to *communicate the behavior expectations.* Write the behavior expectations in advance, making sure the language is appropriate for the students. Communicate behavior expectations firmly, directly, and politely. Be specific. Say, "Ask permission before using someone else's materials," rather than just "Respect others." State *do*s rather than *don't*s ("Raise hands," rather than "No talk-outs"). Demonstrate the expectations. You will have different behavior expectations for different parts of the activity or lesson. One set of expectations will apply while you are giving directions and another set when students are practicing with a partner, for example. Communicate expectations just before they are needed rather than all at the beginning.

It's very important to *follow through with expectations.* Don't state them and then ignore them. Be consistent. For example, if you stated that students must raise their hands, then don't respond to call-outs. Monitor students carefully and acknowledge students for following the stated expectations. Note that if you are a practicum student or student teacher, you must clearly establish your expectations for student behavior. Don't assume that, because the students understand and follow the cooperating teacher's rules, they will automatically behave the same way with you.

Responding to Diversity When Communicating Behavior Expectations

Be a diversity responsive teacher by not only stating behavior expectations but also displaying them in writing, demonstrating them, and using picture clues. Be consistent in language. Use the same terms as when the rule, routine, or social skill was originally taught. This will be helpful for many students, including English language learners.

The Challenging Class

If your class is having difficulty meeting behavior expectations, spend more time clarifying, reviewing, and demonstrating expectations at the beginning of lessons and activities. Check for understanding. Be sure that your manner is appropriately assertive. Follow up with positive and negative consequences. You may need to spend more time formally teaching the rules, routines, and social skills that underlie the expectations.

Acknowledging Appropriate Behavior

Acknowledging appropriate behavior means noticing, and letting students know you noticed, when they are doing the right thing. It means positively responding when they use the social skills you taught them, when they follow the class rules and routines, when they meet behavior expectations. Unfortunately, many of us find it much more natural to notice and respond to inappropriate behavior. We expect and take for granted appropriate behavior. So acknowledging appropriate behavior may take special effort on your part. It's worth that effort as this is a critical management skill.

When you spend most of your time noticing desirable behavior, you strengthen desirable behavior, decrease the incidence of undesirable behavior, let students know what behavior you expect, and create a positive classroom climate for students and yourself. You also teach students to notice and appreciate their own behavioral skills. It's a very powerful management tool. Acknowledge appropriate behavior frequently, specifically, sincerely, fairly, and with an emphasis on socially important behaviors.

It is essential to pay more *frequent* attention to appropriate behavior than to inappropriate behavior. Sprick, Garrison, and Howard (1998) recommend a ratio of 3 to 1, in other words acknowledging desirable behavior at least three times as often as paying attention to undesirable behavior. It isn't wrong to pay attention to students when they are behaving inappropriately; at issue is the ratio or balance.

Acknowledgments are *specific* when they provide informative feedback by describing the appropriate behavior noticed: "When you finished your work early you found a book to read." You can also describe the behavior *and* label it in relation to rules, routines, and social skills: "You followed the rule of respecting others when you listened to Michelle's opinion without interrupting." You can choose to describe the behavior *and* praise it: "Wow! Super job sticking to your work when it was tough." In addition, you can describe the behavior *and* prompt the student to acknowledge himself: "You must be proud of yourself for saying how you felt in a calm way."

Having their appropriate behavior acknowledged shouldn't make students feel manipulated. You need to *sincerely* use words or gestures of encouragement and appreciation. Just as you want to hear those words from family, friends, or employers, students want to hear them from their teachers. Students become immune to repetitive words of praise such as constant "good job" comments (Sprick, Garrison, and Howard 1998). Don't say things that aren't true. If you don't feel sincere, rethink your expectations for students. Also, talk *to* the person when you are acknowledging her behavior ("Ruby, you followed directions the first time asked"). Don't talk *about* the person ("I really like the way Ruby is following directions"). The latter is usually meant as an indirect reprimand of other students (who are not following directions).

Acknowledging appropriate behavior *fairly* means acknowledging all students but not the same behavior in all students and not necessarily with the same frequency. The focus should be on behaviors that are challenging to individuals. Staying on task for two minutes challenges some students. Working with less skilled or less popular partners challenges some students. Acknowledge behaviors that students need to learn and/or use more frequently or consistently. Your intention is to tide them over until the joys or positive natural consequences of the behavior take over, the behavior becomes a deeply ingrained habit, or until the student's own sense of accomplishment is enough to maintain the challenging behavior. Don't praise behaviors that are already easy for individuals, except rarely and randomly. Don't add extrinsic reinforcement for behaviors that are already intrinsically motivated. For example, if a student loves reading he doesn't need your praise for reading.

It's essential to acknowledge *important* behaviors. Consider what behaviors are important in life, at work, in school. Acknowledge independence, cooperation, and kindness to others, not just compliant behaviors like sitting quietly or raising hands. Some examples of behaviors that may be important to acknowledge for your students include ignoring distractions, compromising, standing up for someone being picked on, and taking another perspective.

Responding to Diversity When Acknowledging Appropriate Behavior

Students from different cultural backgrounds or in different age groups vary in the types of acknowledgments they prefer. Some may prefer to be praised as part of a group rather than for individual accomplishments. Some prefer private rather than public acknowledgments. Some prefer warm, personal appreciation, and some prefer more impersonal feedback or encouragement. Be observant of the responses to your acknowledgments and talk to students about their preferences.

Students may also vary in the ratio of attention for appropriate behavior to attention for inappropriate behavior that works best for them. Mathur, Quinn, and Rutherford (1996) recommend a ratio of 5 to 1 for students with emotional or behavioral disorders, that is, attention to appropriate behavior is most effective when given five times for every one time attention is given to inappropriate behavior.

The Challenging Class

If verbal acknowledgments don't always seem to be strong enough for your group, use activity or privilege rewards. The class can earn points for appropriate behavior that can be saved for extra free time, going early to lunch, a walk in the woods, a movie, or whatever they find enjoyable.

Monitoring Student Behavior

Another critical management skill for teachers is monitoring. This is also called active supervision (McIntosh et al. 2004) and "withitness" (Kounin 1970). Monitoring means knowing what's going on in all parts of the classroom (or other environment) with all of your students. Monitoring communicates that you're on top of things. It works wonders in preventing and stopping misbehavior, increasing engagement in learning, and helping you notice appropriate behavior.

You can monitor in a variety of ways: scanning and listening, moving around, positioning yourself to see everyone, and interacting with students. Monitor while presenting or reading to students, visually scanning the whole group and taking care not to be tied to your desk, stool, or projector. Briefly stand near students who are having difficulty paying attention (sometimes called *proximity management*). Move around and check in with students as they do seatwork or work with peers. Position yourself to see the rest of the class when working with small groups or helping individuals. Write on the board before the lesson or use a projector. Supervise transitions and breaks carefully. Stand by the door as students enter or leave the classroom. As you monitor, make eye contact with students, smile at appropriate behavior or frown at inappropriate, and use other nonverbal signals. Interact with students verbally: encourage, remind, redirect, express appreciation, acknowledge appropriate behavior, connect.

Active teacher monitoring is an indispensable critical management skill. Build it into every lesson and activity. Notice how it is related to other critical management skills: careful room arrangement makes monitoring easier; it is an important part of managing transitions; and monitoring will help you in acknowledging appropriate behavior.

Responding to Diversity When Monitoring Student Behavior

Be sensitive to cultural differences as you interact with students through signals, gestures, touch, praise, and so on. Make a special note to check in with students who struggle with starting or completing tasks, who have difficulty working with peers, dealing with frustration, and so on.

Planning for Logistics

A critical aspect of planning the context for teaching and learning is attending to logistics. By logistics we mean housekeeping tasks such as organizing materials and equipment and planning setup and cleanup, as well as arranging for assistants when needed.

Your wonderful, creative lessons and activities won't work if you haven't thought about the organization that will make them happen smoothly. The old saying that the devil is in the details applies here. Some activities and lessons are especially complex logistically, such as those that involve lots of materials or equipment or unfamiliar, messy, and potentially dangerous materials and equipment. This is also true for activities and lessons that have multiple parts, where a great deal of movement and change is required, furniture has to be moved, and additional helpers are needed. Planning for logistics is important for efficiency, safety, protecting learning time, reducing down time, preventing behavior problems, and ending up with a reasonably tidy room.

Planning for materials needed in the lesson or activity is an important part of planning for logistics. Consider the following suggestions:

- Have *your* instructional materials ready, such as your lesson plan outline, computer discs, transparencies, and other visual supports.
- Think about the materials the students will need. Some will be the belongings they keep in their desks or packs, such as pencils, paper, and books. List materials needed on the board and also keep extras available.
- Plan student access to materials kept stored in the classroom, such as dictionaries, math manipulatives, or scissors. Decide how these will be made available (Do you want students to pick them up individually when needed? Do you want selected students to pick them up for their groups? Will you pass them out?).
- Determine how to distribute unique materials. You may have gathered materials just for this lesson or activity such as note-taking guides, books, frogs to dissect, aprons to protect students' clothing, and so on. Decide whether you will put them on student desks during a break, assign students to distribute them as a chore for the week, or use another routine that you've previously taught the students.
- Be sure to have enough materials or plan how students will share them.
- Plan for the products students will create during the lesson or activity, how they'll be turned in, stored, displayed, or taken home.

Another aspect of planning for logistics is readying equipment. Equipment needed might include a television monitor, overhead projector, laptop computer, or FM wireless microphone. If you need to borrow equipment, arrange that ahead of time. Set it up in advance and check that it works. Think about safety and plan procedures if students are to use equipment.

Plan how the room will be set up and also plan for cleanup. Think about what chores will need to be completed, necessary equipment (soap and water, paper towels, extra waste baskets), and how you'll assign cleanup duties.

Another aspect of planning for logistics involves deciding whether you will need help with the lesson or activity from teaching assistants, other school staff, parent volunteers, or student helpers. Decide how you will recruit help and plan exactly what you want them to do.

Managing Transitions

Another highly important, critical management skill is developing procedures for handling transitions. Transitions include movements from place to place inside or outside of the classroom and changes in the type of activity or subject, such as entering the classroom, going from the classroom to the library, moving into small groups, switching from math to science, changing from partner practice to independent work. Transition management incorporates most of the other critical management skills, including room arrangement, stating behavior expectations, monitoring, and so on. It is included as a separate skill because transitions can be a major source of behavior problems if they are unplanned, unstructured, and unsupervised. Following are suggestions to help you support students in smooth transitions:

- Plan ahead for transitions. Think through your day, class, lesson, or activity ahead of time. Note needed transitions and analyze how you want those transitions to happen.
- Decide on directions for major transitions and write them on the board or transparency in advance.
- Prepare students for transitions by telling and writing the schedule for the day, class, lesson, or activity. Warn students in advance of changes ("In 5 minutes I'll ask you to leave your small groups and return to your desks for math timings.").
- Make behavior expectations for transitions clear regarding talking, moving, and so on. If you have taught the students a routine for this transition (for example, for leaving at the end of the day or for lining up), remind them of it.
- Communicate the time allowed for the transition and materials needed for the next activity, if appropriate.
- Begin the next activity on time. Don't fall into the habit of giving repeated reminders to hurry students and don't wait for stragglers if you can avoid it. Provide a reason for making transitions quickly by choosing early arrivers for favored tasks, or by beginning the next activity with an interesting opening, a joke, or riddle, and so on. If much of the class is late, reevaluate the time allowed and/or directly teach the transition routine.

Responding to Diversity When Managing Transitions

- Some students have a hard time making changes. Try providing a personal copy of the schedule, additional time reminders ("In 3 minutes . . ."), or a transition buddy.
- Students who speak little or no English may feel a great deal of anxiety about not knowing what's happening next or why they are leaving the classroom. Help reduce that anxiety by providing a picture schedule that indicates lunch, library, going home, and so on.
- Gilbert and Gay (1989) describe stage-setting behaviors that some African American students use before beginning tasks, such as gathering materials, looking over the whole assignment, and rechecking directions with teacher and peers. It may be helpful to think of stage-setting as part of the transition and to provide for it when stating expectations and time allowed.

Your goal is to make transitions as smooth, relaxed, and efficient as possible. Provide as much or as little structure as your students need.

The Challenging Class

If your class struggles with making transitions and they enjoy competition, divide the class into teams that compete against each other to see who is quickest to make the transition. Teach formal lessons on the most problematic types of transition routines, such as returning to class after recess.

Summary

Teachers need to develop critical management skills and to apply them in lessons and activities. See Chapter 8 for ideas on applying critical management skills when planning partner and small-group work. See Chapter 19 for questions to ask yourself about incorporating critical management skills and an example of a plan with critical management skills written in.

References and Suggested Readings

Cipani, E. 2004. *Classroom management for all teachers: 12 plans for evidence-based practice.* 2nd ed. Upper Saddle River, NJ: Merrill/Prentice Hall.

Colvin, G., and M. Lazar. 1997. *The effective elementary classroom.* Longmont, CO: Sopris West.

Darch, C., and E. Kame'enui. 2004. *Instructional classroom management: A proactive approach to behavior management.* 2nd ed. Upper Saddle River, NJ: Pearson Education, Inc.

Emmer, E., C. Evertson, and M. Worsham. 2006. *Classroom management for middle and high school teachers.* 7th ed. Needham Heights, MA: Allyn and Bacon.

Evertson, C., E. Emmer, and M. Worsham. 2006. *Classroom management for elementary teachers.* 7th ed. Needham Heights, MA: Allyn and Bacon.

Gilbert, S. E., and Gay, G. 1989. Improving the success in school of poor black children. In *Culture, style and the educative process,* ed. B. J. Shade, 275–283. Springfield, IL: Charles C. Thomas.

Grossman, H. 1995. *Classroom behavior management in a diverse society.* 2nd ed. Mountain View, CA: Mayfield.

Herrell, A., and M. Jordan. 2004. *Fifty strategies for teaching English-language learners.* 2nd ed. Upper Saddle River, NJ: Pearson/Merrill Prentice-Hall.

Jones, V., and L. Jones. 2004. *Comprehensive classroom management: Creating communities of support and solving problems.* 7th ed. Boston, MA: Allyn and Bacon.

Kaplan, J. S. 1995. *Beyond behavior modification.* 3rd ed. Austin, TX: Pro-Ed.

Kea, C. 1998. Focus on ethnic and minority concerns: Critical teaching behaviors and instructional strategies for working with culturally diverse students. *CCBD Newsletter,* (March). Reston, VA: The Council for Exceptional Children.

Kerr, M., and C. Nelson. 2006. *Strategies for addressing behavior problems in the classroom.* 5th ed. Upper Saddle River, NJ: Pearson Education, Inc.

Kounin, J. S. 1970. *Discipline and group management in classrooms.* New York: Holt, Rinehart & Winston.

Law, B., and M. Eckes. 2000. *The more-than-just-surviving handbook: ESL for every classroom teacher.* 2nd ed. Winnipeg, Manitoba, Canada: Portage and Main Press.

Lewis, T., S. Hudson, M. Richter, and N. Johnson. 2004. Scientifically supported practices in emotional and behavioral disorders: A proposed approach and brief review of current practices. *Behavioral Disorders* 29: 247–259.

Mathur, S., M. Quinn, and R. Rutherford. 1996. *Teacher-mediated behavior management strategies for children with emotional/behavioral disorders.* Reston, VA: Council for Exceptional Children.

McIntosh, K., K. Herman, A. Sanford, K. McGraw, and K. Florence. 2004. Teaching transitions: Techniques for promoting success between lessons. *Teaching Exceptional Children* 37 (1): 32–38. (References within article for active supervision.)

Rhode, G., W. Jenson, and H. Reavis. 1993. *The tough kid book.* Longmont, CO: Sopris West.

Sprick, R., M. Sprick, and M. Garrison. 1993. *Interventions: Collaborative planning for students at risk.* Longmont, CO: Sopris West.

Sprick, R., M. Garrison, and L. Howard. 1998. *CHAMPs: A proactive and positive approach to classroom management.* Longmont, CO: Sopris West.

Witt, J., A. VanDerHayden, and D. Gilbertson. 2004. Instruction and classroom management: Prevention and intervention research. In *Handbook of research in emotional and behavioral disorders,* eds. R. B. Rutherford, M. M. Quinn, and S. R. Mathur, 426–445. New York: Guilford.

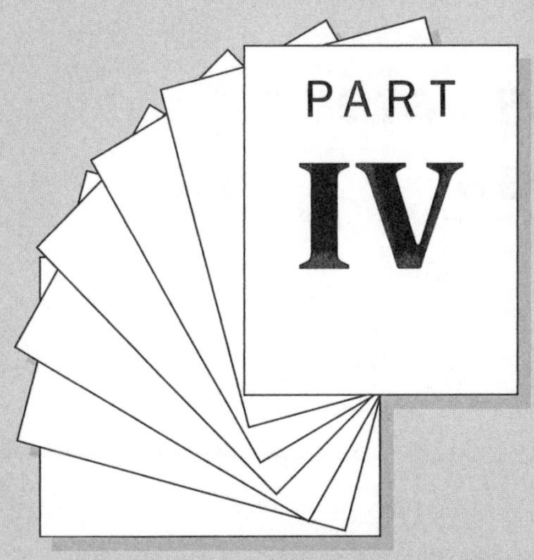

Writing Your Plan

In the first three parts of this book, you learned about what to teach, how to teach, and considerations for planning the context for teaching and learning. Now it is time for you to put together the information you have learned and write your plan.

In the first few chapters of this part of the book, you will learn about two basic types of plans—lessons and activities—and how to figure out when to write which type of plan. You will also learn that lessons and activities have different purposes. Lessons are generally used to provide initial instruction, whereas activities, often in combination with lessons, help students reach longer-term objectives. Both lessons and activities are very important in the instructional process.

You will also learn about specific types of lesson models and how to know when to use each. A lesson model is a specific way of instructing. Informal presentation, direct instruction, and structured discovery are the three lesson models presented in this book. Each model is used for a different purpose and all are effective in helping students learn. Lesson plans for all of these models are relatively easy to learn. By the end of the chapters on each of the models, you will know how to write a new type of plan. Chapter 19 will help you edit your first draft of your plan. This editing step will help ensure that your plan is complete and as responsive to diversity as possible.

This book will conclude with a chapter that will teach you how to use the diversity responsive teaching framework in two ways. First, you will learn how to use it as a brainstorming tool for generating ideas to make lessons and activities diversity responsive. You will also learn to use it as a tool for professional growth that will help you select personal objectives in the area of diversity responsive teaching and analyze the plans you have written.

All of the information you have learned so far in this book will become important as you write your plans. We encourage you to refer back to earlier chapters as you begin writing the specifics of your plan. We want to remind you again that practice will help you become more fluent in writing plans. When you become fluent, writing plans will take less time. Additionally, you may find that you do not need to write as much because many techniques and strategies will become habits and require less thought. We encourage you to use the guides that we have provided you as you write.

Lessons versus Activities

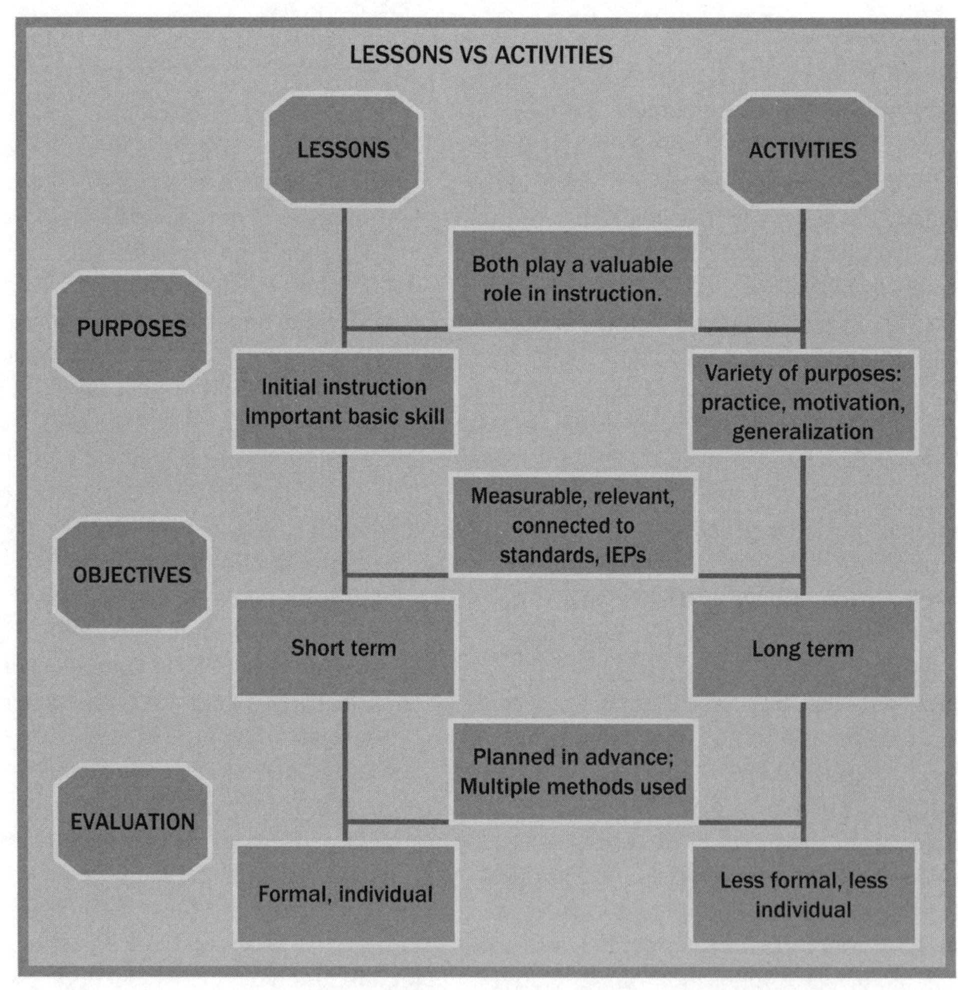

Introduction

It is important to distinguish between lessons and activities because they have different purposes. Although teachers use both lessons and activities to help their students learn, lessons are used to initially teach knowledge and skills. Activities help students to further process, practice, and generalize knowledge and skills. It is crucial to think carefully about your goals for instruction and to decide when to use lessons and when to use activities.

Lessons and activities each require different planning decisions and tasks. When writing a lesson plan, decide the structure of the teaching so that it lines up with the lesson objective that serves as its foundation. Activity plans need to be congruent also; however, these plans often address the logistics of managing materials and student participation and interactions rather than actual teaching. When teachers have no clear distinction between activities and lessons, we have noticed a common problem—forgetting to teach!

Recognizing whether you are going to teach an activity or lesson will help you select an appropriate planning format. Think of the lesson or activity plan format as a form of scaffolding. It provides support in remembering what to include. For example, the format for a direct instruction lesson plan includes a place to write how the teacher will present or teach the new information, followed by a place to write how students will practice. This ensures that new information is taught thoroughly before students are asked to use the information. The lesson plan format ensures that you will not forget to teach.

It can be difficult to clearly distinguish between lessons and activities because lessons typically include various activities. Additionally, because lessons vary in length—a lesson might last 30 minutes or 3 days—it can be difficult to determine when a lesson begins and when it ends; therefore, it is hard to know where an activity fits. However, our objective is *not* that teachers will be 100 percent accurate in deciphering lessons from activities. Our belief is that being aware of the differences between the two will help teachers make good teaching decisions.

Primary Differences between Lessons and Activities

Lessons are different from activities in several ways. As stated earlier, one way to distinguish between the two is to look at their *purposes.* The purpose of a lesson is to provide initial instruction on important skills or knowledge. Activities, on the other hand, may have a variety of purposes—learner motivation, additional experience, elaboration of information, additional opportunities for processing and practice, or integration and generalization of skills and knowledge.

Another way to distinguish between lessons and activities is to look at their *objectives.* A lesson has a specific, measurable, short-term objective, and the teacher's intention is that each student will meet that objective by the end of the lesson. Typically, teachers use activities with lessons to help students progress toward long-term objectives or goals.

Because of the differences in objectives, the type of *evaluation* needed for lessons and activities differs. Teachers follow lessons with formal evaluations of whether each student can independently meet the objective. The evaluations used with activities are often less formal and less individual.

The following sections provide further information and examples to help clarify the key differences between, and elements of, lessons and activities.

Lessons

As previously stated, the purpose of a lesson is to provide initial instruction on important skills or knowledge, and the objective is for each student to meet a specific, measurable, short-term objective by the end of the lesson.

Lesson Example

In this sample lesson, an instructor wants to teach students to spell the plural form of nouns ending in *y.* The objective is that students will write the plural form of 10 listed nouns ending in *y* preceded by a consonant, for example, *berry* to *berries.* The teacher instructs the students by explaining the spelling rule, showing examples, providing practice, and giving feedback. The teacher may also begin by showing examples and then lead the students to discover the spelling rule or pattern. Following the lesson, the instructor evaluates by giving a test as described in the objective.

This is a lesson because the teacher provides *initial instruction* on an *important basic skill;* spends time *teaching;* and intends to *evaluate* the students to see if they have met the *short-term objective following* the lesson.

Definition of Terms

The italicized terms in the previous paragraph are defined as follows:

- *Initial instruction* "Initial" *does not* mean that students have never heard of the topic of the lesson before. They will typically have had some previous introduction, and the teacher will use strategies in the lesson to connect the new learning to prior knowledge and experience. If the students do not have the necessary background, then the teacher has selected the wrong objective or lesson to teach at this time. "Initial" *does* mean that the students need formal instruction before they can use the new knowledge or skill. This can mean that the information is brand new, but it can also mean that the information is being retaught or revisited. It means that students need more than review and practice.

- *Important basic skill* Important basic skills include academic skills, thinking skills, study skills, social skills, vocational skills, and so on. They are considered basic because they are either important for real-life functioning or they are necessary prerequisites for other important skills. (One could make a case that the skill in the previous spelling lesson example is not important in an age of computers with spell-check capabilities.)

- *Teaching* Teaching can take many forms: it can be highly teacher-directed; it can incorporate peers; and it can emphasize discovery. However, teaching means that the teacher does more than organize and provide activities or give directions, hoping that students learn something. If no teaching is necessary, you do not have a lesson. Instead, you have either an activity or a time-filler.

- *Evaluate* When writing a lesson objective, a standard is established against which a student's learning is evaluated. Teachers also decide the method of evaluating learning at that time. They can use many ways to evaluate—not only written tests. If it is unnecessary to evaluate each student's learning, then you are not providing initial instruction on an important basic skill (in other words, you are not teaching a lesson). If your intention is to provide an "experience," you may have an activity, not a lesson. If your intention is to ask students to demonstrate their knowledge or skill with the help of peers or a teacher, you have an ongoing practice activity, not a completed lesson.

- *Short-term objective* Lessons are intended to help students reach a measurable, short-term objective. A series of lessons, often combined with activities, leads to the attainment of long-term objectives or goals. Long and short are not exact terms and cannot be defined precisely. We cannot give exact definitions or numbers, but consider the following example. Mrs. Lopez wants her students to learn to add and subtract fractions with uncommon denominators. She breaks up the long-term objective into several short-term lesson objectives, such as finding least common multiples, converting improper fractions, and so on. She will plan a lesson for each of those short-term objectives. Mrs. Lopez may decide to teach the lesson on least common multiples in 20-minute periods over three days. She considers this one lesson because she is not going to formally evaluate until after the third day. She will, however, want to monitor each student's success before going on to the next lesson. The students will not have received all of the necessary instruction to reach the short-term objective until Day 3.

- *Following* The evaluation of the objective following the lesson may occur immediately after the lesson or may occur one day or several days after the lesson. You may need to provide extended practice before evaluating, or you may have found, through monitoring, that you need to reteach before evaluating. However, if you do not intend to evaluate for weeks or months, you may be planning to evaluate whether students meet a long-term objective or goal, not a short-term lesson objective.

Activities

Activities are not intended to provide initial instruction and do not include the same evaluation as lessons. Activities have a variety of *purposes:* they may lead up to lessons, be part of lessons, follow up lessons, or extend lessons.

Activity Purposes

Activities are designed to provide the following:

- Motivation for students before beginning a series of lessons
- Background information, experience, or an opportunity to recall prior knowledge before a series of lessons. (A lesson typically includes an opening with strategies to motivate students or to help them connect this lesson with prior knowledge. We are differentiating this from longer, more elaborate activities used before a series of lessons.)
- Ongoing practice toward long-term objectives or goals
- Opportunities for students to apply a previously learned skill
- Opportunities for students to generalize previously learned information
- Opportunities for students to integrate knowledge and skills learned from lessons in different subject areas

Although activities are not associated with specific short-term objectives, they are planned with definite intentions. Teachers develop activities as part of their long-term planning and have a clear purpose for activities that help students reach important goals and objectives. Teachers also use activities to help evaluate student needs and progress. Even though activities are not always paired with formal evaluations of individuals, teachers carefully observe their students during activities and examine the products that students create to decide whether additional activities and lessons are needed.

Activity Examples

The following examples illustrate the wide variety of activity purposes:

- Before beginning a series of lessons on magnets, Mrs. Troxel plans an activity. She gives students different types of magnets and materials and has them experiment, make predictions, generate questions, and so on. Her purpose with this activity is to create interest and to motivate the students to learn more about magnets, to make sure each student has experience with magnets before beginning the lessons, and to provide practice on thinking skills. Mrs. Troxel also uses this activity to assess prior knowledge before deciding where to begin lessons.
- Every day Mrs. Chenier writes a sentence on the blackboard that is full of errors. Students are to copy the sentence and fix the errors. This is an activity that provides ongoing practice on proofreading for errors in capitalization, punctuation, spelling, and so on—not to give initial instruction on written mechanics.
- Students have had earlier lessons on how to write letters. You now plan an activity in which students write letters to the agricultural extension agent asking for information on rabbit care (there is a pet rabbit in the classroom). You may choose to review earlier lessons at the beginning of the activity, but you are not providing initial instruction on letter writing.
- Students are making a garden in the schoolyard. They use measuring skills learned in math, information about plant needs for light and water learned in science, and group decision-making skills learned in social skills lessons to select the vegetables to be planted. This is an activity intended to help students integrate and apply skills learned in a variety of subject areas.
- Following Mr. VanHenley's math lessons on the multiplication concept and operation, his students can figure out the answers to single-digit multiplication problems, but they are not always 100 percent accurate and they are very slow. Mr. VanHenley plans a series of practice activities—partner flash card practice and multiplication bingo—to help the students reach the long-term objective of writing answers to multiplication fact problems (0–10) at a rate of 80 digits per minute with no errors. In this case, Mr. VanHenley follows each activity with a timed math fact test to chart individual student progress toward the objective.

- The week before January 15th, Mr. Vandermay shows a video and leads a discussion about Dr. Martin Luther King, Jr., as the first in a series of activities leading up to Dr. King's birthday. His goal is to provide general information about a famous American and to make sure his students understand the upcoming holiday. He has not written a short-term objective and plans no evaluation.

- Mr. Palm plans an activity for his second graders about polar bears. He reads a story and then helps the students put together a book that includes drawings and sentences about polar bears. Mr. Palm is providing initial instruction, in a sense, because his students do not know many of the polar bear facts discussed in the book. However, he does not really care whether each student memorizes these facts and does not intend to give a test on polar bears. Polar bears are a vehicle for providing ongoing practice on listening skills, fine motor skills, writing complete sentences, and so on. As he looks at the students' books, he will monitor progress ("I see that Ralph is still forgetting to put a period at the end of his sentences."), but plans no short-term objective with a formal evaluation. Mr. Palm may have other goals as well—to pique curiosity about animals and nature or to give the students experience in being authors.

- Mrs. Eerkes plans an activity to follow a series of lessons on the Civil War. It will be a simulated debate in Congress on the issue of preserving the union versus states' rights. The students will be divided into two groups and given time to research the issues and to plan their speeches. Mrs. Eerkes has several purposes for this activity: (1) to provide practice in public speaking and cooperative planning and research; (2) to encourage a deeper understanding of the issues involved; and (3) to allow the students to demonstrate their knowledge in an alternative way. She knows that this activity will not allow her to be aware of each student's independent understanding, so she has planned other evaluation methods as well.

- Mr. Floyd plans an art activity in which he will teach his students to tie-dye. He will include many of the elements of lesson planning—step-by-step instruction, demonstrations, and supervised practice. This is considered an activity because tie-dyeing is not an important basic skill (anymore), and because students will each produce a tie-dyed item, but with Mr. Floyd's help. He will not test them later, either by asking them to list the steps in tie-dyeing or by asking them to make a tie-dyed item alone.

Summary

Lessons have been defined very narrowly and activities have been defined very broadly. Lessons have a consistent structure and involve explaining, demonstrating, and supervising student practice. Activities lack one or more of the attributes of a lesson and have many purposes and structures. Both need to be carefully planned.

Selecting the Appropriate Plan

When teaching students, whether in your own classroom or that of a cooperating teacher during a practicum or student teaching, the two basic types of plans that you will need to write are activity plans and lesson plans. Both require careful thought and become easier and less time-consuming to write with practice. As your understanding of important planning components increases, you will be able to make decisions more automatically with fewer details needed in writing.

When you decide on a topic to teach (or are given a teaching assignment by a cooperating teacher), you need to carefully analyze whether you need to write an activity plan or a lesson plan. Ask yourself the questions in Figure 12.1.

Figure 12.1 provides a summary of the decisions that will help you determine when to write a lesson plan and when to write an activity plan.

Figure 12.1 Lesson Plan or Activity Plan?

Ask yourself the following questions:

- Do I need to provide initial instruction?
- Is this an important basic skill?
- Can I write a specific, measurable, short-term objective for this topic?
- Will I need to spend time teaching (rather than only reviewing or giving directions)?
- Will I want to evaluate whether each student can independently meet the objective following the lesson?

If your answer to any of these questions is *no,* write an *activity plan* (see "Activity Plans" in Chapter 14).

Write *preplanning* tasks:

- Activity objective
- Activity description
- Activity rationale
- Prerequisite skills and knowledge; key terms and vocabulary

and

- Activity beginning
- Activity middle
- Activity closing

If your answer to all of these questions is *yes,* then write a *lesson plan* (see "Lesson Plans" in Chapter 13).

Write *preplanning* tasks:

- Connection analysis
- Content analysis
- Lesson objective
- Objective rationale

and

- Lesson setup
- Lesson opening
- Lesson body
- Extended practice
- Lesson closing
- Lesson evaluation

Lesson Planning

Introduction

Putting together a daily lesson is the end result of a complex planning process. This process begins when the teacher determines the overall curriculum to be taught. The curriculum is based on an analysis of student needs, on district or state standards, generalizations or big ideas from the subject area, and on a student's Individualized Education Program (IEP). Once the curriculum for the year or for a particular unit is identified, the teacher divides the content into individual lessons and writes specific lesson objectives, making sure each lesson clearly fits with the goals of the overall curriculum. The teacher finally selects a lesson model—direct instruction, informal presentation, structured discovery—that will work best to meet the objective of a specific lesson.

Teachers use lessons to help students attain a specific short-term objective. Lessons typically have a clear beginning and ending, and they will last a few hours at the most. Lessons are followed by an evaluation of each student's learning in relation to the stated objective(s). Series of lessons that lead to the attainment of long-term objectives or goals are often combined, along with activities, into a unit of instruction. Remember that lessons may be developed for individuals or small groups of students as well as for the whole class.

Lessons can be used to teach specific skills and information directly or to give students the opportunity to discover information on their own or with their peers. The type of content that can be taught through lessons is extremely diverse. Teachers typically use lessons to teach academic content; to develop study skills, social skills, and problem-solving skills; and to promote higher-level thinking.

Examples of Lesson Objectives

The following objectives help demonstrate the wide variety of skills and knowledge that teachers can address in lessons:

- When teased in a role-playing situation, students will talk through each of the five problem-solving steps.
- On a list of 25 sentences, students will circle the complete subject in all sentences.
- Given a list of 10 assignments, students will accurately transfer all of them to an assignment calendar.
- Given five two-step multiplication and division problems, students will write or draw a description of the problem-solving process they used to find the answer.

Generic Components of a Lesson Plan

A lesson plan is a written description of how students will progress toward a specific objective. It clearly describes the teacher's statements and actions, which hopefully result in student learning. All lesson plans include the following eight generic components:

1. Preplanning tasks
2. Lesson setup
3. Lesson opening
4. Lesson body

5. Extended practice
6. Lesson closing
7. Evaluation
8. Editing Tasks

The specific content of the components will vary with different lesson models because each model enables students to progress toward an objective in a different way.

The following descriptions of each component include two parts: the purpose of the component and a summary of the type of content that might be included. Our intent is to help you generate ideas, not to list everything that must be included in each component in every lesson plan. It is up to you to select or generate the specifics that are appropriate for the lesson model, the subject matter, and the students you are teaching. As you plan each component, be sure you plan for the diverse needs of your students.

The components are described here in the order in which they would appear in the lesson plan. This is not necessarily the order in which they will be written. When preparing to write a lesson plan, refer to Chapters 15 through 17 for information about the specific model you will be using. Examples of completed plans are included in Chapters 15 through 18.

Component 1: Preplanning Tasks

The purpose of this component is to help you thoroughly think through the content you will teach and the best way to teach it. This is a good time to think about how this content connects with the larger picture, for example, the state standards and the generalizations or big ideas within the subject area. Generally, this component consists of the following:

- *Connection Analysis* The lesson planning should begin by identifying the *generalization or big idea, state standard,* or *IEP goal* that you will address in your lesson.

- *Content Analysis* The next step is to decide on the specific content you will teach. This is accomplished by completing a thorough content analysis, which helps you think in detail about the content you will be teaching. In turn, this allows you to determine the best way to teach the content.

The term *content analysis* is a general one. The following are various types of content analyses: a *subject matter outline,* a *task analysis* or a *concept analysis,* a *principle statement,* definitions of *key terms or vocabulary,* and a list of *prerequisite skills and knowledge.*

The type of content analysis done depends on *what* is being taught. When you plan to teach a concept, for example, always include a concept analysis. When the point of the lesson is to teach a skill or procedure, you would always include a task analysis. When teaching information about a topic, a subject matter outline works best. A clearly written principle statement is included when teaching about a cause-and-effect or an if-then relationship. All lessons may have a number of key terms and vocabulary that need to be defined in ways the students will understand. A listing of prerequisite skills and knowledge would also be routinely considered as part of a content analysis. This analysis will help determine whether the content is appropriate for the students and will also help you write the objective. A content analysis is a critical preplanning task. Time spent on analyses will save time later, as the rest of the lesson or activity plan will fall into place more easily (see Chapter 1).

- *Objective* Select and write a clear, measurable, worthwhile lesson objective. The objective must contain a behavior, the content, the condition, and the criterion so that you can specify in detail what is to be learned and how you'll know if students have learned it (see Chapter 2).

- *Objective Rationale* Once you have written the objective, you need to actively think about and evaluate its importance and relevance. Reread it and ask yourself the following questions: *Why should my students know how to do this? How will my students benefit from this learning? Does this objective connect to a state standard? Does it relate to an important big idea? Does it lead to an IEP goal?* When you are satisfied with your answers to these questions, you will have an objective rationale. If your answers to these questions help you determine that the objective is not important, write a new one.

Ask yourself the following question: *Does my objective really represent what I want my students to know? For example, do I really care if they can name three types of penguins, or is the purpose actually to practice following directions?* If the purpose is practicing following directions, you would need to write an activity plan, not a lesson plan.

- *Lesson Model* Now you are ready to determine the best way to teach the objective. This decision can be based on the objective itself, the students, the time available, or the type of content being taught (very abstract or difficult, for example). Lesson models presented in this text are direct instruction (Chapter 15), informal presentation (Chapter 16), and structured discovery (Chapter 17).

Avoid making the mistake of selecting activities and methods and then trying to make up an objective for them. Instead, use backward planning.

Component 2: Lesson Setup

The purpose of the setup is to prepare students for the beginning of the lesson. A lesson should not begin until you have the students' attention (for example, they are physically turned toward you, they are listening to you, and so on). Also, you can prevent problems by explaining behavior expectations to students right up front, rather than waiting for problems to occur. Note that you're planning your initial signal and expectations. Write signals for regaining attention and communicating additional or changed expectations into the plan where needed.

- *Signal for Attention* Signal to the students to gain their attention; have them look at you and listen to you so the lesson can begin. In some cases, students are ready, so a simple "Let's get started," or "Good morning" is a sufficient signal for attention. In other cases, stronger signals—such as turning the lights off and on or ringing a bell—may be needed to attract their attention. Wait for attention and then acknowledge it (see Chapter 11).

- *Communication of Behavior Expectations* It is important to explain the rules, routines, and social skills that apply to the current lesson, that is, how you expect the students to act during the lesson. It is not necessary to review all classroom rules, routines, or social skills, just those most pertinent to the current lesson (raising hands, getting help, sharing, for example). Write the statement of behavior expectations in language that is positive, appropriate to the age of the students, specific, and clear. Plan to show, as well as say, the expectations to students. Communicate expectations at each transition within the lesson, rather than all at the beginning (see Chapter 11).

Component 3: Lesson Opening

The purpose of the lesson opening is to help prepare students for the learning to come. You will typically want to let students know what they can expect to learn, why it is important, and how it builds on what they already know. You will also want to get them excited about learning. To plan the lesson opening, select one or more strategies from each of the following categories:

- *Motivate and Focus Students* To motivate and focus students, tell or show them the lesson objective, use an attention-getting "set," and tell the purpose, rationale, importance, or application of the lesson objective.

- *Connect New Learning* To help students see relationships between known information and the new learning, discuss how the learning connects to personal experience and prior knowledge, build background knowledge or context, review earlier lessons or skills, preview upcoming lessons, present an advance organizer, or show a graphic organizer.

An opening generally includes a statement of the objective and the objective purpose. When you state the objective, tell students in their terms what they will know or be able to do at the end of the lesson or activity. The objective purpose lets the students know why the knowledge or skill they are learning is important to them, for example, how it will help them in their daily lives or how it will help them in school. Students respond positively when they understand why they are learning what you are teaching. Openings can be elaborate or simple, but it is important that all lessons (and activities) have one (see Chapter 4 for more ideas).

Component 4: Lesson Body

The instruction, related directly to the lesson objective, occurs in the lesson body. For this reason, Component 4 is considered the heart of the lesson. The majority of planning time and teaching time is spent on the lesson body. The body is where the content is presented through explanations, examples, demonstrations, or discoveries, and where students begin to process and practice the new skills and knowledge.

Although the specifics of the body vary with the lesson model, the lesson body should always include the following:

1. Universal Interventions in Instruction and Management. Remember to design your lesson plan to make it more likely that all your students will be successful. Universal interventions should always be included in lessons and activities as they can benefit all students in the class. The following are some examples of universal intervention strategies:
   a. *Universal design for learning and differentiated instruction.* Plan for building in techniques to provide options for students. Think about options in presentations, how to keep students engaged, and how students can express what they know (see Chapter 3 for ideas).
   b. *Responding to diversity.* Build in strategies that address the cultural, linguistic, and skill variation among students in your classroom. Consider the examples you use, opportunities provided to work with peers, practice opportunities, and how to emphasize vocabulary as examples of responding to diversity. Make sure that the content of your lesson is interesting and meaningful to your students.
   c. *Critical teaching skills.* These are instructional "best practices" and are instrumental in helping students learn.
      - *Explanations, demonstrations, and directions.* Carefully think through how to present and explain lesson information. Be sure that you have incorporated strategies that will make it easier for all of your students to learn the information you are presenting. Plan to present information in a variety of ways (see Chapter 5 for ideas).
      - *Visual supports.* Providing visual supports (pictures, diagrams) can help students better understand and learn the information you present. They are generally very helpful to all students and should be included wherever needed (see Chapter 5 for ideas).
      - *Active participation strategies.* Plan frequent opportunities to involve students in the lesson and to rehearse and process the new learning. Use a variety of strategies (see Chapter 6 for ideas).
      - *Checks for understanding.* These are specific active participation strategies designed to help teachers monitor student progress toward an objective. A teacher's goal is to check individual student learning throughout the lesson. Consider carefully the strategies you select to help you monitor whether students understand the material you present in your lesson. The most effective checks for understanding are those active participation strategies that enable each individual student to respond and receive feedback (see Chapters 6 and 7 for ideas).
      - *Practice strategies.* Provide opportunities for students to practice the newly learned skill or information under the supervision of a teacher. Practice opportunities within the lesson body differ in relation to the model of instruction you use. Remember to include a variety of practice ideas so that students stay motivated and interested (see Chapter 7 for ideas).
   d. *Critical management skills.* These techniques are classroom management "best practices." Techniques for preventing management problems are extremely important at various points in the lesson body (in addition to other lesson components). Use such techniques when you want to gain student attention, when students work together in partners to practice a newly acquired skill, or when students are using manipulatives, for example (see Chapter 11 for ideas).

2. Selected Interventions in Instruction and Behavior. These accommodations and modifications are generally incorporated into lessons and

activities to help one student or a few, and they will not be necessary or appropriate for all students in the class. These strategies, when incorporated into lessons and activities, help students be successful in spite of the challenges they may have. For example, they can help students who are challenged in the areas of focusing attention, learning and showing what they know, or following rules (see Chapters 9 and 10 for ideas).

In summary, the lesson body is the section of the lesson where the teaching takes place. It is important to present information in multiple ways, such as verbally, by demonstrating, and in writing. Visual supports can add interest and clarity to the presentation of information. Keeping students involved in the lesson and monitoring their progress are additional important elements that occur within the lesson body.

Component 5: Extended Practice

The purpose of the extended practice component is to plan for developing high levels of accuracy and fluency and providing application opportunities so students can generalize the skill or knowledge. (This is not the same as the initial supervised practice that may have been included in the body of the lesson.) Students will usually need extended practice opportunities prior to evaluation. These opportunities are often provided through activities, seatwork, and homework that help students master, transfer, and retain the information or skill. Monitoring this practice will provide students with important performance feedback and help you determine when students are ready to be evaluated. You will need to make decisions in this component about the following:

- *Practice opportunities.* Describe the plan for providing practice opportunities during and following the lesson. These are in addition to supervised practice. Remember that distributed practice (many short practices) is more effective than massed practice (one long practice). Some students may need a great deal of extended practice, whereas others may need enrichment activities. Be sure that students have an opportunity to practice individually prior to evaluation (see Chapter 7 for ideas).
- *Related lessons or activities.* It is useful to determine and list the other lessons or activities that will build on this objective and provide opportunities to generalize, integrate, and extend the information.

Component 6: Lesson Closing

The lesson closing helps students tie the material together. It may follow the body of the lesson, or it may follow extended practice. A lesson closing may include a review of the key points of the lesson, opportunities for students to draw conclusions, a preview of future learning, a description of where or when students should use their new skills or knowledge, a time for students to show their work, and a reference to the lesson opening (see Chapter 4 for more ideas). Lesson closings can be elaborate or simple, but you always need to include one.

Component 7: Evaluation

The purpose of the evaluation component is to let you and your students know if learning has occurred. It also helps you determine whether it is appropriate to build on the current lesson or whether you need to reteach or change the lesson model, methods, or materials.

The lesson evaluation is actually planned when the lesson objective is written. Look back at the objective to be sure the evaluation matches the objective, and then describe when and where the evaluation will occur. For example, if the objective is to "write a paragraph with a topic sentence," you might plan to have the students write the paragraph tomorrow morning in class. The paragraphs must not be the practice paragraphs they wrote with peer or teacher help. Remember that evaluations need to be of each individual student's independent performance. Do not confuse teaching and testing.

Monitor the students during the body of the lesson and during extended practice to give yourself an idea of when to formally evaluate. It makes no sense to give students a test that you know they will fail. Students may be evaluated again later (on a unit test, for example). They may also be evaluated on an ongoing basis. For example, you could evaluate paragraph construction in their journal writing. Learning must always be evaluated following the lesson, regardless of other evaluations planned. This evaluation is essential for deciding what to do next (see Chapter 7).

Component 8: Editing Tasks

Editing tasks are addressed in detail in Chapter 19. The three editing tasks are:

Editing Task #1—*Add critical management skills.* Go back through your plan and incorporate critical management skills. In the appropriate spots in your plan, note the following: any room arrangement changes, signals for attention, communication of behavior expectations, planned acknowledgments of appropriate behavior, monitoring of student behavior, planning for logistics, and management of transitions (see Chapters 11 and 19).

Editing Task #2—*Double-check for universal and selected instructional interventions.* Make adjustments in any of the following: use of principles of universal design; responses to linguistic, cultural, and skill diversity; strategies to ensure a clear presentation; use of active participation strategies including checks for understanding; and the use of visual supports (see Chapters 3, 6, and 7). Review the selected instructional interventions that you have included. Be sure they are necessary and will meet the needs of the students for whom they were selected (see Chapter 9).

Editing Task #3—*Evaluate congruence.* The final task is to examine your plan for congruence. It is imperative that the various components of a lesson match, that is, that the body of the activity and the evaluation both match the lesson objective. The same is true of an activity plan, (the middle of the activity should match the activity objective). Making your plan congruent helps ensure that students are evaluated on what they were taught and what they practiced (see Chapter 19).

Steps in Writing a Lesson Plan

Writing a lesson plan requires a series of decisions. Even before starting to write the actual lesson plan, you must decide what exactly you will teach and how best to teach it. Experienced teachers are able to do more thinking and less writing when they plan lessons because of their experience. They do, however, often write fairly detailed plans when they prepare to teach new content. This helps them to think through the best way to teach the information they will present. In general, the best way to become fluent in writing lesson plans is to practice. As experience grows, teachers will need to write less because certain aspects of the lessons will become second nature.

Include all of the generic components presented in this chapter in every written lesson plan until you gain the necessary experience to reduce your written planning. The order in which you will write the various components of the plan, however, does not necessarily correspond to the order in which they appear in this chapter or to the order in which you will present them to the students. For example, it makes more sense to write the lesson body before the lesson opening (or activity middle before the beginning), but you would obviously present the lesson opening to the students before the lesson body (activity beginning before the activity middle). It is also important to note that, although Components 2 through 7 are the only ones actually presented to the students, the preplanning tasks component and the editing tasks component are equally as important.

Sequence for Writing the Components of a Lesson Plan

The following is a suggested sequence for writing the components of a lesson plan:

1. Component 1: Preplanning Tasks
2. Component 4: Lesson Body
3. Component 5: Extended Practice
4. Component 7: Evaluation
5. Component 3: Lesson Opening
6. Component 6: Lesson Closing
7. Component 2: Lesson Setup
8. Component 8: Editing Tasks

Writing a Useful Plan

When you write a plan for a lesson or an activity, it is important that your finished product not include every word you are going to say. A detailed list of main ideas is much preferred for a couple of reasons. First, when you force yourself to determine what the key ideas are, the essential points of your lesson become very apparent to you and can greatly assist you in presenting information clearly. Secondly, if you are writing plans for others to read, remember that your instructor, cooperating teacher, supervisor, principal, or substitute must be able to follow your main ideas.

Even your complete plan of key ideas will likely be too long to use as a reference as you teach. You can make a shorter, outlined version so you can refer to it with a quick glance. This can be done easily with your word processor by saving and printing key sections of your plan. Another idea is to use a set of index cards or to list the main steps that you will follow in presenting your lesson or activity right on the board for a reference. We encourage you to experiment until you find a tool that works well for you.

How to Write a Reader-Friendly Plan

- Use an outline format whenever possible (major headings, subheadings, bullets, numbers, and indenting).
- Label the transitions from one part of the lesson or activity to another. State directly what is going to happen (for example, "transition to lab stations" or "explain partner rules").
- Use a variety of font sizes and appearances (uppercase and lowercase, bold, and underline).
- Use key words and phrases rather than long narratives.

It is impossible to make a rule that determines how much detail to include in your plan. It is safe to say, however, that any explanation that may be complex or have the potential to be confusing should be put in writing to help ensure it is complete, accurate, and clear. For example, if you are going to teach your students how to write topic sentences, you would not simply write, "Explain topic sentences." This is too brief because the key information you need to emphasize during the lesson is not planned. You would have to rely solely on your memory to ensure that you present the key information your students need to know. It can be very difficult to remember and clearly present all of the key information when you are up in front of a room full of students. You will not want to write every single word you will say to the students either. Something in between is preferable. The following example outlines key information.

Topic Sentences

- Usually, (not always), the first sentence
- Describes main idea
- Tells what the paragraph is about

Summary

Teachers write lesson plans for topics in all subject areas. Variations in lesson plans result from the specific characteristics of the model of instruction being used in the lesson. Regardless of the lesson model however, important components must be included in all lesson plans. The content within the component will vary somewhat depending on the model used.

References and Suggested Readings

Arends, R. I. 2004. *Learning to teach.* 6th ed. New York: McGraw-Hill.

Borich, G. 2000. *Effective teaching methods.* 4th ed. Columbus, OH: Merrill, an imprint of Macmillan Publishing.

Callahan, J. F., L. H. Clark, and R. D. Kellough. 2002. *Teaching in the middle and secondary schools.* 7th ed. Part 2, Module 4. Columbus, OH: Merrill/ Prentice Hall.

Cartwright, P. G., C. A. Cartwright, and M. E. Ward. 1995. *Educating special learners.* 4th ed. Boston: Wadsworth.

Cruickshank, D. R., D. L. Bainer, and K. K. Metcalf. 2006. *The act of teaching.* 4th ed. Boston: McGraw-Hill College.

Joyce, B., M. Weil, with E. Calhoun. 2004. *Models of teaching.* 7th ed. Boston: Pearson.

Lasley II, T. J., T. J. Matczynski, and J. B. Rowley. 2002. *Instructional models: Strategies for teaching in a diverse society.* 2nd ed. Belmont, CA: Wadsworth/Thomson Learning.

Moore, K. D. 2005. *Effective instructional strategies: From theory to practice.* Thousand Oaks: Sage Publications.

Orlich, D. C., R. J. Harder, R. C. Callahan, and H. W. Gibson. 2001. *Teaching strategies: A guide to better instruction.* 6th ed. Boston: Houghton Mifflin.

Wood, J. 2006. *Teaching students in inclusive settings: Adapting and accommodating instruction.* 5th ed. Upper Saddle River, N.J.: Pearson.

Activity Planning

Introduction

Teachers typically use a wide variety of activities during the school day. Some of these activities are necessary routines to organize and manage all of the tasks that need to be done, such as correcting homework or getting ready to go home. Others are meant as fun or relaxing activities to provide a break for students, such as listening to music or singing a song. Certain activities occur daily, such as math timings. Others may happen only occasionally, such as watching a fun video. This chapter is not about how to plan these types of activities, except in those cases where the activity is quite complex, such as morning opening activities.

This chapter is about how to plan for activities that are directly related to the curriculum—activities that introduce, extend, supplement, or enrich lessons. The purpose or rationale for any given activity may not be immediately apparent to an observer, but it is very clear to the teacher.

Purposes of Activities

As discussed in Chapter 12, teachers use activities that relate to the curriculum with various purposes in mind. Activities can often provide the following:

- *Motivation* for students before or during a series of lessons (for example, planning class fundraising activities during a unit on economics).
- *Background information* or enrichment of the students' knowledge and experience before or during a series of lessons (for example, taking a field trip to a salmon hatchery while studying resource conservation).
- *Ongoing practice* toward long-term objectives, such as playing math games to increase fluency on addition facts or completing art activities that provide practice using fine motor skills or following directions.
- Opportunities for students to *apply* or *generalize* a previously learned skill (for example, having students plan and maintain a daily meal and snack plan that meets good nutrition requirements).
- Opportunities for students to *integrate* a variety of skills learned from lessons in different subject areas (having students practice their writing skills by writing letters to the editor of the local newspaper about pertinent social issues being discussed in social studies, for example).
- *Differentiation of instruction* by dealing with the same content but at different levels. For example, an activity could involve setting up different poetry tasks at various stations and assigning students to stations based on their skills and interests.

It is important to note that various components of a *lesson plan* may have the same purposes as noted for activities; for example, the opening of a lesson may be intended to motivate students. In addition, lessons always include practice activities (see supervised and extended practice components), and they sometimes incorporate activities to supplement the presentation of information. For example, a teacher may show a videotape about the main parts of the heart and their functions during a lesson on the circulatory system. When activities are part of a daily lesson, they should be included within the lesson plan itself. When activities are part of a series of lessons or unit, or when activities are long and complex, it will be helpful to write a separate activity plan.

Teachers typically decide what activities to use while planning units of instruction. Teachers may also plan additional activities based on their assessments of student progress. For example, teachers may find that students need more practice in identifying adjectives than originally planned.

Generic Components of an Activity Plan

An activity plan is a written description of exactly what the teacher will do and say to help students prepare for and complete an activity. The plan may consist of a set of questions to ask the students, a set of explanations that help tie the current activity to other learning, or step-by-step procedures and directions.

All activity plans contain the same generic components, even though the content of each component will vary greatly, depending on the type of activity planned. For example, a plan to show and discuss a videotape will look very different from an activity plan for a complex art project. The following explains the purpose of each component and suggests the kinds of decisions that need to be made in each. This is designed to help guide you through the steps for planning your activity. When you are ready to actually write an activity plan, refer to Figure 14.1, "Writing an Activity Plan."

Component 1: Preplanning Tasks

Typically, teachers will develop various activities and lessons to help students progress toward long-term objectives. Keeping this in mind, the preplanning component of the activity plan helps you think through how the current activity connects with important learning outcomes.

One essential part of this component involves developing a thoughtful connection between the objective of the activity and its purpose. This process begins by identifying the *activity objective.* This is the long-term objective within which the current activity fits. This objective is specific and needs to include all four essential components. In addition, be sure you can identify the *generalization* or *big idea,* the *IEP goal,* or the *state standard* to which the objective connects.

Remember that an activity objective is different from a lesson objective because students will not necessarily meet the objective by the end of the activity. An example of an activity objective is having students write a paragraph that includes a topic sentence, three supporting detail sentences, and one closing sentence. Students may not be expected to meet the objective for a number of weeks or months. In summary, activity objectives are generally considered long-term objectives, whereas lesson objectives are considered short-term objectives.

Another important part of this component involves selecting an activity that will help students progress toward the long-term objective and then writing an *activity description.* Once you have decided on the objective, brainstorm activities that will bring about this outcome. Be creative. Consider variety, novelty, and student interests. Think about the diversity in your classroom and what kinds of activities would be flexible enough to provide opportunities for all students to be challenged and successful. Select an activity that best fits the objective and the students (or you may choose to plan several alternative activities to meet student needs).

Note that if you are a practicum student or student teacher, your cooperating teacher may already have decided on the topic and the type of activity. For example, she may ask you to plan an art activity that will fit with the unit on Northwest Native Americans or to find a book to read to the students that introduces the theme of friendship.

Once you have selected the activity, write a short description (one or two sentences) that summarizes it. This task will help you distinguish between the desired outcome (objective) and the actual activity. An activity description might appear as follows: "Give students packets of color-coded sentence strips. Each packet includes one topic sentence strip and three supporting detail sentence strips. Working in pairs, students will place supporting detail sentences under each topic sentence strip."

Avoid making the mistake of selecting an activity first and then trying to justify it by making up an objective and rationale. Remember to use backward planning. Choose the objective first and then select an activity to help students achieve the objective.

The final task in thinking about the objective is to construct an *activity rationale.* This is a description of how the current activity will help students progress toward the objective. When you plan the rationale, you may wish to refer to the broad purpose for the activity (for example, to motivate, enrich, practice, integrate, apply, or generalize).

The rationale provides the important connection between the long-term objective and the current activity. It requires thinking through carefully why students need to do the activity. Rationales such as "I thought it would be fun . . ." or "I happen to have this videotape . . ." are definitely questionable. Activities ought to be fun and motivating, of course, but they also need to result in important learning. An activity rationale might look like the following: "This activity is intended to provide ongoing practice in identifying topic and supporting detail sentences. Physically moving the topic and detail sentence strips may make the connections more concrete to the students. In addition, the opportunity to talk through decision making with a peer partner may increase understanding."

Note that the activity rationale is really a rationale for the current activity rather than for the long-term objective. The rationale for the long-term objective would have been determined when the objective was written.

Examples of Activity Objectives, Descriptions, and Rationales

Example #1

- *Activity objective* Students will write answers to addition facts (with sums from 0–20) at the rate of 80 digits per minute with no errors (State Mathematics Standard: "Add, subtract, multiply, and divide whole numbers").
- *Activity description* Students will play a bingo game in which math fact questions (for example, 5 + 3 = ?) are called out and students cover the correct answer on their bingo card.
- *Activity rationale* The game format is intended to increase interest and motivation in gaining accuracy and fluency on math facts.

Example #2

- *Activity objective* Students will describe the contributions of at least three Americans who were important in ending slavery (State History Standard: "Examine and discuss historical contributions to U.S. society of various individuals and groups from different cultural, racial, and linguistic backgrounds.").
- *Activity description* I will read a story to the students about Harriet Tubman and ask questions that will help them identify the important contributions she made in helping people escape slavery through the Underground Railroad.
- *Activity rationale* Reading to the students provides an alternative method of gaining background information, and it helps the students with reading difficulties. This story is only one of the activities that will be used to teach about Harriet Tubman. Students will also watch a videotape and search the Internet for information.

The other main preplanning task is to think through necessary *prerequisite skills or knowledge,* as well as *key terms and vocabulary.* It is very important to carefully consider what information or skills your students need to be successful in the current activity. Review, teach, or provide scaffolds or supports as appropriate. It is equally important to identify key terms and vocabulary words that need to be defined and taught. Be sure that you define terms using language your students will understand.

Component 2: Activity Beginning

The purpose of the activity beginning is to prepare students for participating and learning in the new activity. The activity *setup* includes both a signal for attention and a statement of behavior expectations. An *opening* is also included in the activity beginning.

You will need to decide on a signal for gaining the attention of the students at the beginning of the activity, as well as methods of regaining attention during the activity. Plan your expectations for student behavior during the beginning of the activity and explain how you will communicate them to the students (see Chapter 11).

It's very important that you think about how you will help students understand the purpose of the activity, and how it connects with long-term objectives, with their prior knowledge, and with their personal experience. It may be necessary to build background knowledge for them. You will also want to capture their interest right away and motivate them to participate. Write your plan for the *opening* (see Chapter 4).

Component 3: Activity Middle

The activity middle is a specific description of what the students and the teacher will do during the activity. This will be the most detailed and longest section of the plan and must be thought through carefully.

The planning decisions in this section will be very different depending on the type of activity. However, certain planning elements should always be considered because they will help meet the diverse needs of the students. One key element is to provide information both verbally and visually, which is an example of a *critical teaching skill.* For example, write the rules for a game on a poster as well as saying them to the students, or demonstrate the preparation of a microscope slide as well as providing a list of procedures (see Chapter 5). Another key element is to incorporate *active participation* by all students during the activity. For example, when asking questions during a story, have students say their response to a neighbor rather than calling on only one or two volunteers. Many active participation strategies serve as *checks for understanding* so that you can monitor student learning. For example, students can hold up fingers to show how many syllables they hear in a word (see Chapters 6 and 7). A third element is to plan provisions, that is, *accommodations* that consider individual strengths and weaknesses. These might include allowing options, such as (1) having students work individually, with partners, or in small groups, or (2) allowing students to make a presentation rather than writing a report (see Chapter 9 for many additional ideas).

It's important to remember the following:

- Provide information verbally, in writing, through demonstrations and with pictures.
- Incorporate active participation and checks for understanding.
- Plan provisions for individual differences through universal and selected interventions.

Think about your activity—what you will be doing, what the students will be doing, and what you will need to communicate to your students. If the students will be listening to or watching something (readings, films, or demonstrations, for example), you will need to plan a set of questions to ask or a series of explanations to make. If the students will be creating something (writing, drawing, or building, for example), you will need to plan a set of directions to give and perhaps plan to show an example of a finished product. If the students are going to be doing something (such as performing experiments or playing a game), you will need to plan a set of procedures or rules and perhaps plan to demonstrate the process.

You may need to develop one or more of the following:

- *A set of questions* Plan questions to ask before, during, and after reading a story, playing a musical selection, or taking students on a nature walk. It can be difficult to ask good questions spontaneously. Planning some of the questions in advance will help you ask clear and thought-provoking ones. It will allow you to plan appropriate questions for your English language learners. It will also help you think through the purposes of the questions. For example, when you read a story with your students, you may want to ask questions to emphasize vocabulary words, predicting, the meanings of figures of speech, making inferences, summarizing, main ideas, or character, setting, and plot.
- *A series of statements or explanations* Prior to a presentation, explain that the videotape they are about to see presents three major factors that contribute to child abuse and that, when the video is over, they need to be prepared to discuss them. Telling students what to watch or listen for will help them focus. Planning these statements in advance will ensure clarity and brevity.
- *A list of directions* Provide step-by-step directions for the book covers students will be making for the short stories they have written. Displaying the directions in writing, as well as stating the

directions to the students, is very important and will save much repetition. Planning the directions in advance will ensure clarity and completeness.

- *A sample of a finished product* Provide an example of a completed book cover. Seeing a completed product can be very helpful in understanding what to do and what is expected. Be sure to clarify whether students' products need to look exactly like the sample, or whether you are looking for variety and creativity. If the steps in making the product are complex, consider showing samples of the product at various stages of completion.

- *A list of procedures* List procedures for how to experiment with each magnet, how to find partners or form groups, how to share tasks, where to get or how to use materials or equipment, and so on. In addition to stating the procedures, show the written list and demonstrate them.

- *A list of rules for a game* List rules for the quiz show game the students will be playing to review social studies information prior to their test. Again, providing a written summary of the rules as well as stating them and demonstrating them is a good idea. Be sure to plan all needed rules to avoid confusion, arguments, and wasted time.

Plan how you will check for understanding after explaining directions, procedures, rules, and so on. For example, you may ask specific questions—"What do you do first? How do you find your partner?"—and call on selected individuals or ask for written or signaled responses. Simply saying, "Does everyone understand?" or "Any questions?" is not effective (see Chapters 6 and 7).

Component 4: Activity Closing

The activity closing helps students tie it all together. Decide whether it will be important to review key ideas and to preview future lessons or activities. It may be necessary to provide an opportunity for students to draw conclusions, describe their problem-solving processes, or show what they created. You may wish to formally assess progress toward a long-term objective. Activity closings do not necessarily need to be time-consuming and elaborate, but should provide a meaningful ending of some kind (see Chapter 4).

Component 5: Editing Tasks

Editing tasks are addressed in detail in Chapter 19. They are summarized here. The purpose of the editing tasks is to build in critical management skills, double-check that you included appropriate universal and selected instructional interventions, and to check for congruence. All of these tasks help finalize your plan.

Editing Task #1—*Add critical management skills.* Write in room arrangement changes, signals for attention, communication of behavior expectations, planned acknowledgments of appropriate behavior, monitoring of student behavior, planning for logistics, and management of transitions (see Chapters 11 and 19).

Editing Task #2—*Double-check for universal and selected instructional interventions.* Be sure that you have included necessary interventions. Think about principles of universal design, clarity of presentation, use of active participation strategies and checks for understanding, and the use of visual supports (see Chapters 3 through 9 and Chapter 19). Selected interventions should address the needs of one or a few students.

Editing Task #3—*Evaluate congruence.* Look carefully at congruence. Remember that the various components of activities must match (for example, the activity objective and the activity middle). Congruence ensures an emphasis on the activity objective throughout the plan. In addition, congruence helps students move toward the objective you selected, ensuring that students are evaluated on what they were taught and what they practiced. Turn to Chapter 19 for directions on how to evaluate congruence.

Steps in Writing an Activity Plan

When you first learn how to write an activity plan, it is important to include all of the generic components in every plan. The order in which you write the components however, will not necessarily correspond to the way in which you would present them to your students. For example, it makes more sense to write the activity middle before the setup, but when the activity is presented to the students, you would obviously present the opening before the middle. Remember that while Components 2 through 4 of your activity plan are the only ones that will actually be presented to students, the preplanning tasks and editing components are of equal importance and should be completed in writing.

Sequence for Writing the Components of an Activity Plan

The following is the suggested sequence for completing the components of an activity plan:

1. Component 1: Preplanning Tasks
2. Component 3: Activity Middle
3. Component 4: Activity Closing
4. Component 2: Activity Beginning
5. Component 5: Editing Tasks

Writing a Useful Plan

Remember that when you write your activity plan, it is important that your final draft serve as a useful resource for you and those who observe you. (See "How to Write a Reader-Friendly Plan" in Chapter 13 for guidance.)

Summary

You can plan many types of activities for your students, but they should all have a clear purpose. Be sure you can state the important objective that the activity will help your students meet.

Figure 14.1 summarizes each component in an activity plan.

Figure 14.1 Writing an Activity Plan

The content of the components in Figure 14.1 tells what typically would be included in each component of an activity plan.

COMPONENT 1: PREPLANNING TASKS

Prepare the following:

- *Activity objective* State the long-term objective for the activity as well as the generalization or big idea, the IEP goal, or the state standard that is being addressed.
- *Activity description* Prepare a brief summary or description of the activity itself.
- *Activity rationale* Describe how the current activity helps students progress toward the long-term objective.
- *Prerequisite skills or knowledge* and *key terms or vocabulary* Describe those needed for success in the activity.

COMPONENT 2: ACTIVITY BEGINNING

Prepare the following:

- *Setup* This includes an initial *signal for attention* to make sure students are listening and the *communication of behavior expectations,* which informs students how to act during the beginning of the activity.
- *Opening* An opening shows students how this activity connects to yesterday's lesson, to personal experiences, or to prior knowledge. It may be used to build background knowledge. The opening also helps to motivate or focus the students (stating the activity objective and rationale, for example).

continued on next page

Figure 14.1 Writing an Activity Plan (continued)

COMPONENT 3: ACTIVITY MIDDLE

Prepare the following:

- A description of what you need to communicate to the students. Depending on the type of activity, you may need one or a combination of the following: a set of questions, a list of statements or explanations, a list of rules, a list of procedures, a sample of a finished product, and a list of directions.
- A description of how you will effectively communicate this information to the students (use of critical teaching skills, visual supports, demonstrations, checks for understanding, diversity strategies, active participation, and so on).

COMPONENT 4: ACTIVITY CLOSING

- Prepare a description of how you will end the activity. Your closing may involve a class review, students drawing conclusions, teacher previews of future learning, students showing work, or an evaluation procedure (if appropriate).

COMPONENT 5: EDITING TASKS

1. *Add critical management skills.* Go back through your plan and incorporate critical management skills. In the appropriate spots in your plan, note the following: any room arrangement changes, signals for attention, communication of behavior expectations, planned acknowledgments of appropriate behavior, monitoring of student behavior, planning for logistics, and management of transitions (see Chapters 11 and 19).
2. Be sure that you have considered *universal instructional interventions* (universal design, critical teaching skills, and responding to cultural, linguistic, and skill diversity). Remember to add in *selected instructional and behavioral interventions* as needed for one or a few students.
3. *Evaluate congruence.* Make sure the various components match. Also make sure to address and emphasize the objective throughout. (See Chapter 9.)

Sample Plans

Look at the framework for diversity responsive teaching (DRT) as you examine the sample plans at the end of this chapter. Ask yourself how the plan incorporates responses to diversity in *what* is taught, *how* it's taught, and the *context* for teaching and learning. We'll give you a start in thinking about how various parts of the plan fit with various components of the framework. We encourage you to look for additional examples of each component and to think about what changes you believe would make this plan even more likely to support all students' success.

Notice that "The Underground Railroad" activity plan is an example of teaching content *about* diversity and of making sure that all *contributors* and *perspectives* are included. Two examples of planning the *how* are: *congruence* in how the key idea stated in the objectives are developed throughout the plan (questions emphasize key ideas) and the variety of *question* types (high-level and low-level) used. Finally, using *whole class behavior points* (in a challenging class) is an example of responding to diversity when planning the *context*.

Note that the Tic-Tac-Toe spelling activity will be reviewed in Chapter 19.

Tic-Tac-Toe Spelling

This is a large group activity plan.

I. PREPLANNING TASKS

A. Prerequisite skills or knowledge: How to play Tic-Tac-Toe

B. Key terms or vocabulary: NA

C. Long-term objective: Given a list of 15 words that contain one to three syllables and end in "–ing," students will write (or spell orally) all words correctly. Students are given lists that match their skill level (one, two, or three syllables, for example). State writing standard: spell age-level words correctly.

D. Activity description: A Tic-Tac-Toe game where partners quiz each other on their spelling words. Correct responses result in placing an X or O on the Tic-Tac-Toe board.

E. Activity rationale: This game is intended to provide students a fun way to practice and memorize their spelling words. This format also provides practice in giving and taking constructive feedback.

F. Materials: poster of game directions, transparency of grids and rules, worksheets with 25 Tic-Tac-Toe grids on each.

II. ACTIVITY BEGINNING

A. Setup

1. Signal for attention: "Attention, please."
2. Behavior expectations: "While I'm giving directions, keep eyes on me and raise hands to ask/answer questions unless I ask you to call out."

B. Opening

1. Review: "You are studying words that end with '–ing'. Call out some examples."
2. Motivate: "We're going to play Tic-Tac-Toe Spelling today."
3. Objective and purpose: "Tic-Tac-Toe Spelling will help you memorize correct spelling of words, so you can use these words in your writing; you won't need to look up words in a dictionary."

III. ACTIVITY MIDDLE

A. Post written game directions:

1. Exchange spelling lists with your reading partner.
2. Partner 1 (*X*) asks Partner 2 (*O*) a word from her list.
3. Partner 2 spells. If correct, Partner 2 places an *O* on a Tic-Tac-Toe square.
4. If wrong, Partner 1 says "The word _____ is spelled _____. How do you spell _____?"
5. Partner 1 places a check if correct or a minus if incorrect by the word spelled.
6. Reverse the roles. Keep playing until time is up.

B. Explain directions for the game using poster and transparency of Tic-Tac-Toe grids and sample word lists.
   - Demonstrate with teaching assistant as I explain
   - Explain that checks and minuses are to keep track of words they know and to make sure all words are asked.

C. Check for understanding of all directions: I choose two students to come to the front and model the game procedure as I ask other selected students specific questions such as "Who goes first?" "What does the asker do now?"

D. Distribute Tic-Tac-Toe grids. "Trade spelling lists with your partner."

E. Play the game: Play for 20 minutes. Complete as many games as possible.

CFU = After each step, stop and ask a question and request a unison verbal or signal response ("What would you say if I spelled cat 'kad'?" "What does he write if the word isn't spelled correctly?" and so on.)

IV. ACTIVITY CLOSING

A. Preview: "Tomorrow, we'll do another practice activity to help you memorize your spelling words."

B. Practice one final time: "Pick one misspelled word from your list (if no words are misspelled, use "challenge words") and spell it correctly 3 times."

The Underground Railroad

I. PREPLANNING TASKS

A. Activity objective(s):

1. Students will explain orally, or in writing, the complex workings of the Underground Railroad (U.R.) to include relevant dates, individuals involved, numbers of slaves rescued, as well as the impact that the U.R. had on slave trade in America.

2. Students will summarize in writing (or in an oral report), key contributions made by Harriet Tubman as a key player in the Underground Railroad, including a description of who she was, where she lived, how she became involved, and her contribution to helping free slaves.

B. Activity description: I will read a story about Harriet Tubman and the U.R. My plan is to have students listen for specific information that they will use in a follow-up project. I will help them focus their attention on the information I want them to learn by telling them what to listen for in advance of reading each section. I'll help students process the information they are hearing by using active participation strategies such as table group and partner discussions. I will then follow up with questions designed to check for understanding regarding the key ideas I want my students to learn.

C. Activity rationale: This story will help students move toward the activity objectives. I typically use the after-lunch story to add breadth to topics being studied in other curricular areas, such as social studies. I selected this particular story because it ties in nicely with our current unit on immigration in which we look at the reasons that various groups of people came to America and their experiences once they arrived. We have just begun our study of American citizens of African descent and are investigating the issues that lead up to the abolition of slavery.

D. Materials: *Traveling on the Underground Railroad* by Steven Everett and vocabulary words (write on the board before the activity).

II. ACTIVITY BEGINNING

A. Signal for attention: Flicker lights (students are returning from recess).

B. Behavior expectations: (1) Stay in seats; (2) Look at me; (3) Listen to the story; and (4) Follow my directions the first time asked. Remember that you are earning points toward a cooking activity.

C. Opening

1. Connecting statements. Say, "We have been studying the reasons why various groups of individuals traveled to America. Yesterday we talked about how the arrival of African Americans was unique. They came here not by choice, but rather by force. Their arrival in America did not represent an escape to "the land of the free," but rather the beginning of a life of slavery—property of "masters" living in the South—being dreadfully mistreated."

2. Focusing statements. Say, "Thankfully, as you know, a significant number of slaves made it to freedom because of the U.R. Today you will hear more about Harriet Tubman, an African American woman, and how she helped slaves escape on this railroad. You'll also learn about how the U.R. worked. The U.R. was not really a railroad. It was the name used to describe all of the secret places and ways by which slaves traveled to escape from captivity in the South."

III. ACTIVITY MIDDLE

A. Reminders to myself:

1. Draw name sticks to help ensure that a variety of students answer questions.
2. Mark whole-class behavior points throughout activity when students are following directions.

B. Review terms: read definitions and show pictures to emphasize meaning. Say, "There are some very specific vocabulary words that will help you better understand how the U.R. worked. I've written each word and its definition on the board."

1. Procedure for teaching key vocabulary:

   a. Say each word clearly and have students repeat.

   AP = Choral read

   b. Explain each word; use photographs.

   - **Underground railroad:** the name used to describe all of the secret places, routes, and ways by which enslaved people traveled to escape from captivity in the South. *Show photographs of secret places and routes taken by slaves.*
   - **Conductor:** guides for the people escaping. *Show photographs.*
   - **Station** or **depot:** business or home where escaping people were hidden. *Show photographs* and *emphasize the difference between a station or depot* they may know about (train or bus).
   - **Passengers:** the runaway slaves. *Show photographs.*

   c. Leave words on board for students to use as a reference.

   d. Acknowledge appropriate behavior and give behavior points here.

C. Setup for story: say, "You will need to listen carefully as I read this story to you. You'll hear what it was like to be a slave; how the U.R. got started; and how it worked. You will also hear about Harriet Tubman and why she is to be so admired."

D. Begin reading story. (I'll walk around as I read and check in more often with those students who may have difficulty attending.)

1. Section 1: pages 1–6

   a. Before reading, say, "Listen to find out why the slaves wanted to run away, why they were punished."

   b. After reading, ask, "What kind of 'offenses' were the slaves punished for? Why did the slaves want to run away to the North?"

   AP = Discuss with table groups, call on individuals (name sticks).

   c. Acknowledge appropriate behavior and give behavior points here.

2. Section 2: pages 7–12

   a. Before reading, say, "Listen to find out how the U.R. worked and what the various parts of the U.R. were." (Refer back to key terms on the board.)

   b. After reading, ask, "How did the U.R. work? What were the roles of the conductor and of the stations? What was a typical trip on the U.R. like?"

   AP = Turn to a partner
   CFU = Call on selected individuals.

3. Section 3: pages 13–20

   a. Before reading, say, "Find out how and when Harriet Tubman first used the U.R."

   b. Acknowledge appropriate behavior and give behavior points here.

   c. After reading, ask, "What events led to Harriet Tubman's first trip on the U.R.? What was the scariest part of her trip?

> ***AP/CFU*** = Have students discuss with table groups; then call on selected individuals; other students thumbs up or down to agree or disagree.

4. Section 4: pages 21–34

   a. Before reading, say, "You will learn how and why Harriet Tubman became involved in helping others use the U.R."

   b. After reading, ask, "Harriet Tubman decided to help others use the U.R. Why? Why did she continue to help for so long even though it was so dangerous?"

   c. Acknowledge appropriate behavior and give behavior points here.

> ***AP*** = Turn to a partner
> ***CFU*** = Call on individuals.

IV. ACTIVITY ENDING

A. Explain future connections.

B. Preview the follow-up writing assignment about H. Tubman and the U.R. They'll need facts to use so . . .

   1. Have them construct a concept map with as many facts as possible about U.R. and Harriet Tubman. (They frequently use concept maps as a way to organize facts and information as a review.) Give them three minutes to write; then give them two minutes to compare with a neighbor.

      a. Selected intervention: Have Ellen help Paul fill in his map.

Preface to the Lesson Models

 Introduction

A lesson model is an overall teaching approach that teachers use to guide student learning in a specific way toward the attainment of a lesson objective (Arends 2004). In Chapters 15, 16, and 17, we provide information about three important models—direct instruction, informal presentation, and structured discovery. Chapter 18 features examples of how to use direct instruction and structured discovery to teach specialized content: concepts, social skills, and learning and study strategies.

The three models selected for this book were chosen for several reasons. First, they are reasonably easy for teachers to implement, and are very effective when used correctly. Next, certain models of instruction may work better than others for teaching certain types of content, and we want you to feel comfortable teaching all kinds of content. Finally, they represent variety (from direct to less direct) in their approach to teaching which clearly addresses the fact that not all students learn in the same way.

According to Mercer et al., teachers need to make instructional decisions based on the differential needs of their students. This means that teachers must offer a continuum of teaching methods, including "explicit" and "implicit" instructional approaches, because of the diversity found in classrooms today. They point out that "an allegiance to one method of teaching reduces the range of appropriate instructional choices for teachers and students" (1996, 226). We offer some basic models in this book that can serve as the beginning of a repertoire of a necessary variety to meet the needs of diverse learners.

 Selecting a Model to Use

Students are guided toward a specific lesson objective in different ways, depending on the lesson model used. Some models, such as direct instruction and informal presentation, are best used to teach basic knowledge and skills. Some models, like structured discovery, may be used to promote inductive thinking and problem-solving skills. Because of their varied purposes, a thorough understanding of the characteristics of various lesson models can help teachers determine which particular model will work best for a particular lesson or activity.

A lesson model should always be selected after the lesson objective is written. Decide first where you want students to go (the lesson objective), and *then* decide how to help get them there (the lesson model). Once you have selected the model to use, be sure your written plan reflects the essential elements of the chosen model. For example, if you are writing a direct instruction lesson, the plan should detail how you will explain and demonstrate information, how you will check for understanding, and what types of practice opportunities you will provide, as these are some of the key elements of the direct instruction model. Although all lesson plans contain the same eight components, the content of the components will differ depending on the lesson model you use.

Responding to Skill Diversity When Selecting a Lesson Model

Using a variety of methods and models increases effectiveness and adds variety to your teaching. Because the different methods and models have unique purposes and characteristics, it is important to select them carefully. Carefully consider the content and students you are teaching as you choose methods and models. In addition, variety creates interest for your students and can also make teaching more interesting and fun for you.

Consider these variables when selecting lesson models and methods:

- Evaluate the level of structure that the students need to be successful. Do not assume that all students learn best with, or even prefer, unstructured approaches.

- Recognize that students with learning and behavioral problems often require very explicit instruction. This needs to be followed by focused, active practice with immediate feedback.

- Use the most time-efficient models and methods if the students have fallen behind in the curriculum.

- Evaluate the amount of academic learning time that each student would have in the lesson or activity. For example, having groups of students work together to bake cookies may sound like a good way to practice measurement skills; however, when you look closely, you may see that, in an hour-long activity, Joanne spent 30 seconds measuring one tablespoon of cinnamon. This isn't much practice!

- Be sure that students have the necessary skills to be successful in the methods you are using. For example, decide whether they have the needed social skills for small-group projects. These skills may need to be directly taught in advance.

- Small-group instruction may frequently be needed in a classroom of students with diverse achievement levels. Students should be carefully assessed on specific skills to form short-term skill groups. It is important to keep assessing and reforming groups as necessary.

Responding to Cultural Diversity When Planning Lessons

Many cultural variables have implications for the selection of lesson models and the use or structuring of project- or center-based activities. As you plan lessons (and activities), consider the teacher's role, the pacing of instruction, the amount of talk and movement, the specificity of directions, and other features. When selecting lessons (and activities), consider the following about your students:

- Comfort with initiating their own projects, and choosing what or how to learn

- Tolerance for structure or lack of structure

- Ease with working independently or with peers

- Experience with sitting quietly or with maintaining high activity levels

- Comfort with the teacher as a co-learner or as an authority

- Desire for feedback or direction independent of or dependent on the teacher

- Beliefs about asking for help or questioning the teacher

- Preference for learning from peers or from adults

Organization of Chapters 15 through 17

We will provide detailed information about direct instruction, informal presentation, and structured discovery models in each of these chapters. A basic description introduces each model. Next, we describe typical uses for the model and discuss some key elements of each model in "Key Planning Considerations." Finally, Figure 15.1 through Figure 17.1 provide summaries of how to write the actual lesson plans. These figures are to be used as guides. Our intent is for you to read carefully *all* of the information provided about each model and use it as a reference when you write your plans. The summaries can serve as reminders of the key information that needs to be included in the written plans. Refer to Chapter 13 for information about generic lesson components.

The content of each component included in each specific model is essential to defining the model. Teachers can add, rearrange, or omit certain component content. However, have a good rationale for doing so. Varying the critical elements of the model too much will result in something other than the model that was chosen.

Note that before you select a specific lesson model to use, complete the following preplanning tasks:

- Determine the specific content to be taught in the lesson and analyze that content.
- Write the lesson objective.
- Write the lesson rationale.
- Now, select the model and refer to the appropriate chapter for more information.

Summary

It is important to know a variety of methods and models. Selection will be most effective when you consider your students' needs as well as their interests and strengths. When you provide variety in your presentations and the methods you use, it may automatically create interest for your students. Variety is the spice of life, as the old saying goes!

References and Suggested Reading

Arends, R. I. 2004. *Learning to teach.* 6th ed. Boston: McGraw-Hill.

Joyce, B, M. Weil, and E. Calhoun. 2004. *Models of teaching.* 7th ed. Boston: Pearson.

Mercer, C. D., H. B. Lane, L. Jordan, D. H. Allsopp, and M. R. Eisele. 1996. Empowering teachers and students with instructional choices in inclusive settings. *Remedial and Special Education*, 17 (4): 226–236.

Direct Instruction

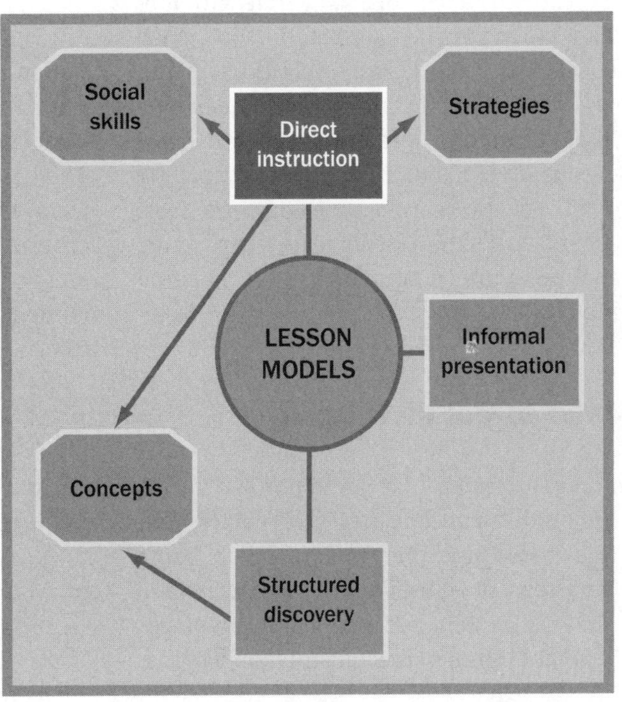

Introduction

Direct instruction is often summarized as "I do it; we do it; you do it." That is, the teacher demonstrates the skill, the teacher and students do the skill together, and the students do the skill by themselves. Another phrase used to describe direct instruction is "model-lead-test." It means the teacher shows and tells, leads the students in practicing, and then evaluates the students. Both phrases imply that the teacher is carefully guiding the learning of the students. This is precisely the intent of direct instruction. Direct instruction is explicit teaching.

Direct instruction lessons are teacher-directed, and the lesson events focus on moving students toward a specific objective. Teachers begin by clearly stating the lesson objective and the lesson purpose to the students. They then explain and demonstrate the information or skill to be learned, using many examples. Students are given a variety of opportunities to practice the new knowledge or skill. Teachers carefully supervise the students' practice, which may occur within small groups or with a partner. The final supervised practice stage is always individual student practice. This allows teachers to see how each student is progressing.

Teachers provide students with feedback on their performance as they monitor the supervised practice opportunities. This helps ensure that students are accurately practicing the new information or skill. Careful monitoring also allows teachers to determine whether or not to reteach and when to evaluate.

In the direct instruction approach, teachers present information in small steps so that students can master one step before moving to the next. The direct instruction lesson results in students demonstrating their new skill or knowledge independently, without help from anyone.

Note that there are two types of direct instruction. One type, often called "Big D. I.," refers to published programs that provide scripted lessons, such as Reading Mastery I and II Fast Cycle (Engelmann and Bruner 1995). In this chapter, we will describe the other type, commonly referred to as "little d. i." In both types of direct instruction, teachers explicitly guide students toward learning specific objectives. When teachers write the lesson plan, they create the explanations, directions, and other material contained in "little d. i."

Uses of Direct Instruction

Direct instruction lessons play an important role in teaching basic skills, concepts, rules, strategies, procedures, and knowledge that lends itself to being presented in steps or subskills. The following are some examples of content and topics that can be appropriately taught through direct instruction lessons:

- *Procedures* are a series of steps that lead to the completion of a task. Examples include how to: measure in feet, read a map, serve in volleyball, convert fractions to whole numbers, initiate a conversation, react to teasing, resist peer pressure, complete makeup assignments due to absence, get help, or what to do with completed work.

- *Strategies* are a specific type of procedure. They are techniques that help students learn, study, or get organized, including how to read text with comprehension, take notes from text readings, take multiple-choice tests, proofread assignments, or create concept webs of main ideas. (See Chapter 18 for information on strategy instruction.)

- *Principles* are relational rules and are usually stated as cause–effect or if–then relationships. The following are examples of principles: If a sentence is a question, then it should end with a question mark; if $A(B + C) = D$, then $AB + AC = D$; when a *CVCe* word has a silent *e* at the end, it makes the previous vowel say its name; and when a sentence includes three or more related items, a comma belongs after each item.

- *Concepts* are categories of knowledge. Examples include triangle, peninsula, noun, socialism, migration, ecosystem, or plot.

Direct instruction lessons also play an important role in lessons that emphasize higher-level thinking. Higher-level thinking cannot occur without having basic facts and information about which to think. The content taught in direct instruction lessons may form the foundation for lessons that emphasize critical thinking and problem solving. The following are some examples of how higher-level thinking is dependent on knowledge of basic skills and information:

- Mr. Garcia wants his students to use the Internet as one resource for their country analysis. He first teaches them computer-access skills through direct instruction.

- Ms. Parker wants her students to design their own science experiments to test certain hypotheses. She first teaches them steps in the scientific method through direct instruction.

Direct instruction lessons also play an important role in the use of certain teaching methods (Arends 2004). For example, if you want to use cooperative learning groups or discussions in your lessons and activities, you will need to directly teach students skills such as reaching consensus, taking turns, active listening, and paraphrasing.

Key Planning Considerations

When writing the body of the direct instruction lesson, carefully consider and plan in detail the presentation of information, the demonstration, and the supervised practice. The content analysis, which plays an important role in the lesson body, must be planned carefully as well.

Content Analysis

The content analysis of a direct instruction lesson varies according to the content you are teaching. When planning a "how-to" lesson, the content analysis will include a task analysis. When teaching a principle, you will write a clearly stated principle statement. Finally, when teaching a concept through direct instruction, include a concept analysis. Note that the task analysis, principle statement, or concept analysis will be presented and taught as part of the lesson body (see Chapter 1).

Presentation of Information

In the presentation of information section of the direct instruction lesson body, the teacher presents the information students need to know to meet the lesson objective. The presentation should include a description of the content to be taught (the *what*) and how the new skill or knowledge will be explained (the *how*). It is important to present all of the information necessary for understanding the new knowledge or skill through explanations, descriptions, definitions, and specific examples and nonexamples. The presentation of information section of the lesson body can occur before, during, or after the demonstration part (see the next section).

Typically, the information in this section of the lesson is presented both in writing (on a transparency, a whiteboard, a poster, or a handout) and orally. Any explanation that may be complex or have the potential to be confusing should be put in writing to help ensure it is complete, accurate, and clear. Also include descriptions of various visual supports that can add interest and help clarify information. Critical teaching skills such as active participation strategies, including checks for understanding, are also very important parts of the presentation of information section, and should be planned out carefully. (See Chapters 3–7 for additional information on these topics.)

Appropriate parts of the content analysis play a very important role in the instruction that occurs during the body of a direct instruction lesson. For instance, a teacher directly shows and explains a task analysis to the students. The same is true of a concept analysis or a principle statement. This is also the time and place when the teacher introduces and teaches key terms if they were not taught in the opening. A well-planned content analysis can help the lesson body take shape.

When the body of the lesson is written, include enough detail to prevent being "caught off guard" during the lesson. Do *not* simply write in the plan, "I will explain the steps" or "I'll define each term." It is necessary to plan *how* you will explain—namely, by listing in the plan the key points or ideas you want to convey and the examples you want to include. Write out the definitions of key terms so that they are clear and complete. It is very difficult to spontaneously explain, describe, or define in a clear way. Often the ideas that seem most simple and obvious to the teacher are the most difficult to explain.

Remember that it is hardly ever appropriate to ask students to provide the initial explanations of the new information, because it is very important that initial explanations are accurate and clear. You can involve students by asking them to review prerequisite knowledge or skills before the presentation of information. They could also be asked for their ideas and examples after the necessary information has been presented.

Carefully plan how you will check for understanding of the information. If you are presenting a great deal of new information, incorporate checks for understanding and opportunities for student processing after each step or part of the information. Calling on one student to paraphrase or give an additional example will not reveal whether all of the students understand. Include active participation strategies that will allow you to check for understanding of all students.

Demonstration

Before, during, or after the presentation of information, teachers need to demonstrate—show or model—the new knowledge or skill. Demonstrating can mean showing a *product* (for example, "Here is an example of a paragraph that includes a topic sentence and supporting details"), or modeling a *process* ("Watch as I make this foul shot," or "Listen as I think out loud while developing my topic sentence"). Using a skit or role play can also effectively demonstrate a new skill. In most all cases, the "doing" portion of a demonstration is accompanied by the teacher thinking aloud so student can hear what she is thinking. Use visual supports during the demonstration to emphasize key points. During the demonstration portion of the lesson body, teachers will probably show examples or demonstrate specific steps, but it is essential that they model the whole product or process as well.

Teachers or other experts, rather than students, should demonstrate the skill or process to provide a correct model for students to follow. This reduces the chances that students incorrectly practice the new skill. You can ask students to demonstrate later in the body of the lesson (see supervised practice for further information).

Note that teachers commonly forget to teach before asking students to practice. It is essential that teachers provide complete explanations, many examples, and many demonstrations. If you find this unnecessary, you are most likely planning a review or practice activity rather than a direct instruction lesson. Another common error teachers make out of eagerness to promote active participation and involvement is to ask students to do the initial teaching. If students can do the initial teaching, you most likely have planned an activity rather than a lesson. You can keep students engaged in many ways without neglecting your responsibility to teach clearly and accurately.

Supervised Practice

The supervised practice portion of the lesson body provides an important link between the lesson body and the components that follow. After presenting and demonstrating the lesson information, provide the students with opportunities to practice the new skill or information. Provide this practice under your guidance and supervision. Careful observation of student practice can help you judge whether or not your students understand the information that you presented. Lead, prompt, and give corrective feedback immediately.

The three levels of supervised practice provide varying amounts of scaffolding. They are as follows:

- *Whole-group supervised practice* In this type of practice, the teacher involves the class as she demonstrates the skill again ("What do I do next, everyone . . . ?"). This is a good place to encourage quick-paced active participation and gradually withdraw prompts.

- *Small-group or partner supervised practice* During small-group or partner practice, the teacher again monitors carefully while students practice. Students must be given very clear directions about how they are to divide up the work and practice ("Partner 1 reads the steps and Partner 2 does the computation; on the next problem, switch roles."). Peers provide support for each other in these first attempts at performing the new skill.

- *Individual supervised practice* The final and *essential* level involves asking each student to practice alone while the teacher monitors and corrects ("Work on the next 5 sentences and I'll come around and check your work.").

Some key ideas to remember about supervised practice are: (1) always include individual supervised practice; (2) do not move on to supervised practice if checks for understanding show that students are confused; (3) make sure the practice activities provided for supervised practice are congruent with other parts of your lesson; (4) provide supervised practice after each step or part when content is very difficult; and (5) remember that supervised practice is not the formal evaluation. (See Chapter 7 for more information on supervised practice.)

Figure 15.1 Writing a Direct Instruction Lesson

When preparing direct instruction lessons, you will typically include the following content within the different components:

COMPONENT 1: PREPLANNING TASKS

The preplanning tasks section is a cover sheet for the rest of the lesson plan. Include the following:

- *Connection analysis* Identify the generalization or big idea, the IEP goal, and/or the state standard addressed in the plan.
- *Content analysis* May include a task analysis, a concept analysis, or a principle statement, key terms and vocabulary, and a list of prerequisite skills or knowledge.
- *Objective* Possible objectives for a direct instruction lesson could be for students to demonstrate, list, rewrite, give an example, identify, state reasons, label, use a strategy, or compute.
- *Objective rationale* To help clarify the value of the objective.

COMPONENT 2: LESSON SETUP

The lesson setup is the first component of the lesson plan that is actually presented to students. Include the following in the lesson setup:

- *Signal for attention* This is the initial signal for attention. Examples of signals include playing music, flicking lights, or saying, "Let's get started."
- *Statement of behavior expectations* These are the initial expectations. An example would be to say, "If you need help, you may ask your partner."

COMPONENT 3: LESSON OPENING

The lesson opening should effectively prepare the students for new learning. Include the following in the lesson opening:

- A strategy designed to generate interest in the lesson and to relate new learning to prior knowledge.
- A way to state the objective so students know what they will learn. In a direct instruction lesson, students are told directly what they will be expected to do or know following the lesson.
- A statement of the objective purpose, so students know why the new learning is valuable and useful.

COMPONENT 4: LESSON BODY

The lesson body looks like a series of repeated steps. First, teachers "show and tell"; next, check for understanding; next, conduct supervised practice with feedback; then, provide more "show and tell"; and so on. For less

continued on next page

Figure 15.1 Writing a Direct Instruction Lesson (continued)

complex lessons, teachers will "show and tell" all steps and then provide supervised practice. Provide the following in the lesson body:

- Teacher "show and tell." The *presentation of information* and an accompanying *demonstration* is necessary to enable the students to learn the content or perform the skills being taught (or the first step in a sequence). This should include many, varied examples. Do not forget to include visual supports.
- Strategies that will be used to promote *active participation.* For example, students may compare answers with a partner, write answers on a piece of scratch paper and hold it up for you to see, or respond in unison.
- Techniques that will be used to *check for understanding.* These should involve overt responses on the part of the students (that is, they do or say something) so you can determine if students are progressing toward the objective. For example, students may use thumbs up or thumbs down to signify they agree or disagree.
- *Supervised practice* opportunities. You will always include individual supervised practice, but you may choose to include whole-group, partner, or small-group practice as well. For example, you may first provide practice for the whole group ("Let's do one more problem together"). Next, students work with a partner ("You will practice the next six problems with your partner. Each of you take turns working three problems while thinking out loud, and your partner will check for accuracy"). Finally, students work alone ("Try the next two problems by yourself, and I will come around and check your answers").
- *Universal and selected interventions.* Decide which strategies you will build in or add on to help all students be successful. For example, use an elaborate opening to build background knowledge, individual behavior contracts, large-print worksheet, picture directions, or expanded partner practice.

COMPONENT 5: EXTENDED PRACTICE

Extended practice is one of the key elements in the direct instruction lesson. Students will need additional practice to develop the accuracy and fluency necessary for the application and generalization of the new skill or knowledge. Seatwork and homework are types of assignments that provide extended practice opportunities, and they should match the individual supervised practice in the body of the lesson. Checking or observing these assignments carefully will let you know when formal evaluation should occur. Long-term extended practice is typically provided in the form of activities (see Chapter 14 for detail). Include the following in writing the extended practice:

- List additional practice opportunities, including assignments and homework. Be sure that final practice activities provide students with an opportunity to practice alone. One diversity strategy to consider in this component is variation of extended practice opportunities. Some students will need a great deal of extended practice, whereas others will need far less. Emphasize application and generalization.
- A list of lessons and activities, if appropriate, that will build on the objective and additional opportunities for students to generalize, integrate, and extend the information.

COMPONENT 6: LESSON CLOSING

The lesson closing in a direct instruction lesson will occur in one of two places. If extended practice is assigned as in-class work, the teacher may close the lesson after the assignment has been completed. If extended practice is

Figure 15.1 Writing a Direct Instruction Lesson (continued)

assigned as homework, the lesson closing will occur immediately following the lesson body. When preparing the lesson closing, include the following:

- One or more strategies for closing the lesson. Frequently selected strategies for closing the direct instruction lesson are a review of key points of the lesson, a description of where or when students would use their new skills or knowledge, a time for students to show their work, or a reference to the opening. Plans that involve students in the closing are especially effective.

COMPONENT 7: EVALUATION

The evaluation component of the direct instruction lesson is planned when the measurable lesson objective is written. Evaluation is designed to determine individual student progress in relation to the lesson objective, which means the student does not receive help from peers or teachers during the evaluation. Careful monitoring of progress during supervised and extended practice activities will help teachers determine when students are ready to be evaluated. When preparing the evaluation, include the following:

- A description of the evaluation. You may want to include a sample in the case of a paper and pencil test, and may want to tell when and how the evaluation will occur if not immediately following the lesson. An example would be to write, "Later in the day, during other activities, I will ask each student individually to draw an example of a right triangle for me, and I'll check them off on my class list if they do it correctly."

COMPONENT 8: EDITING TASKS

Remember to use editing tasks to evaluate your plan: (1) Write in critical management skills; (2) Double-check for instructional interventions; and (3) Evaluate congruence (see Chapter 19).

Sample Plans

Look at the framework for diversity responsive teaching (DRT) as you examine the sample plans at the end of this chapter. Ask yourself how the plan incorporates responses to diversity in *what* is taught, *how* it's taught, and the *context* for teaching and learning. We'll give you a start in thinking about how various parts of the plan fit with various components of the framework. We encourage you to look for additional examples of each component and to think about what changes you believe would make this plan even more likely to support all students' success.

Notice that the lesson "Summarizing What You Read" includes *carrier content* about diversity (a story about a friend with a hearing impairment) and focuses on *similarities* as well as *differences* (the friends have many interests in common). The lesson plan "How to Write A Cover Letter" emphasizes *connections* and *importance to students' lives* (getting a summer job). Both of these are responses to diversity when planning *what* to teach.

All three lessons include numerous examples of responding to diversity when planning how to teach. The "Summarizing What You Read" plan includes a variety of strategies in the *opening* (activating background knowledge, stating objective and purpose, and reviewing of prior learning). The plan on "How to Write a Cover Letter" is a good example of using *universal design for learning* (the teacher explains, shows, and writes the information, and includes response options in the objective). The "How to Get Help on In-Class Tasks" plan shows authentic exercises in *supervised practice* and includes an excellent variety of practice opportunities in *extended practice*.

The lesson "How to Get Help on In-Class Tasks" teaches a classroom routine as a *universal behavioral intervention*. Notice that "How to Write A Cover Letter" is an example of a lesson in which the content is personally interesting and relevant to students, which may work to prevent behavior problems. Some *critical management skills* are included in "Summarizing What You Read." All of these are responses to diversity when planning the *context* for teaching and learning.

References and Suggested Readings

Arends, R. I. 2004. *Learning to teach.* 6th ed. Boston: McGraw-Hill. (See Chapter 8 in particular.)

Borich, G. 2004. *Effective teaching methods.* 4th ed. Columbus, OH: Merrill, an imprint of Prentice Hall. (See Chapter 5 in particular.)

Carnine, D., J. Silbert, and E. J. Kame'enui. 2004. *Direct instruction reading.* 4th ed. Upper Saddle River, NJ: Merrill.

Eggen, P. D., and D. P. Kauchak. 2006. *Strategies and models for teachers: Teaching content and thinking skills.* Boston: Pearson. (See Chapter 9 in particular.)

Engelmann, S., and E. Bruner. 1995. *Reading mastery 1/11 fast cycle.* Columbus, OH: Macmillan/McGraw-Hill.

Lasley II, T. J., T. J. Matczynski, and J. B. Rowley. 2002. *Instructional models: Strategies for teaching in a diverse society.* 2nd ed. Belmont, CA: Wadsworth/Thomson Learning.

O'Brien, J. 2000. Enabling all students to learn in the laboratory of democracy. *Intervention in School and Clinic* 35 (4): 195–205.

Rosenberg, M. S., L. O'Shea, and D. J. O'Shea. 2002. *Student teacher to master teacher: A practical guide for educating students with special needs.* 3rd ed. Columbus, OH: Merrill, an imprint of Prentice Hall. (See Chapter 6 in particular.)

Smith, P. L., and T. J. Ragan. 2004. *Instructional design.* 3rd ed. Columbus, OH: Merrill, an imprint of Prentice Hall.

Witzel, B. S., C. D. Mercer, and M. D. Miller. 2003. Teaching algebra to students with learning disabilities: An investigation of an explicit instruction model. *Learning Disabilities Research & Practice* 18 (2): 121–131.

Summarizing What You Read

This is a direct instruction lesson for a small reading group.

I. PREPLANNING TASKS

A. Connection analysis: *State Reading Standard #2:* The student understands the meaning of what is read. *Component 2.1:* comprehend important ideas and details. *Benchmark 1:* demonstrate comprehension of the main idea and supporting details; students summarize ideas in their own words.

B. Content analysis

1. Task analysis: How to Summarize What is Read
   a. Read the passage.
   b. State the main idea in a few words or a sentence.
   c. State the supporting details in a few words or sentences.
   d. Tips: Use your own words, and as few words as possible.
2. Prerequisite skills: Know how to identify the main idea and supporting details, and how to paraphrase.
3. Key terms or vocabulary: **Summarize**—to tell about something in as few words as possible.

C. Objective: Given a task analysis of how to summarize and three paragraphs of grade-level reading material, students will summarize each paragraph in their own words (say the main idea and two supporting details in no more than two to three sentences).

D. Objective rationale: Summarizing helps comprehension, and puts material read into manageable form for future use.

E. Materials: *Three transparencies* (one for reviewing terms, two that include the task analysis at the top and reading passages about similarities between hearing and non-hearing children on the bottom), and an *evaluation handout* for each student.

F. Room arrangement: Desks in groups of four; make sure all can see the board and screen.

II. LESSON SETUP

A. Initial signal for attention: Play music (tape recorder).

B. Initial behavioral expectations: Eyes on me; participate (point to T-chart: "What does participating look like and sound like?").

III. LESSON OPENING

A. Activate background knowledge: "Has anyone told you about a TV show or a movie they saw? What did they say? Did they tell you every single word that was said and everything that happened? Or, did they summarize?" **AP** = Call on individuals

B. Pre-teach vocabulary: Point to and read definition of *summarize* on board. "I could summarize or tell about in a few words, the story we read last week by saying it was about a girl who sailed around the world and found a monkey and brought it home."

C. Statement of objective; objective purpose:

1. "Today you will learn how to summarize what you *read*."
2. "This will help you better understand what you read and make it easier to use what you read (for a book report, for example)."

D. Review prerequisites: "To summarize, you must know the main idea and supporting details."

1. Show transparency #1. Review definitions: **main idea** and **supporting details. AP** = Choral read definitions.
2. Show sample paragraph. Have students find the main idea and details. **AP** = Tell a partner, call on nonvolunteers.

IV. LESSON BODY

A. Presentation of information

1. Show transparency #2 (task analysis and paragraphs). "The paragraphs are about a boy who has a friend who is deaf."
2. Explain that summarizing involves following a series of steps; give examples and nonexamples of the tips in the task analysis.
3. **AP** = "State steps in your own words to your partner"; **CFU** = Call on selected nonvolunteers to say steps.

B. Demonstration

1. Do a think-aloud of the task analysis (using Paragraph 1): "First I read the passage. Then. . . ."
2. Draw a graphic organizer while thinking aloud (concept map of connected circles).
3. End with, "My summary is: Li and his two best friends like to do the same things. They like to play baseball and to draw pictures."
4. Repeat the think-aloud with Paragraph 2. **AP** = "Signal with your fingers the # of the step I'm on."

C. Check for understanding

1. Show Paragraph 3 and then 4: **AP** = Choral read. "Count off for Numbered Heads Together in your table groups."
2. Ask, "What is the main idea?" and so on. Call on selected students from each group to respond. **AP** = Thumbs up if you agree.

D. Supervised practice

1. Show transparency #3 (task analysis and paragraphs).
2. "Work with a partner on the next four paragraphs."
   a. "The first person reads and summarizes, while the second person checks. Switch after each paragraph."
   b. "What does the first person do? And then . . . ?" **CFU** = Call on selected nonvolunteers.
   c. Remind students of the rule about giving feedback politely (behavior expectations).

3. I monitor and give feedback on summaries and acknowledge polite feedback when I hear it.
4. "Summarize the next three in writing by yourself" (individual supervised practice).
5. Monitor and give feedback. Make sure I hear each student summarize at least one paragraph.

V. LESSON CLOSING

A. Signal for attention with bell.

B. Review the importance of the skill by asking students to explain the value of summarizing. "If your family asks you what you learned today, what will you say . . . everyone? **AP** = Choral respond. If they ask you why summarizing is important, what will you say? Think about it. . . ." **AP** = Tell your partner.

C. Review steps. "Close your eyes and picture the list of steps." Open your eyes and read them.

VI. EXTENDED PRACTICE

A. Form cooperative learning groups for science.

1. Each member has three paragraphs of written material on the senses.
2. Members will orally summarize paragraphs to the group.
3. I monitor and provide feedback.

VII. EVALUATION

Throughout the day, I'll have individual students summarize three paragraphs of appropriate grade-level reading material to me. The paragraphs are about Curtis Pride and Marlee Matlin. This fits in with our unit on famous people with disabilities. I will check students off if they can do it without prompting.

How to Write a Cover Letter

This is a direct instruction lesson for secondary students.

I. PREPLANNING TASKS

A. Connection analysis: *State Standard, Writing 2.2:* Write for a broad range of purposes including to apply for jobs.

B. Content analysis

1. Task analysis: *Components of a Cover Letter* (see lesson body).
2. Prerequisite skills: Writing paragraphs and letters; prior practice with writing about their education and accomplishments.
3. Key terms or vocabulary: **Cover letter**—a letter that accompanies a resume; **Qualification**—a quality, ability, or accomplishment that makes a person suitable for a particular position

C. Objective: Given a personal fact sheet and a job description, students will write or dictate a cover letter that includes two addresses, an opening, a body with at least one paragraph, and a closing, and provides a convincing argument for being hired.

D. Objective rationale: This lesson will help students learn the basics of writing cover letters to send along with resumes, which will in turn help them in their search for a summer job.

E. Materials: *Transparencies:* (1) graphic organizer of unit, (2) cover letter/purpose of cover letter, (3) components and samples of cover letters, (4) blank cover letter template; posters. *Student handout packets:* copies of transparencies, templates, job descriptions; and students' fact sheets from last week's lesson.

F. Reference: http://www.naz.edu/dept/career_services/coverletters.html

II. LESSON SETUP

A. Signal for attention: Turn on overhead projector.

B. Behavior expectations: Follow along and participate; raise your hand and wait to be called on before speaking; and show respect (listen when others speak).

III. LESSON OPENING

A. Review prior learning.

1. Say, "This lesson is part of the job search unit. We're learning about job searches because many of you will soon be applying for summer jobs."
2. Show a graphic organizer of the unit (transparency #1) with "writing cover letter" highlighted.
3. Remind them of last week's lesson on how to write a resume. Show an example of a resume.

B. Statement of objective; objective purpose.

1. Say, "Today we will learn how to write a basic cover letter to accompany a resume."
2. Say, "A well-written cover letter will increase your chance of getting a job."

C. Preview the purpose of a cover letter.

1. Show transparency #2 with Part 1: Robby's cover letter, and Part 2: "Purpose of a Cover Letter."
2. Read Robby's cover letter (applying for a construction job).
3. Explain "Purposes of a Cover Letter"—to introduce yourself, summarize your qualifications, and so on.
4. Think aloud how the letter matches the purposes. Ask students to find other examples, such as "Where does the writer summarize his qualifications?"

> ***AP*** = Talk to partner

IV. LESSON BODY

A. Presentation of information and demonstration (of product)

1. Pass out the packet of handouts. Students will follow along and take notes as I present information and assign practice.
2. Show transparency #3 (Part 1: Components of a Cover Letter; Part 2: Sample cover letter).
3. Read "Components of a Cover Letter" and explain each, using examples from the sample cover letter at the bottom of the transparency.

> ***AP*** = Students follow along on their own copies

   I. Addresses
      a. Writer's address (including city, state, zip) in the upper right corner
      b. Company or organization's address in the left margin

   II. Opening paragraph
      a. State what you are seeking (your objective), and match it to their needs.
      b. Say something positive or flattering about the business.

   III. Body of the letter is one or two paragraphs describing your education, skills, and accomplishments.
      a. Emphasize how you can help the organization. Use any important "buzz words."
      b. Highlight skills you have that match their needs.

   IV. Closing paragraph
      a. State a plan of action, such as they call you or you call them, to arrange a meeting.
      b. Thank them for their consideration and note enclosures or attachments, such as a resume.

4. Have students take out whiteboards. Ask specific questions about parts of the letter ("What goes in the opening?") and where parts of the task analysis are found ("Where do you talk about your accomplishments?").
5. Repeat with another example if needed (Gail's cover letter).

> ***CFU*** = Students write responses

B. Demonstration (of process)

1. Show transparency #4 (blank cover letter template) and posters of job descriptions and personal fact sheet.
2. Using my fact sheet and job description do a think-aloud of each component while filling in the template ("Next, I write the opening . . . I need to state the job I'm interested in, . . ." and so on). They copy what I write on their partially completed template.

> ***CFU*** = Call on selected nonvolunteers.

3. Ask specific questions about parts of the letter ("What did I put in my opening?").

C. Individual supervised practice

1. Hand out the personal fact sheet of an imaginary person.
2. Pass out a job description (superhero, rock star).
3. Have students write a cover letter using a template.
4. I monitor and give feedback to each student.

V. EXTENDED PRACTICE

A. Have students select sample cover letters from my file and label the components.

B. Have students find a sample job description in my file and write a cover letter without a template.

VI. LESSON CLOSING

A. Group review of practice

1. Have students share successes and trouble spots of writing cover letters.

B. Preview tomorrow's evaluation: "Tomorrow we will write our own, personal cover letters using our own information and a realistic job description."

VII. EVALUATION

Once the extended practice activities are finished and I have given feedback, then students will write their own, personal cover letter (as described in the objective).

How to Get Help on In-Class Tasks

This is a direct instruction lesson for teaching a classroom routine.

I. PREPLANNING TASKS

A. Connection analysis: This is part of a series of lessons focused on the general rule "Use your time wisely." IEP goal: Ken will seek help appropriately when frustrated with assignments.

B. Content (task) analysis: See presentation of information.

C. Objective: Students will correctly follow the routine for getting help when they encounter difficulty on an in-class task in three out of three observations.

D. Rationale: This procedure will prevent wasted time and help students be more independent and efficient in getting help.

E. Materials: Poster, PowerPoint slide, handouts of steps, worksheets, class list, and clipboard.

F. Rehearsal: Practice skit with assistant and practice demonstration with Ken and Rich before class.

II. LESSON SETUP

A. Signal for attention: "Eyes up here, let's get started."

B. Behavior expectations: Follow the active listening guidelines (point to poster showing written guidelines with picture cues).

> ***CFU*** = Ask students to demonstrate each guideline.

III. LESSON OPENING

A. Attention-getter: Do skit with teaching assistant. She has arm up in air, obviously for a long time. Just when she puts arm down to rest, the teacher looks up and helps someone else with a hand raised.

B. Objective and purpose: Has this happened to you? Today you'll learn a better procedure to get help. This procedure is important because your time won't be wasted, it's more fair, and you'll learn to help each other and yourselves. It's part of our rule "Use your time wisely."

C. Application: Use this routine when doing assignments in class by yourself or in groups.

IV. LESSON BODY

A. Presentation of information

1. Show steps of task analysis on poster.
2. Explain and give examples of each step. Have each step fly in on PowerPoint slide.

> ***AP*** = Ask students to paraphrase each step to partner before going to next one.

3. Task analysis: How to get help on in-class tasks.
   a. If you run into difficulty, try helping yourself:
      I. Look at examples, reread directions, or use resources such as glossary.
      II. Try again.
   b. If you still need help:
      I. Ask peers (if allowed).
      II. Use signal to teacher (stand book up on desk or write group name on board).
   c. While waiting for help:
      I. Plan question to ask (not just "I don't get it").
      II. Skip problem and go on if possible.

B. Demonstration
   1. Hand out copies of steps and tell students to check off the steps as they see me demonstrate them (AP).
   2. Sitting in student desk with math worksheet, I think out loud the steps ("I'm stuck on this one. Let's see, is there an example like this at the top of the page . . ." and so on). **CFU** = Call on selected students at random to describe each step I followed.
   3. Demonstrate incorrectly with social studies questions (don't reread directions, call out "I can't do this" in whiny voice). **AP** = Have students tell partner errors. **CFU** = Call on students at random to correct me.
   4. Demonstrate correctly with Ken and Rich (who often have trouble with this). We pretend to be working on a group project. Include the steps of asking peers for help and writing group name on board. Ask class which steps they checked off.

C. Supervised practice
   1. Leave up poster.
   2. Give students very challenging worksheets with unfamiliar format and no oral directions.
   3. Tell them to use the procedure when they need help.
   4. Provide positive and corrective feedback on following the steps, to each student.

V. LESSON CLOSING

A. Refer back to opening skit: What could I do differently? Would I feel different?

B. Application: Ask students to think of a time when they are likely to need this procedure and visualize themselves using it.

C. Review: Read steps in unison from poster.

VI. EXTENDED PRACTICE

A. Leave poster up. Ask students to review steps before each period for which they'll be needed the next three days.

B. Occasionally give computer time points to students who follow steps. (Try to catch Ken and Rich doing it right the first day.)

C. Don't help students until they follow the steps—point to the poster as reminder.

D. Reteach individuals and provide cards with steps to check off, for their desks, as needed.

E. Ask class for feedback after the third day. Are they getting help faster? Are they helping themselves or each other more often?

VII. EVALUATION

During the following week, observe students as they work on tasks and check them off as they follow the routine without prompting, at least three times. (Don't forget Ken's progress monitoring chart for IEP goal.)

Informal Presentation

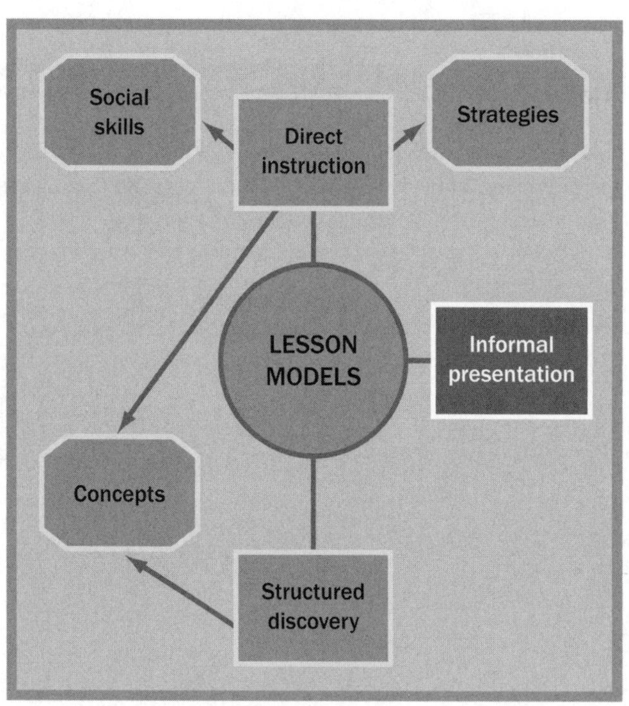

 Introduction

The purpose of the informal presentation model is to deliver information to students in a clear and concise manner. Arends (2004) suggests that this teacher-directed model is the most popular one used in schools today. He also suggests that its popularity is no surprise, because it provides a very effective way to help students acquire the array of information they are expected to learn. The main idea of this model is that the teacher first tells the students what they are going to be told, then tells them, and finally tells them what they were told (Moore 2005). Careful planning can make these lessons effective in all subject areas with either large groups or small groups of students who are of varying ages and abilities (Arends 2004).

An effective informal presentation lesson is designed to lead students to a specific objective. The lesson content is delivered in a clear, interesting manner, and the main ideas of the lesson are emphasized through the use of an advance organizer (Ausubel 1960), graphic organizers, visual supports, and so on. With this model, students are kept actively involved in the lesson and in rehearsing the new information in a variety of ways, such as asking and answering questions, summarizing concepts, discussing key ideas with a partner, or constructing examples. At the end of this type of lesson, students will be able to explain, compare and contrast, define, describe, or apply the new information.

This lesson model provides several advantages. For one, this type of lesson significantly benefits students who have reading or reading comprehension problems, as it can serve as an accommodation for them. They are able to gain necessary information without having to rely solely on written material. This model is also very time-efficient. Instructors can teach large groups as well as small groups of students the same information at the same time.

Uses of Informal Presentation

Teachers generally use the informal presentation model to teach declarative information. That is, they teach knowledge about something or that something is the case, rather than how to do something (Arends 2004; Smith and Ragan 2005). Factual information, principles, and concepts are examples of various types of declarative knowledge.

Teachers can organize declarative information in different ways, depending on the type of information. For example, if you are going to teach a principle, plan a clear principle statement in advance and communicate it to the students during the lesson. Many supporting examples accompany the thorough explanation of the principle. Key ideas regarding factual information are best organized as a subject matter outline for use in an informal presentation lesson. This framework provides the teacher with a mechanism by which to evaluate what information to include. It can help teachers ensure that the content they will present is related and relevant.

The informal presentation model is appropriately used to present a wide range of topics. Here are some examples of specific content topics organized into two of the categories of declarative knowledge:

- *Factual Information.* This category of knowledge includes such topics as the history of the stock market, community helpers, differences between poetry and prose, the story of Anne Frank, and mammals.

- *Principles.* This type of knowledge includes ideas such as drinking alcohol can cause alcoholism; when the economy is sluggish, interest rates generally go down; birds migrate when the weather changes.

The following examples illustrate the variety of purposes the informal presentation model can address:

- Mrs. McBride includes content about sexually transmitted diseases (STDs) in a unit she teaches as part of her health class curriculum. She begins the unit with an informal presentation lesson on types of STDs and criteria used to classify them. In this case, Mrs. McBride is using this lesson to *present new information.*

- Ms. Wines uses an informal presentation lesson to teach her students about various types of cloud formations. This information is to be used as background information for a series of lessons on causes of weather. Ms. Wines is using an informal presentation lesson to *teach background information* for future lessons.

- Mrs. Davis follows a student reading assignment about the causes of the civil war with an informal presentation lesson. The purpose of the lesson is to *help clarify previously studied information.* She clarifies the information her students gained from the reading assignment.

- Mr. Chin prepares an informal presentation lesson to *conclude a series of lessons* on the civil rights movement. He plans to summarize a number of key points and generalizations for which his students will be held responsible.

- Mrs. Brown uses an informal presentation lesson about volcanoes—complete with a working model—as an introductory lesson to a unit on landforms. The purpose of the lesson is to teach specific content and to *help create interest* in the upcoming unit.

- Ms. Bishop teaches informal presentation lessons on several aspects of computer technology. The computer content changes far more rapidly than student textbooks are replaced, so the information in her textbooks is often outdated. Ms. Bishop reads extensively to stay current in her field, but the written material she reads is not appropriate for her students. In this case, Ms. Bishop uses informal presentation lessons to *present information not readily available in other sources,* such as textbooks.

 Key Planning Considerations

Informal presentation lessons are not difficult to plan if the teacher begins with a thorough understanding of the content to present. When planning the lesson, give special consideration to the following elements:

Content Analysis

The content analysis for an informal presentation lesson will often include a subject matter outline. Whenever the goal is to teach about something (rather than to teach how to do something) and to teach factual information, a subject matter outline can be an effective way to organize the information to be presented. A well-planned subject matter outline will be used in the lesson body, where it will be called a presentation outline.

Careful preparation of the subject matter outline can be of great benefit. First, it can help ensure that you select content that directly relates to the objective to be accomplished, as well as the knowledge structure of the discipline. It can also help prevent errors in accuracy and ensure that the information to be presented is clear. Finally, the outline simplifies lesson body planning because it is used to guide the presentation delivery portion. Various active participation and diversity strategies, visual supports, and presentation techniques will become the main focus of the lesson body planning rather than organization of the content.

A carefully written subject matter outline (presentation outline) can be an excellent resource for your students as well. You may choose to show the outline to the students during the presentation, or you may give them a copy, or partial copy, to use as a note-taking guide. Another option would be to give them the outline to use as a study guide. They can add more information to it from readings, interviews, videos, Internet sites, or other sources.

There is no set rule about the amount of detail to include in the outline. Provide enough detail to ensure a clear presentation, but not so much detail that the presentation loses focus. Strive to prepare an outline that is detailed, yet brief. Single words and short phrases should serve as cues for information that has been committed to memory. These are preferred to lengthy sentences or narrative (Esler and Sciortino 1991). The outline, which should not be read, should serve as a reminder of what will be said.

When you are going to teach a principle, include a principle statement in the content analysis. Remember that principles are relational rules that prescribe the relationship between two or more concepts. When teaching principles using the informal presentation model, a principle statement serves as the organizer for the presentation.

Be sure that you plan in advance how to explain the principle to your students. Begin by writing out the complete principle statement, including the condition and the result or the action that needs to be taken. It can be difficult to correctly or accurately explain the principle spontaneously during the lesson or activity. Next, carefully consider which words are best used as part of your explanation. Finally, be sure that you plan many, varied examples to illustrate the principle. It is important that your students can *apply* the principle to unknown examples (Smith and Ragan 2005).

Content Knowledge

All teachers find themselves in the position of needing to teach lessons on topics they have never taught before. When this happens to you, be prepared to spend some time learning the content before you begin planning how you will teach it. It would be difficult, if not impossible, to prepare a complete, accurate presentation outline for use in the lesson if you do not fully understand the subject matter. Your study of the content will help you in choosing interesting and meaningful examples, making relevant comparisons, and connecting information to real-life applications. When using the informal presentation model, thorough content knowledge is absolutely essential. The time you spend learning will be time well spent as it will likely result in increased student learning.

Using this model also makes it important to understand how the content fits into the knowledge structure of the discipline from which it comes, because all disciplines have key concepts, generalizations, or "big ideas" that define them as distinct from other disciplines. These concepts form a knowledge structure—perhaps best conceptualized as one enormous subject matter outline—that provides an organized way to think about and study the information within the discipline, such as categorizing it and showing relationships among categories (Arends 2004). When teaching content from a particular discipline, students learn best if they can see how it fits into the big picture.

Advance Organizer

Use advance organizers to orient students to a new learning task—to focus attention and organize student thinking (Schmidt and Harriman 1998; Arends 2004). The organizer can be a picture, diagram, or statement the teacher makes. For example, use oral introductions to a lesson, written questions presented at the beginning of a chapter in a text, study guides, or graphic organizers as advance organizers (Schmidt and Harriman 1998). Use various visual supports, such as photographs, to help further clarify, explain, or demonstrate the content of the advance organizer, as needed.

Advance organizers play an important role in providing students with cognitive scaffolding. First, they help students see how the content they will learn fits into the big picture. Explanations about how the content is organized and how it will be presented further assist students to understand. The preview that the advance organizer provides is a valuable aid to comprehension.

The advance organizer may be seen as the equivalent of the chapter introduction in a textbook. It is generally more abstract than the content of the current lesson (it contains an overriding organizational idea into which the information to come will fit). An example of a verbal advance organizer is, "There are many types of families, but they all have in common the caring for and support of individual members." Designing the organizer can help you plan a presentation that is aligned with this important big idea.

The advance organizer will generally be presented in the lesson opening. The teacher may begin by using one strategy to address prior knowledge, such as a review of previous related lessons, followed by the presentation of an advance organizer. This way, the information to come is linked to prior knowledge. An advance organizer may help students utilize their prior knowledge, but it should also be designed to relate directly to the information that follows it.

The following are examples of advance organizers:

- Mrs. Dyson explains to her students that opera themes reflect the composer's interpretation of the social climate of the time.
- Mrs. Garcia opens her presentation on the westward movement by stating, "Human migration follows new economic opportunities and/or political upheavals."
- Mr. Lundquist explains the commonalities among sonatas, prior to playing recordings by various composers.
- Ms. Tatupu shows a diagram of drugs classified into six types—stimulants, depressants, hallucinogens, inhalants, narcotics, and cannabis products—before providing information about specific drugs.

Checks for Understanding and Active Participation

You need to actively engage students during informal presentations. They should not be passive listeners. Also carefully monitor their understanding as you present. A variety of techniques can be used to check for understanding. These checks should occur throughout the presentation and just prior to moving to extended practice or other activities. Many active participation strategies are appropriate for this purpose. For example, you could periodically stop during the presentation and ask students to write summary statements, or use response cards to signal agreement or disagreement. The important thing is to make sure that students do not leave the presentation with misinformation or misunderstandings.

Presentation Delivery

Clarity of presentation is a must in this model. The following suggestions will help you to present information clearly:

- Use cues in the delivery to help students identify key ideas or important points ("Write down this definition in your notes," or "The first three . . . are . . .").

- Stop at certain points during the presentation and give students an opportunity to review their notes and ask questions.
- Repeat key points.
- Use visual supports to help clarify information (video clips, CD segments, slides, posters, charts, and so on).

The delivery of this lesson is unique because the teacher is "on stage." A good way to prepare for this type of lesson is to practice the delivery before presenting it to the students. You could practice in front of a mirror or teach the lesson to the empty classroom after school. Strive for movement around the room, as well as varied voice inflections, facial expressions, and gestures (R. Keiper, pers. comm., October 2001).

The length of the presentation will depend on the students. Two factors to consider are age and attention span. In a primary classroom, the limit for this type of lesson may be five minutes, whereas the teacher's presentation may last 15 minutes in a high school classroom (Ornstein and Lasley 2004).

Extended Practice

The informal presentation lesson is always followed by extended practice opportunities. The information presented in the lesson body is explored, applied, emphasized, and enriched in the extended practice component of this lesson. Students may study or practice the information in more depth, or they may have an opportunity to synthesize various skills with the knowledge learned in the current lesson. During this portion of the lesson, check individual student progress and decide when the students are ready for evaluation. Carefully select, plan, and monitor extended practice activities. Here are some examples of extended practice tasks:

- Mr. Reed delivers a presentation on genetic engineering that is followed by small-group discussions of ethical considerations.
- Mrs. Bedell first presents basic information about different types of families around the world. Students then complete various "center" activities where they read, write, draw, and interview peers about their families.
- Mrs. Cline presents information about cell division. Students then go to their lab stations to perform experiments.
- Mr. Springer teaches an informal presentation lesson about parts of a research paper. Students then go to the library to begin collecting resources for their own papers.
- Cooperative groups brainstorm scenarios about emergencies prior to Mrs. Wood's presentation on using 911.

Figure 16.1 Writing an Informal Presentation Lesson

The following list describes what is typically included in each component in an informal presentation lesson plan.

COMPONENT 1: PREPLANNING TASKS

The preplanning tasks section is a cover sheet for the rest of the lesson plan. Include the following in this section:

- *Connection analysis* Identify the generalization or big idea, the IEP goal, and the state standard addressed in the plan.
- *Content analysis* Include a *subject matter outline* (which will become the presentation outline) or principle statement, key terms and vocabulary, and necessary prerequisite skills or knowledge.

Figure 16.1 Writing an Informal Presentation Lesson (continued)

- *Objective* In addition to the content objective, a learning strategy objective may be included (such as taking notes from a lecture).
- *Objective rationale* To help students know why the lesson is valuable.

COMPONENT 2: LESSON SETUP

Include the following in the lesson setup:

- *Signal for attention:* Turn on overhead projector, ring a bell, or raise your hand, for example.
- *Statement of behavior expectations:* "Please raise your hand before speaking."

COMPONENT 3: LESSON OPENING

A lesson opening should be planned carefully, so it will effectively prepare the students for the new learning. An advance organizer is an integral part of the lesson opening in this model. Include the following in preparing a lesson opening:

- A strategy designed to generate interest in the lesson, relate new learning to prior knowledge, or build background knowledge.
- A way to state the *objective* in words your students understand, so they know exactly what they will be expected to know and do.
- A statement of the *objective purpose,* so students know why the new learning is valuable.
- An *advance organizer* and a plan for presenting it. Another visual support may also be included.

COMPONENT 4: LESSON BODY

The lesson body is the detailed presentation outline (the subject matter outline prepared as a preplanning task), along with questions, active participation and diversity strategies, and checks for understanding. Include the following when preparing the lesson body:

- *Presentation outline* (use the subject matter outline).
- A plan for making the presentation delivery smooth and interesting (use of voice variations, humor, interesting examples and analogies, summaries, and so on).
- *Active participation* strategies that will be used to keep students involved, such as giving opportunities to discuss content with peers.
- Techniques that will be used to *check for understanding.* Plan relevant and stimulating questions in advance and response strategies that involve everyone.
- *Visual supports* for use throughout the lesson body. You may provide *graphic organizers* such as study guides or presentation outlines (complete or partial).
- *Selected Interventions*. Consider individual student needs and plan necessary accommodations. For example, provide a note-taker or a completed outline for students who have difficulty taking notes.

continued on next page

Figure 16.1 Writing an Informal Presentation Lesson (continued)

COMPONENT 5: EXTENDED PRACTICE

The informal presentation lesson always includes relevant extended practice activities, such as following a presentation with a discussion or writing assignment. All extended practice opportunities must relate directly to the lesson objective and the information presented in the lesson body. Provide individual practice during this component because students will be evaluated on their individual performance in relation to the lesson objective. You will need to monitor these assignments or activities carefully so you will know when formal evaluation should occur. Include the following when preparing this component:

- A plan for providing extended practice immediately following the presentation or within a day or two. Some extended practice options include reading related materials, watching a video about the topic presented, gathering additional information by doing library research, conducting experiments in the lab, developing questions from the information presented to be used in a team game, and participating in a debate.

COMPONENT 6: LESSON CLOSING

The lesson closing generally follows the lesson body if the extended practice activity is a homework assignment. The closing could also occur after extended practice if practice opportunities are to be completed in class immediately following the lesson body. The closing would then follow the in-class practice. Consider the following when preparing the lesson closing:

- A strategy for closing the lesson. Selected closing strategies for the presentation lesson frequently refer back to the opening (the advance organizer), and provide review of the key points of the lesson. The closing may also provide an opportunity to preview future learning, describe where or when students should use the new knowledge, give students one last chance to ask questions, or have students compare their notes with a partner.

COMPONENT 7: EVALUATION

Teachers may conduct a lesson evaluation immediately after the presentation with a paper and pencil test. More commonly, teachers evaluate after providing extended practice opportunities. By carefully monitoring practice activities that occur after the actual informal presentation, you will be able to tell when students are ready for the lesson evaluation. The evaluation specified in the lesson objective is used to "test" whether individual students have attained the specific objective. When preparing a plan, include a description of the evaluation.

COMPONENT 8: EDITING TASKS

Remember to use editing tasks to evaluate your plan (see Chapters 13 and 19).

1. Write in critical management skills.
2. Double-check for the use of effective instructional interventions.
3. Evaluate congruence.

Sample Plans

Look at the framework for diversity responsive teaching (DRT) as you examine the sample plans at the end of this chapter. Ask yourself how the plan incorporates responses to diversity in *what* is taught, *how* it's taught, and the *context* for teaching and learning. We'll give you a start in thinking about how various parts of the plan fit with various components of the framework. We encourage you to look for additional examples of each component and to think about what changes you believe would make this plan even more likely to support all students' success.

Responding to diversity when planning *what* to teach is addressed in both lesson plans. First, the Rosa Parks lesson is *about* diversity. It also addresses *skills for a diverse world* as the theme of social justice emerges. In the "Portion Distortion" lesson, students will explore foods that represent their various cultural backgrounds, an example of *completeness* in *what* is taught.

There are examples of planning for diversity in *how* to teach in both lessons. Take a look at the variety of *visual supports* (real food and containers), and scaffolds (partial and complete note-taking guides) used in the "Portion Distortion" lesson. The "Rosa Parks" lesson includes *multiple objectives* (content knowledge and writing), *activating and building background knowledge* (student experience with protest), and the use of *selected interventions* for Bettie (who is deaf) and Stan (who has writing difficulties).

Look at the behavior expectations in the lesson setup for the "Rosa Parks" lesson. Notice that the teacher has clarified how the rule for polite listening applies in this lesson. This rule allows for diverse *perspectives* in showing respect. Examine the extended practice component of the "Portion Distortion" lesson. Notice the transition from the teacher presentation to the activity stations and the movement between activity stations. Has the teacher planned all critical management skills necessary to prevent behavior problems or wasted time? Would you add anything?

References and Suggested Readings

Arends, R. I. 2004. *Learning to teach.* 6th ed. Boston: McGraw-Hill. (See Chapter 7 in particular.)

Ausubel, D. P. 1960. The use of advance organizers in the learning and retention of meaningful verbal material. *Journal of Educational Psychology* 51: 267–272.

Callahan, J. F., L. H. Clark, and R. D. Kellough. 2002. *Teaching in the middle and secondary schools.* 7th ed. Part 11, Module 9. Upper Saddle River, NJ: Merrill.

Eggen, P. D., and D. P. Kauchak. 2006. *Strategies for teachers: Teaching content and thinking skills.* 5th ed. Boston: Allyn and Bacon. (See Chapter 10 in particular.)

Esler, W. K., and P. Sciortino. 1991. *Methods for teaching: An overview of current practices.* 2nd ed. Raleigh, NC: Contemporary Publishing Company.

Herrell, A., and M. Jordan. 2004. *Fifty strategies for teaching English-language learners.* 2nd ed. Upper Saddle River, NJ: Prentice-Hall. (See Chapter 2 in particular.)

Joyce, B., M. Weil, with E. Calhoun. 2000. *Models of teaching.* 6th ed. Boston: Allyn and Bacon. (See Chapter 13 in particular.)

Kame'enui, E. J., D. W., Carnine, R. C. Dixon, D. C. Simmons, and M. D. Coyne. 2002. *Effective teaching strategies that accommodate diverse learners.* 2nd ed. Columbus, OH: Merrill, an imprint of Prentice Hall.

Moore, K. D. 2005. *Effective instructional strategies: From theory to practice.* Thousand Oaks: Sage Publications. (See Chapter 7 in particular.)

Ornstein, A. C., and T. J. Lasley. 2004. *Strategies for effective teaching.* Boston: McGraw-Hill. (See Chapter 5 in particular.)

Schmidt, M. W., and N. E. Harriman. 1998. *Teaching strategies for inclusive classrooms: Schools, students, strategies, and success.* San Diego, CA: Harcourt Brace College Publishers.

Smith, P. L., and T. J. Ragan. 2005. *Instructional design.* 3rd ed. Hoboken, NJ: Wiley Jossey-Bass Education. (See Chapter 8 in particular.)

Stringfellow, J. L., and S. P. Miller. 2005. Enhancing student performance in secondary classrooms while providing access to general education curriculum using lecture format. *TEACHING Exceptional Children Plus* 1(6).

Rosa Parks and the Civil Rights Movement

This is an informal presentation for a large group of students.

I. PREPLANNING TASKS

A. Connection analysis
   1. Primary state standard: *History:* Identify and analyze major issues, movements, people, and events in U.S. history from 1870 to the present with particular emphasis on growth and conflict (for example, industrialization, the civil rights movement, and the information age).
   2. Additional standards:
      a. *Writing standard:* Produce a legible, professional-looking final product.
      b. *Social studies:* Investigate a topic using electronic technology, library resources, and human resources from the community.
   3. *Big Idea:* Problem/Solution/Effect (Kame'enui et al. 2002)

B. Content analysis: *Subject matter outline* (see presentation outline).

C. Objective(s): In a five-paragraph written report, students will explain three or more facts about Rosa Parks (education, birth date, and so on), the events that led to the Montgomery, Alabama, bus strike, and the results of the boycott. (A prepared rubric given to the students will provide more specific detail; for example, include an introduction, conclusion, and so on in the report.)
   1. They will work toward this objective for several days (the first few days will involve fact-finding, and the second few days will involve report writing). The students will also practice word-processing skills and Internet search skills.

D. Objective rationale: Knowing about Americans who have had a significant impact on events in the United States contributes to overall general knowledge. It is also important for students to see how activists can inspire change without violence.

E. Materials: Report rubric, presentation outline, transparencies of newspaper articles and photographs, and note-taking guides.

II. LESSON SETUP

A. Signal for attention: Turn on overhead projector.

B. Behavioral expectations: "Remember our rule about polite listening. Sometimes that means not talking at all while someone is presenting and sometimes it means responding. During this lesson, polite listening will include calling out a response if you feel strongly about something you hear."

III. LESSON OPENING

A. Review prior learning: "Yesterday, we began to talk about America prior to the civil rights movement; talked about segregation and the treatment of African American people . . . ."

B. Preview:
   1. "Today, we will begin to study the civil rights movement, how it began, and why it was so important. We will start by learning about one individual whose bravery made a big difference for African Americans."
   2. "Have any of you taken a stand for something you believe in, at a cost to yourself? I remember when some students left school to attend an antiwar protest . . . think about that during our lesson today."

C. Objective and purpose.

1. You will learn about the Montgomery, Alabama, bus boycott, an important event in the civil rights movement. You will also learn about the remarkable woman who inspired the boycott.
2. You will gather information about this woman from a variety of resources and write a five-paragraph report about her and the boycott. The report will be graded, both on the content of the report and the quality of the product. (Show transparency of rubric.)
3. The purpose of the lesson is to teach the history of race relations and to learn how one person can make a difference.

D. Advance organizer: Many important events played a role in changing the relationships between African Americans and white citizens of the United States.

IV. LESSON BODY

A. Prepare for the presentation.

1. Pass out two variations of the note-taking guide (one blank with only headings and subheadings, and one completed outline for Stan who writes very slowly and misses key ideas).
2. Say, "During my presentation, listen for and write down the key ideas and facts that I present. You will add to those ideas later when you do some additional research. For now, the goal is to gather some basic information."
3. Make sure I allow time for Bettie to read the transcriber's notes and see photos.

B. Show the presentation outline. **AP** = students take notes throughout; pause periodically to let them compare.

- **a.** Event leading to the Montgomery, Alabama, bus boycott (show photographs #1–2).
- **b.** Who and when? Rosa Parks was riding home from work on December 1, 1955 (show photo #1, on bus).
- **c.** Where? Cleveland Avenue bus line in Montgomery, Alabama.
- **d.** What happened? Rosa Parks refused to give up her seat in the front row of the "colored section" to a white man who could find no seat in the section reserved for whites.
- **e.** The event defied local ordinances and Alabama state statutes requiring segregation in transportation.
- **f.** Parks was arrested, jailed, and eventually convicted of violating segregation laws. She was fined $10, plus $4 in court costs (show photo #2, in court).
- **g.** The black community in Montgomery was outraged.
- **h.** Ask, "What happened on the bus? When did it happen? How do you think she felt? Has anything like this happened to you?" and so on. **AP** = Students turn to partner. **CFU** = Call on selected nonvolunteers.
- **i.** The Montgomery, Alabama, bus boycott (show photos #3–4 and newspaper article #1).
- **j.** Protesters formed the Montgomery Improvement Association (MIA) (show photo #3 of MLK).
- **k.** MIA was formed under the leadership of Dr. Martin Luther King, Jr., a minister who recently moved to the city.
- **l.** MIA urged sympathizers not to ride segregated buses and helped them find other transportation.
- **m.** The boycott (show photo #4 of empty buses and people walking), which lasted 381 days, began as a one-day demonstration on December 5, 1955 (show article #1 about the boycott).
- **n.** Ask, "What organization was formed by protestors? Who gave leadership to the group? How is this protest similar to and different from protests during the American Revolution?"

> ***AP*** = Students turn to partner to discuss questions.

o. Result of the boycott (newspaper articles #2–4).

p. In November 1956, a federal court ordered the Montgomery buses to be desegregated (article #2).

q. On December 20, 1956, federal injunctions served on city and bus officials forced them to comply (#3).

r. On December 21, 1956, Dr. King and Rev. Glen Smiley, a white minister, shared the front seat of a public bus; the boycott was a success (#4).

s. Ask, "What were the results of the boycott? Was it successful? Do protesters use boycotts today?" Call on individuals.

C. "Tomorrow we'll focus on Rosa Parks. Who was this brave woman? What led her to that day on the bus in Montgomery?"

CFU = Call on selected nonvolunteers to answer questions.

AP = Pause and have students compare notes after each section.

V. EXTENDED PRACTICE

A. Explain today's activity.

1. With your reading partner, generate a list of questions about Rosa Parks and the boycott about which you would like more information.
2. Look for answers in books and on the Internet.
3. Partner #1 records; Partner #2 is On-Task Supervisor. (Pair Gail with Leon.)

VI. LESSON CLOSING

A. Summarize: The boycott was the first large-scale, organized protest against segregation that used nonviolent tactics. Rosa Parks's personal act of defiance helped start something good.

B. Ask for questions. Ask for comments about their experience with acting for social justice.

C. Preview: "Tomorrow we will see a video and learn more about Rosa Parks, beginning with her early life."

VII. EVALUATION

A. Checkpoint #1: Collect and check their notes for accuracy after the videotape tomorrow.

B. Checkpoint #2: Collect and grade the five-paragraph report.

C. Checkpoint #3: Students will be asked about information stated in the objective on the unit test.

Source: Parks, Rosa Louise, Microsoft® Encarta® Online Encyclopedia 2001 (http://encarta.msn.com). © 1997–2001 Microsoft Corporation. (Information contributed by Paul Finkelman, B.A., M.A., Ph.D. Professor of Law, University of Akron School of Law. Author of *Slavery and the Founders: Race and Liberty in the Age of Jefferson.* Coeditor of The Macmillan Encyclopedia of World Slavery.)

Note that excellent examples of documents (such as photographs of newspaper articles written during the boycott) are available at the following site: http://www.archives.state.al.us/teacher/rights/rights1.html.

Portion Distortion: Americans' Love Affair with Food

This is an informal presentation lesson for a large group of students.

I. PREPLANNING TASKS

A. Connection analysis: *State Standard Health & Fitness:* Develop and monitor progress on personal nutrition goals based on national dietary guidelines and individual needs.

B. Content analysis

1. Subject matter outline: Portion Distortion and Standard Serving Size (see lesson body).
2. Prerequisite skills: Knows the terms *USDA Food Pyramid, food product label information,* and *serving size.*
3. Key terms and vocabulary: **Portion distortion**—misjudging standard portion size, believing standard portions are larger than those recommended by USDA

C. Objective: On an in-class test, students will list examples of standard serving sizes for five foods, each from a different part of the USDA Food Pyramid, and a common object that approximates the standard serving (for example, three ounces of meat is about the size of a deck of cards).

D. Objective rationale: Knowing what standard serving sizes look like can help students better judge the amount of calories they are taking in when eating meals or snacks. This can help with weight management.

E. Materials: Presentation outlines, transparencies, recording sheets, foods. (Remember to include a variety of foods familiar to students. Use their meal journals.)

II. LESSON SETUP

A. Signal for attention: "Attention please."

B. Behavioral expectations: Participate (answer questions, take notes) and be respectful (eyes on speaker, listening).

III. LESSON OPENING

A. Generate interest.

1. Think about weight control for a minute. Which is more important—to watch what you eat or how much you eat? (Seventy-eight percent of Americans believe that what they eat is more important in managing their weight than the amount of food they eat.) **AP** = *Cover, then ask for a show of hands.*
2. Both are important: It is possible to gain weight by eating small portions of foods that are high in calories, and also possible to gain weight by eating large portions of foods that are low in calories. For example, a ½ cup serving of pasta may contain the same calories as four cups of green beans.

B. Objective and purpose:

1. The purpose of this lesson is to help you make better choices for selecting the amounts of food you eat.
2. Today you will learn standard serving sizes and how to determine portion sizes for foods you eat so you can adjust your own eating habits. (Too little food can be just as serious a health problem as too much.)

C. Advance organizer: People tend to eat the portions they are given or what is on the plate. This tendency can lead to being overweight or obese and subsequent health problems. Knowledge of serving size can help prevent these problems.

IV. LESSON BODY

A. Delivery reminders.

1. Move around the room; make eye contact with *all* students.
2. Use verbal cues such as "First . . . , next . . ." to help students focus on important points.
3. Stop after each section for a brief summary.

B. Pass out note-taking guides. **AP** = notetaking.

1. Provide Jan with an outline that also includes some detail.
2. Partner John with Ada for the review of notes.

C. Show presentation outline (on transparency).

- The Problem With Too Much Food.
  - Problems of obesity
  - Heart disease, stroke
  - Diabetes, increased risk of cancer
- Statistics
  - 55 percent of Americans are clinically overweight
  - 1 in 4 Americans are obese
- Factors that contribute to obesity (American Institute for Cancer Research)
  - Eating out (poster of fast food restaurant logos, such as the golden arches)
  - Concept of portion distortion

D. Pause and have students compare notes with a partner periodically. **(AP)**

E. Review key points by asking specific questions, such as, "What problems are caused by being overweight or obese?"

> ***CFU*** = Call on selected nonvolunteers (do this throughout presentation).

- The Food We Eat (portion sizes)
  - Standard serving size (show transparency #2).
    - The *USDA Food Guide Pyramid shows:*
      - Approximate number of servings to eat per day
      - Various categories of food
      - That number of servings (and therefore calories) varies by body size and level of exercise (key idea)
    - How to find out the *standard serving size:*
      - Look at containers (show cans of soup, box of scalloped potatoes)
      - Estimate with fresh foods and fast foods.

- *Portion Distortion*—the American Dietetic Association (show transparency #3).
    - Definition (people are either unaware of or have a distorted idea of the standard serving size).
    - The American Dietetic Association Survey.
        - People were asked to estimate standard serving sizes of eight different foods, including pasta, green salad, beans, and mashed potatoes.
        - The results revealed that 1 percent answered all questions correctly, 63 percent missed five or more questions, and 31 percent estimated only *one* serving size correctly.
    - Results of portion distortion (larger and larger portions, with more and more people becoming overweight).

F. Ask, "What are standard serving sizes? What is portion distortion? How does portion distortion contribute to weight gain?" **(CFU)**

- How to Avoid Portion Distortion (transparency #4).
    - Measure foods as possible
        - Read labels.
        - Count foods (for example, potato chips) or measure (milk).
    - Estimate portions when measuring is not possible.
        - Explain portion sizes as compared to common objects (for example, 3 ounces of meat is approximately the same size as a deck of cards or a computer mouse, and a serving of cheese is about the size of an adult thumb).
        - Demonstrate with *real objects.*

H. Ask, "What are two ways to avoid portion distortion?" **(CFU)**

V. EXTENDED PRACTICE

A. In-class activity stations. There are five stations with different foods at each. (The goal is to have students see that "eye-balling" something is often not accurate. Measuring out and learning which common object represents the serving size is better.)

1. Distribute recording sheets.

2. Explain the directions.

a. Read the standard serving size.

b. Estimate the amount of food that constitutes a standard size by pouring it into bowl (how much cereal is ½ cup, for example).

c. Measure out the portion accurately.

d. Think of a common object of similar size.

e. Record it on a recording sheet.

f. Group 1 begins at Station 1 and so on. (Show transparency of group membership.)

3. Explain and demonstrate group roles (written on board) with a student who rehearsed with me in advance.
    a. Member #1 reads and estimates, Member #2 measures, Member #3 thinks of a common object of similar size, and Member #4 records.
    b. The roles switch at each new station (Member #1 becomes #2 and so on).
4. Ask specific questions about directions and group roles.

B. Homework assignment: Identify 10 of your favorite foods—including fast foods—that cannot be easily measured. Determine portions and come up with common objects about the same size.

VI. LESSON CLOSING

A. Explain that portion size in the United States is a cultural phenomenon and is not representative of the world.

B. Assign homework (see extended practice).

VII. EVALUATION

On the Nutrition Unit Test to be given next week, students will list examples of standard serving sizes for five foods, each from a different part of the USDA Food Pyramid, and a common object that approximates the standard serving.

Structured Discovery

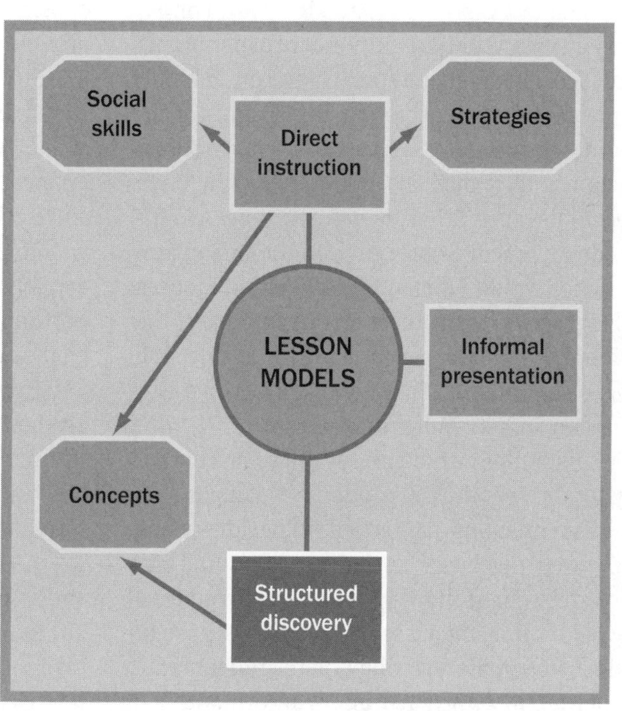

Introduction

The structured discovery model is one in which students "discover" information rather than having a teacher tell it to them. The discovery from the lesson is a planned one (that is, students discover a correct answer). What they discover is the lesson objective that the teacher predetermines. Students are led to the specific objective in a convergent rather than divergent manner. Structured discovery utilizes an inductive rather than deductive approach to learning. This model will help round out the repertoire of beginning skills needed to plan lessons.

Structured discovery lessons have a number of similarities to direct instruction lessons. The purpose of both lesson models is having students reach a specific academic objective. The major difference between them is the route that students take to reach the objective. The most significant differences between the two models are found in the lesson body. In the structured discovery lesson, the teacher prepares the students for the discovery by presenting examples and perhaps nonexamples for them to explore. In a direct instruction lesson, the teacher is telling and showing the information that the students need to know to reach the objective. The rest of the lesson body is quite similar in both types of lessons. The teacher follows the students' discovery by summarizing, reviewing, and providing additional practice with the new learning (supervised practice). The same methods also follow the show and tell component in a direct instruction lesson.

Structured discovery is often confused with the inquiry method or model of instruction. Students "discover" in both models, but the purpose and outcome of the discovery vary significantly. The major goal of structured discovery is for students to learn academic content, whereas the major goal of inquiry is for students to experience and practice the actual process of making a discovery (Arends 2004). For example, students may conduct air pressure experiments to discover facts about air pressure. On the other hand, the goal may be for students to practice making accurate scientific observations. In this case, magnetism, or some topic other than air pressure, might have been selected because the topic is solely a vehicle for having students practice observing. In the first example, the teacher would write an objective that focuses on knowledge of air pressure. In the second case, the teacher would write a long-term objective for the skill of making observations. Therefore, inquiry fits our definition of an activity rather than a lesson.

An understanding of the intent of the structured discovery model lays the foundation for using it successfully. The previous paragraphs have described what structured discovery *is* and how it compares to other models. The following tells what structured discovery is *not*. It is *not* a lesson without purpose or focus. It does *not* create a setting where students randomly experiment with materials or information. It also is *not* a time when teachers encourage students to come up with any "creative" idea or conclusion that comes to mind. A teacher would *not* be successful if students had a great deal of fun "discovering," but did not discover the information needed for the next day's science lesson. Structured discovery is a model that teachers select when they want to teach content knowledge. The lesson process is an added benefit—a secondary objective—not the major one.

Uses of Structured Discovery

The primary objective in a structured discovery lesson is always an academic one. Teachers may choose to use this model for teaching principles or concepts in any content area. Examples of specific topics that could be taught using structured discovery include the definition of a noun, rules for punctuation, what magnets will pick up, when you should call 911, and typical locations of cities.

Teachers have several reasons for selecting a structured discovery lesson to teach particular academic content. One reason is increased student motivation. The challenge of "making the discovery" can create an exciting situation for the students and, therefore, may hold their attention more readily. When preparing to teach a topic that students may find uninteresting (for example, a grammar rule), consider using a structured discovery lesson. It might provide just the right motivation.

Structured discovery lessons may also be selected because they promote higher-level thinking skills. Most educators agree that all students need opportunities to develop their ability to reason and solve problems. Structured discovery lessons are one way to provide this practice. Older students or highly capable students may need even more of these opportunities and will likely be especially excited and challenged by structured discovery lessons.

Note that, in addition to the primary short-term academic objective in the lesson plan, you may wish to include a long-term objective that addresses "thinking," such as problem solving, analysis, asking relevant questions, or drawing conclusions.

A third reason to use a structured discovery lesson is to enhance retention. Students may be more apt to recall what they learned when they have been given the opportunity to figure out something for themselves.

Structured discovery lessons are a valuable teaching tool, but they are not always appropriate. This type of lesson should obviously never be used when the safety of students is an issue. It would not make sense, for instance, to have students discover how to use a Bunsen burner safely or how to effectively break a fall from a balance beam. Additionally, this type of lesson would not be used when damage to materials or equipment may result. For example, it would be inappropriate for students to discover how to turn off a computer.

A structured discovery lesson should also not be used when it is likely that a student will fail. It would not make much sense, for example, to have students discover how to solve long division problems. It is fairly predictable they would flounder in failure as they repeatedly practiced the wrong way to compute long division problems. It may make sense, however, to have them discover math concepts such as "division." A structured discovery lesson also would not be a good choice when the time involved in making the discovery outweighs the benefit of the discovery itself. It may be possible, for instance, for students to eventually discover how to solve long division problems. However, the time it would take to make such a discovery would most likely decrease the value of making the discovery.

A thorough content analysis can help determine when a structured discovery lesson would be a good choice. Using some good common sense will help here as well.

Key Planning Considerations

Structured discovery lessons require very careful planning to help ensure that students will learn information accurately. These lessons have a high probability of resulting in student confusion. It is especially important to consider the following areas.

Content Analysis

Structured discovery lessons can be used to teach a variety of types of content. Therefore, the content analysis of this lesson will vary. If the objective is for students to discover a concept, write a concept analysis. If students are to discover a principle, include a clearly stated principle statement.

Assessing Prerequisite Skills and Knowledge

Lesson readiness can be determined in two steps. First, it is necessary to analyze the prerequisite skills or knowledge to be successful in the current lesson. Secondly, there must be an assessment as to whether or not the students know it. For example, you plan a structured discovery lesson on adjectives. You know that students must be able to identify nouns to understand adjectives. Therefore, you test your students on noun identification.

Gathering assessment information can be either fairly simple (correcting papers from yesterday's assignment), or more complicated (writing and administering a formal pretest). However, individual students must be assessed regardless of the level of difficulty.

Writing the Objective

The short-term academic objective written for the structured discovery lesson is no different from an objective written for lessons using other models. The important thing to remember about structured discovery objectives is how they should *not* be written. They should not, for example, say something like, "Students will discover. . . ." Objectives for all lessons must state what the students will know or do at the end of the lesson. The means to the end is not stated in the objective (see Chapter 2 for more detail).

Stating the Objective to Students

Although you will not begin the structured discovery lesson by telling the students the outcome of the learning because that would spoil the discovery, it is important they understand what they will learn. During the lesson opening for example, you could tell students they are going to learn about a scientific law or a grammar rule. Save any specifics about the law or rule for later.

Setting Up the Discovery

Teachers usually begin the lesson body component of the structured discovery lesson by presenting examples and nonexamples of the content to be learned. Next, "set up" the discovery by telling students directly what they are to discover (for example, "The underlined words in these sentences are adjectives. See if you can write a definition for adjective").

Selecting Examples and Nonexamples

Be sure to carefully select examples and nonexamples for these lessons. It is best to start with the clearest, purest examples and nonexamples because of the potential for confusion during the discovery phase. Successive examples can be more abstract or more difficult to discriminate. Present examples and nonexamples in the form of individual problems, words or scenarios, pictures, demonstrations, and so on.

Sometimes it is not necessary to include nonexamples. For instance, if you plan a lesson in which students are to discover the relationship between adjectives and nouns, you will not need nonexamples because you are not teaching students to distinguish between an adjective and other parts of speech.

A careful content analysis will help you determine whether or not nonexamples are needed.

Planning Questions and Prompts

It is a good idea to plan in advance how to guide the discovery. What will you do, for example, if students seem completely baffled by the initial explanation and examples? Writing down specific questions, statements, or clues will be beneficial, as they will serve to prompt students' thinking. You may also plan visual cues.

Supervised Practice

One of the tricky parts of a structured discovery lesson is determining whether or not all of the students have really "discovered." The teacher must take an active role in helping students draw correct conclusions before the end of the discovery part of the lesson.

Follow this by having students practice the new learning under supervision. It is very important to remember that the part of the lesson where the students "discover" is *not* supervised practice. For example, after the students have discovered principles of air pressure, you would want to provide new problems or demonstrations that would allow them to apply the principles they have learned. As students practice, you must monitor to be sure they are using the "discovered" information accurately.

Behavior Expectations

Students often work together with partners or in small groups during the "discovery" portion of the structured discovery lesson. Remember that students may need to be taught or reminded of specific behaviors necessary for working successfully with others. When lessons involve using or sharing materials or equipment, you must address behavioral expectations as well. You may also need to consider students' tolerance for working through feelings of frustration and confusion, as the probability of this happening is greater in this type of lesson.

Figure 17.1 Writing a Structured Discovery Lesson

The following list describes what is typically included in each component in a structured discovery lesson plan.

COMPONENT 1: PREPLANNING TASKS

The preplanning tasks section is a cover sheet for the rest of the lesson plan. Include the following when preparing the preplanning tasks:

- *Connection analysis* Identify the generalization or big idea, the IEP goal, and the state standard addressed in the plan.
- *Content analysis* This may be a concept analysis or principle statement, key terms and vocabulary, or necessary prerequisite skills and knowledge.
- *Objective* Remember that the objective represents the learning outcome, not the learning activities or process. For example, you would not write, "Students will discover. . . ." Possible objectives for a structured discovery lesson could be for students to describe, state a principle, identify, define, or give examples.
- *Objective rationale* To help you clarify the value of the objective.

Figure 17.1 Writing a Structured Discovery Lesson (continued)

COMPONENT 2: LESSON SETUP

The lesson setup is the first component of the lesson plan that is actually presented to students. Include the following when preparing the lesson setup:

- *Signal for attention:* Use a hand signal, or say, "Listen, please."
- *Statement of behavior expectations:* Have eyes on me; follow directions; take turns with your partner.

COMPONENT 3: LESSON OPENING

The lesson opening should effectively prepare the students for the new learning. Include the following when writing the lesson opening:

- A strategy designed to generate interest in the lesson, relate new learning to prior knowledge, or to build background knowledge.
- A way to state the objective in words your students will understand so students know what they will learn. Be careful not to give away the discovery, however.
- A statement of the objective purpose, so students know why the new learning is valuable.

COMPONENT 4: LESSON BODY

The lesson body is a detailed, step-by-step description of the teaching that will be done (that is, what the teacher and the students will be doing). Include the following:

- An explanation of how to set up, monitor, and review the discovery.
- *Examples and nonexamples* that lead students to discover the definition, principle, and so on, that you are teaching. Be sure to repeat, review, and *check for understanding* of the essential learning to ensure that all students have "discovered" the correct information. Include *supervised practice* with feedback as well.
- *Active participation* strategies, such as partner work, to keep students engaged.
- Additional *universal interventions* throughout the lesson body, for example, (1) use cues, concrete objects, and leading questions when presenting examples, (2) give explicit directions and demonstrate how students should share tasks in partner or group work, and (3) increase the amount and types of extended practice (see Component 5).
- *Selected interventions* to meet the needs of one or a few students.

COMPONENT 5: EXTENDED PRACTICE

Extended practice opportunities help students develop levels of accuracy and fluency high enough to ensure they can generalize the skill or knowledge. Some students may need a great deal of extended practice, whereas others may need enrichment activities. Include the following when writing extended practice:

- A plan for providing extended practice immediately following the lesson or soon thereafter.

continued on next page

Figure 17.1 Writing a Structured Discovery Lesson (continued)

- A list of lessons or activities that will build on this objective. Any additional opportunities students will have to generalize and extend the information should be included as appropriate. You may have planned a structured discovery lesson to teach information that students will need in a lesson to follow (for example, "Today's structured discovery lesson, designed to teach the definition of a noun, provides the background information necessary for tomorrow's direct instruction lesson on common and proper nouns").

COMPONENT 6: LESSON CLOSING

The lesson closing may follow the body of the lesson or it may follow extended practice. Include the following within the lesson closing:

- A strategy for closing the lesson. You may wish to include a variety of activities in your lesson closing, including (a) a review of key points of the lesson, (b) opportunities for students to draw conclusions, (c) a description of where or when students should use their new skills or knowledge, and (d) a reference to the lesson opening.

COMPONENT 7: EVALUATION

Plan the lesson evaluation when writing the objective, so the evaluation matches exactly what is stated in the objective. Remember that evaluation is not necessarily a paper and pencil test. Also, remember that its purpose is to determine how individual students are progressing toward the lesson objective, which means the student does not receive help—from peers or the teacher—during the evaluation. Don't forget to test with new examples. Careful monitoring during supervised and extended practice activities will help you decide when evaluation should occur.

COMPONENT 8: EDITING TASKS

Remember to use editing tasks to evaluate your plan (see Chapter 19).

1. Write in critical management skills.
2. Double-check for the use of effective instructional interventions.
3. Evaluate congruence.

Sample Plans

Look at the framework for diversity responsive teaching (DRT) as you examine the sample plans at the end of this chapter. Ask yourself how the plan incorporates responses to diversity in *what* is taught, *how* it's taught, and the *context* for teaching and learning. We'll give you a start in thinking about how various parts of the plan fit with various components of the framework. We encourage you to look for additional examples of each component and to think about what changes you believe would make this plan even more likely to support all students' success.

The lesson "Punctuating a Series" provides a good opportunity to plan for diversity in *what* is taught. A teacher could easily use information about the local culture or community events as carrier content in the sentences used in this lesson. Can you think of how this could be done with a group of students you know?

The following are examples of planning for diversity in *how* to teach as they appear in both plans. In the "Punctuating a Series" plan, the teacher has planned numerous *prompts* to support students in making the discovery if they have difficulty. This plan also provides for careful *monitoring* (teacher moves around and listens to students as they work in groups) during their discovery time. The "Magnetic Attraction" lesson shows an example of groups of four students with assigned roles and clearly taught *directions* (written, presented orally and demonstrated).

The lesson "How to Punctuate A Series" includes a *selected intervention* (behavior contract) for Garth. The teacher uses precorrection, encouragement, and a reminder of the reward he's working toward. Notice the many materials to manage in the "Magnetic Attraction" lesson. What would you do to plan for logistics to prevent behavior problems?

References and Suggested Readings

Arends, R. I. 2004. *Learning to teach.* 6th ed. New York: McGraw-Hill. (See Chapter 11 in particular.)

Cruickshank, D. R., D. L. Bainer, and K. K. Metcalf. 2006. *The act of teaching.* 4th ed. Boston: McGraw-Hill College. (See Chapter 8 in particular.)

Guillaume, A. M. 2004. *K–12 Classroom teaching: A primer for new professionals.* Upper Saddle River, N.J.: Pearson.

Jacobsen, D. A., P. Eggen, and D. Kauchak. 2002. *Methods for teaching.* 6th ed. Columbus, OH: Merrill Prentice Hall. (See Chapter 7 in particular.)

Joyce, B., M. Weil, and E. Calhoun. 2004. *Models of teaching.* 7th ed. Boston: Pearson. (See Chapter 3 in particular.)

Kame'enui, E. J., D. W. Carnine, R. C. Dixon, D. C. Simmons, and M. D. Coyne. 2002. *Effective teaching strategies that accommodate diverse learners.* 2nd ed. Columbus, OH: Merrill Prentice Hall.

Kellough, R. D. 2000. *A resource guide for teaching: K–12.* 3rd ed. Columbus, OH: Merrill.

Orlich, D. C., R. J. Harder, R. C. Callahan, and H. W. Gibson. 2001. *Teaching strategies: A guide to better instruction.* 6th ed. Boston: Houghton Mifflin Co.

Rosenberg, M. S., L. O'Shea, and D. J. O'Shea. 2002. *Student teacher to master teacher: A practical guide for educating students with special needs.* 3rd ed. Columbus, OH: Merrill, an imprint of Prentice Hall. (See Chapter 6 in particular.)

Magnetic Attraction

This is a large- or small-group, structured discovery science lesson.

I. PREPLANNING TASKS

A. Connection analysis: *State Science Standard, Science 2.2:* Think logically, analytically, and creatively.

Benchmark 1: Examine data to verify a conclusion in a simple investigation. *Big Idea:* the scientific method of forming and testing a hypothesis.

B. Content analysis

1. Principle: Magnets pull objects made of iron or steel.
2. Prerequisite skills and knowledge: Use a recording sheet.
3. Key terms and vocabulary: **Attract** = pull together, **repel** = push apart

C. Objective: Students will write, in their own words, the principle that if an object contains steel or iron, then it will be attracted by a magnet. (An additional objective is that students will infer a principle from available data.)

D. Objective rationale

1. Knowing how magnets work can help students appreciate the various uses of magnets, such as to sort materials (scrap yard), find direction (compass), hold items in place (electric can opener), pick things up (sewing pins).
2. Knowing how to draw conclusions from examining data is a skill that can be applied to many situations. This is an application of the scientific method.

E. Materials and equipment: Small box of pins; 10 bags of small objects for five groups of four students, with two bags per group (note that objects have been selected carefully and the only thing the examples have in common is that they are or are not made of steel or iron); 10 magnets (two per group); and 20 copies each of two worksheets (#1 is double-sided and consists of three parts: Part 1 includes the activity directions, group member roles, and space for listing groups of objects–"pulled," and "not pulled"; Part 2 includes pictures and descriptions of six new objects and it includes Part 3, the evaluation).

II. LESSON SETUP

A. Signal for attention: "Let's get started."

B. Behavior expectations: Sit in seats, eyes on me, listening.

III. LESSON OPENING

A. Motivate, get students to focus on lesson topic.

1. Demonstrate magnetic puppets moving on stage.
2. Ask, "How do you think the puppets are moving?" (Puppets have thumbtacks or paperclips on their feet, and the magnet moving underneath them makes them move).
3. After the answer is discovered, ask, "Have you ever played with a magnet? What were you able to do with it?" **AP** = tell a partner, call on individuals.

B. State the objective and purpose.

1. Say, "Today we are going to discover a rule about which objects magnets can attract (pull). This will help you understand how magnets help us." (Demonstrate key term by spilling a small box of pins and picking them up with a magnet.)

IV. LESSON BODY

A. Set up the discovery.

1. Show transparency (activity directions, roles, and discovery goal), and explain and demonstrate. (Leave transparency on, as a reference.)
2. Directions for using the materials and testing objects.
   a. Take objects from the bag.
   b. Touch your magnet to each object.
   c. Sort. Which objects are pulled by the magnets? Put these in a group. Which objects are not pulled by the magnet? Put these in another group.
   d. Record findings on the worksheet provided (demonstrate on transparency).
   e. Write a rule about what magnets pull.
3. Ask, "What do you do first, everyone . . . ? Second, everyone . . . ?" and so on. **AP** = Unison response, call on selected nonvolunteers.
4. Directions for group roles (they know these roles): recorder, on-task supervisor, reporter, and sorter.
5. Ask, "What does the recorder do?" and so on (leave transparency up). **CFU** = Call on selected nonvolunteers.
6. Distribute bags and worksheets and written directions for discovery.

B. Monitor the discovery. Have early finishers write predictions about which other objects magnets would pull or not pull.

C. Review the discovery. Throughout: table groups discuss **(AP)** and I call on reporters **(CFU).**

1. Ask, "What did you find out about your magnet and objects?"
2. Ask, "How are the objects in the 'pulled' group alike?" (same color? shape? size?).
3. Ask, "What rule did you make about which objects your magnets pulled?"
4. Write rule on board (if the rule is incorrect, demonstrate by testing it).

D. Individual supervised practice.

1. Test the discovery.
   a. Pass out new bags of objects, magnets to each student (eight objects and one magnet).
   b. Read directions for Part 2 on the worksheet. Sort objects using a written description of the object property (aluminum, steel). Write a rationale, such as made of steel; then "test" to see if you are right.
   c. Ask: What do you do first? Where do you explain why you put an object in a certain pile? and so on. **CFU** = Call on selected nonvolunteers.
   d. Have students complete worksheets individually. I monitor, prompt, and provide feedback.
   e. When finished, collect materials and have students get back together as a large group.

V. LESSON CLOSING

A. Review: Today you discovered what magnets attract. What do they attract? What is the rule about what magnets attract? **CFU** = Call on selected nonvolunteers.

B. Preview: Tomorrow you will learn about the force field surrounding magnets.

VI. EXTENDED PRACTICE

A. Explain that they can have more practice in centers (with new objects) if needed.

VII. EVALUATION

A. Ask students to write principle statement (see objective) and turn them in. This is their "ticket to recess."

How to Punctuate a Series

This is a structured discovery lesson for a large or small group.

I. PREPLANNING TASKS

A. Connection analysis: *State Writing Standard:* The student writes clearly and effectively, applies capitalization and punctuation rules correctly. *IEP Goal:* Trish will use correct punctuation (commas, periods, quotation marks) in writing samples. *Big Idea:* the writing process (Kame'enui et al. 2002).

B. Content analysis

1. Principle statement or rule: When a series occurs in a sentence, commas are placed after each item except the last.
2. Prerequisite skills: Recognize commas
3. Key terms:
    a. **series**—three or more related items listed consecutively in the same sentence
    b. **punctuate**—using marks or characters to make the meaning clear

C. Objective: Given 10 sentences, some of which contain a series, students will place all commas correctly.

D. Objective rationale: Knowing basic punctuation marks helps students produce written products that are accurate and clear.

E. Materials: one transparency and two worksheets. (Remember to show Garth his behavior chart before class, point out he's close to earning TV time at home. Remind him that he can earn points during seatwork for staying on task and ask him to show me what that looks like.)

II. LESSON SETUP

A. Signal for attention: "Let's begin."

B. Behavioral expectations: Eyes on me, raise hand, and wait to be called on.

III. LESSON OPENING

A. Review prior learning: Review already learned punctuation marks: period, question mark, semicolon, apostrophe.

B. Statement of objective, objective purpose: Today you will learn one of the uses for the comma—a basic punctuation rule—knowing this rule helps make your writing clear.

IV. LESSON BODY

Reminder to myself: As I monitor seatwork, be sure to mark points on Garth's behavior chart.

A. Set up the discovery
   1. Show transparency: 10 correctly punctuated series and five sentences that need punctuation and the discovery goals. Show only sentences #1–10 for now. (Leave transparency up on overhead during discovery phase.) Example sentences include:
      a. Tammy, Larry, Johnny, and Sherry are members of my family.
      b. My horses' names are Josie, Thunder, and Lucky.
      c. Mt. Baker, Mt. Rainier, and Mt. St. Helens are volcanoes in Washington State.
   2. Say, "Look carefully at the commas in these sentences. They are used to punctuate a series. Your job is to make two discoveries. See if you can figure out (1) a definition for a series, and (2) a rule for how to use commas to punctuate a series."
   3. Explain partner work expectations for making the discoveries:
      a. Work with Study Buddy (Review what on-task looks like and sounds like for buddy work.)
      b. Roles: one person is the recorder for Task 1, then switch; both contribute ideas

B. Monitor the discovery
   1. While students work, circulate and listen to their discussions. Ask what they are finding or thinking. **(CFU)** (Check in with Alice and Mary frequently.)
   2. Prompt, if necessary, by asking questions such as: "How many words make up the series?" "What words are related?" "What words make up the series?" "Where is the first comma? Second?"
   3. Stop when all or most partner groups seem to have made the discoveries.

C. Review the discovery
   1. Ask students to tell their discoveries. I write them on the board.
      a. Definition of series
      b. Rule for punctuating a series
   2. Uncover sentences #11–15 on transparency.
      a. Work through sentences and have students talk me through where to put commas.
      b. Ask specific questions such as "Which words make up the series in this sentence?" "The first comma goes after what word, everyone . . .?"

> ***AP*** = Students write definition and principle in their language notebook.

> ***CFU*** = Call on selected nonvolunteers.

> ***CFU*** = Call on recorders.

D. Supervised practice (individual)
   1. Pass out worksheet #1 (give Lidia a large print version) which includes 15 sentences such as:
      a. Katherine Michael and Robby are the children of Gail and Leon.
      b. Trigger Fury Flicka and Blaze are the names of famous horses.

2. Direct students to add commas to the first five sentences.
3. I will move around the room and make sure each student is accurate in placing commas, and will give feedback to everyone.

V. EXTENDED PRACTICE

A. Seatwork assignment: Assign last 10 sentences on worksheet #1 as more practice, if students are not yet fluent. I'll grade and pass back tomorrow prior to evaluation.

VI. LESSON CLOSING

A. Final review: Students explain how to use commas in a series. **AP** = Tell a partner
B. Preview tomorrow's lesson: They will learn another use for commas.

VII. EVALUATION

A. Evaluation time: After supervised practice today or after extended practice.
B. Evaluation task: Worksheet #2 with 10 sentences, each containing a series of items to be punctuated. (Use sentences about topics that are of high interest.)
   1. Examples of some of the sentences are:
      a. Sea otters whales starfish and barnacles are found at the beach.
      b. Our school has a gym a music room and a lunchroom.
      c. Pizzas made with sausage peppers olives pepperoni and mushrooms are delicious.

Teaching Specialized Content

Introduction

This chapter explains how to teach concepts, social skills, and learning and study strategies. We have included this information in a separate chapter because this content requires somewhat specialized planning. Effective instruction for concepts, social skills, and learning and study strategies is not qualitatively different from teaching other content. It is really more of a difference in instructional emphasis. For example, when planning to teach about concepts, you emphasize using examples and nonexamples; when planning social skill and strategy lessons, you emphasize demonstrating processes and using think-alouds. We have included basic information about each type of content as well as key planning considerations for each.

Teaching Concepts

Regardless of the content area you teach, you will find yourself teaching concepts. Sometimes concepts are taught within a lesson or activity; other times they are taught in separate lessons or activities. For example, teachers would most likely teach the concept of "main idea" in a series of lessons and activities. They might teach the concept of peninsula, on the other hand, within another lesson.

Concepts Defined

Concepts are categories of knowledge. For example, "island" is a concept. There are many specific examples of islands, such as Lopez, Barbados, and Greenland. They all belong to the "island" category because they have certain attributes in common, that is, they are all land masses completely surrounded by water. Teaching concepts is much more efficient than solely teaching specific examples (Cummings 1990). A geography teacher does not need to teach every island in the world separately, because teaching concepts allows students to generalize. If students understand the concept of islands, they will recognize new places as being islands if they have the necessary traits.

To check your understanding of "concept," consider the following examples and nonexamples:

Examples	**Nonexamples**
President	Harry Truman
Rocking chair	My grandma's black rocker
Impressionist art	Van Gogh's "Starry Night"
Planet	Mars

To determine if something is a concept, see if you can think of more than one example of it. In other words, "lake" is a concept because there are many examples of it—Michigan, Samish, Placid, Geneva, Victoria, and others. Mars is not a concept because there is only one Mars. Other examples of concepts are friendship, soft rock, fairness, appropriate spectator behavior, on-task, tessellation, mammal, and tiny.

Types of Concepts

Concepts vary according to how concrete or abstract they are, how broad or narrow they are, and the type of definition they have. It is important to think about the type of concept to be taught when deciding how to teach it.

Some concepts are very concrete, such as table or flower. Some are very abstract, such as truth or love. Many fall in between, like polygon, family, or adverb. The more concrete a concept is, the easier it is to teach and to learn.

Some concepts are very broad, such as living things. Some are very narrow, such as elephants. Between these two extremes, there are a series of concepts in a hierarchy, as in the following example: living things, animals, mammals, land mammals, large land mammals, large land mammals living today, elephants.

When teaching a particular concept, it is important to fit it into a hierarchy of broader and narrower concepts. For example, "We have been learning about geometric shapes. Today we are going to learn about one type of geometric shape—the triangle. In later lessons we will learn about different kinds of triangles, such as equilateral triangles."

Typically, instructors should not teach a very narrow concept, such as "elephant," through a formal concept lesson (unless, perhaps, the students are training to be wildlife biologists). Of the many, many concepts, it is necessary to select those that are most important and useful for the students to learn.

Concepts also vary according to how they are defined. For example, "table" is defined in terms of one set of attributes, that is, a table has a flat surface and at least one leg. This is called a *conjunctive concept.* Other concepts—called *disjunctive*—are defined in terms of alternative sets of attributes. For example, a citizen is a native or naturalized member of a nation (Martorella 1994, 161). A strike in baseball is a swing and a miss, a pitch in the strike zone, or a foul ball (Arends 2004, 329). A third type of concept—*relational*—is defined in terms of a comparison, such as the concept of "big." A mouse is big in comparison with an ant, but it is not big compared to a dog. The concept "big" has no meaning except in relation to something else.

As you analyze a concept and select examples or nonexamples in preparation for teaching, it is important to recognize whether you are teaching a conjunctive, disjunctive, or relational concept.

Concepts may be taught using the direct instruction model or the structured discovery model. The direct instruction model uses a deductive approach, whereas the structured discovery model uses an inductive approach. Each model requires different steps initially. However, the last two steps are the same in both models.

Direct Instruction Model

The following steps illustrate how concepts are taught using the direct instruction model:

- Teacher (T) names and defines the concept.
- T states the critical and noncritical attributes of the concept while showing examples and nonexamples of the concept.
- T provides new examples and nonexamples and asks students to discriminate between them.
- T asks students to explain their answers, that is, to refer to critical attributes present or absent.

Structured Discovery Model

The following steps illustrate how instructors teach concepts using the structured discovery model:

- Teacher (T) names (usually) the concept.
- T shows examples and nonexamples.
- T asks students to examine the examples and nonexamples and to identify critical and noncritical attributes.
- T asks students to define the concept or explain the concept rule.
- T provides new examples and nonexamples and asks students to discriminate between them.
- T asks students to explain their answers, that is, to refer to critical attributes, present or absent.

Teaching concepts using the direct instruction model provides less opportunity for confusion or misconceptions and is more time-efficient. This model is useful when students have little prior knowledge of the concept.

Teaching concepts using the structured discovery model may provide an approach that is more interesting or motivating to students, and that provides practice in inductive thinking skills. This model is useful in helping students refine their understanding of familiar concepts.

Students typically have some prior knowledge and experience of a concept before it is taught. It is helpful to assess and to build on each student's knowledge. Also, it is important to ascertain whether the student has formed inaccurate concepts because of limited experience, such as thinking that all people who speak Spanish are from Mexico, all fruits are edible, or all islands have people living on them.

Both direct instruction and structured discovery models are effective for teaching concepts. Each model has advantages. First, determine the concept to teach, and write the objective. Then, weigh the advantages of both models. Select the one that best meets the needs of the students.

Key Planning Considerations

Concept Analysis

A careful concept analysis is essential for effective concept teaching. A concept analysis includes a definition, critical and noncritical attributes, and examples and nonexamples of the concept.

Developing a definition at an appropriate level for the students is important. Dictionary definitions are not always the best to use. A better source may be the glossary of content area textbooks. The language and complexity of the definition must be suitable for the students. For example, the definition of "mammal" or "square" would be stated differently for first-grade students than for tenth-grade students.

When analyzing a concept, list the critical and noncritical attributes that will be most helpful in distinguishing that concept from similar ones. Critical attributes are essential characteristics of a concept. For example, "four sides" is a critical attribute of a square. However, when defining a concept, any one critical attribute is necessary but not sufficient to defining the concept. A square must have four sides, but the sides must also be of equal length. Noncritical attributes of a concept are those that are not necessary. Whether the length of those equal sides is three miles or three inches is unimportant. Size is a noncritical attribute of a square. A square is a square whether it is big or small.

Carefully select examples and nonexamples to bring out all of the critical and noncritical attributes of the concept. It is important to begin with the "best" examples, the examples that are the clearest and least ambiguous. Gradually introduce examples and nonexamples that are more difficult to differentiate. For example, do not begin with a platypus as an example of a mammal, or with a rhombus as a nonexample of a square (Howell, Hosp, and Hosp, forthcoming).

You will need many examples and nonexamples, because you must use different sets for the initial presentation, the practice, and the evaluation. This ensures that students have not merely memorized the examples and that they understand the concept and its attributes.

When presenting examples and nonexamples, use cues such as underlining, colors, and arrows to emphasize critical attributes. Gradually fade the cues.

Objective

Think carefully about what your students need to learn to understand and use the concept you are teaching. Possible objectives for concept lessons include (1) defining the concept, (2) listing critical attributes of the concept, (3) recognizing examples and nonexamples of the concept, (4) stating why something is an example or nonexample, (5) producing examples, (6) stating similarities and differences between related concepts, (7) using the concept in a novel way, or (8) producing a graphic organizer of the concept.

Opening

When opening concept lessons, it is very important to assess what students already know about the concept and to find out if students have any misconceptions about the concept. It may be useful to brainstorm or conduct "think-to-writes" (writing down everything you know about reptiles in two minutes, for example). Use these strategies to help students connect the new learning with prior knowledge. When possible, help students make connections to personal experience. For example, if you are going to teach the concept "democracy," ask about the students' experiences in electing the class president. It is also best to use some type of organizer that shows the relationship of the concept you are teaching to broader and narrower concepts or to related concepts, such as islands and peninsulas. Remember that you would not state a specific objective that includes the definition of the concept at the beginning of a discovery lesson.

Closing

Some options for closing a concept lesson include (1) reviewing the concept definition, critical attributes, and best examples; (2) discussing related concepts or previewing future lessons on related concepts; (3) reviewing the purpose of learning the concept; (4) describing how students can use their knowledge of the concept in the future; (5) asking students to show their graphic organizers or new examples; and (6) asking students to expand or correct their "think-to-writes". To summarize, concepts are categories of information found in all content areas. They can be taught using direct instruction or structured discovery lesson models. A carefully designed concept analysis can help students develop a clear understanding of the concept they are studying.

Teaching Social Skills

What are social skills? The term *social skills* encompasses many categories and examples. The term includes very broad cognitive-behavioral skills, such as interpersonal problem solving, anger management, and empathy. Social skills also include narrow, specific interpersonal skills such as accepting compliments or greeting others. Teachers may need to teach social skills required for classroom success, such as listening, following directions, asking for help, or waiting for help; cooperative social skills for working in groups, such as taking turns, sharing, or disagreeing appropriately; social skills for employment, such as asking for directions or sharing tasks; social skills needed for making friends, such as starting conversations or joining activities; and skills for dealing with conflict, such as responding to teasing or an accusation, accepting *no*, staying out of fights, negotiating, or accepting consequences.

Why teach social skills? Some students come to school skilled at making friends, getting along with adults, expressing feelings, and understanding the feelings of others. But some could use help in learning to work or play with others, to resolve conflicts, and to manage feelings. A few students may already be rejected by others, are dangerously aggressive or withdrawn, and are in desperate need of help in developing social skills. Because social competence is essential for success in school and in life, many schools are beginning to take a proactive, universal approach by making social skills instruction a regular part of the curriculum, as well as providing more intense, selected instruction for those individuals who need it. You will likely need to teach social skills to at least some of your students (see Chapter 10 for more information on social skills).

Choosing the Lesson Model to Use

Teaching social skills is similar to teaching other procedures or how-to lessons. You begin with a task analysis of the skill and then teach the steps using direct instruction. As in all direct instruction lessons, you will include a presentation of information component in which you explain and give examples for each step. You will demonstrate the use of the social skill and you will ask the students to practice the social skill by acting it out in a role play. You will evaluate whether each student has met the lesson objective by having the student demonstrate the skill in another role play.

Note that when teaching social skills, it is critical to attend to generalization. For this reason, it is very important to follow initial direct instruction lessons with planned activities (see Chapter 15). This gives students the opportunity to apply the skill in a variety of contexts. You may plan an activity to practice a social skill, such as discussing a controversial topic to practice disagreeing politely. You may also teach social skills as an objective in activities with other purposes. For example, you could use the sample activity plan, "Tic-Tac-Toe Spelling" at the end of Chapter 14, to practice the social skills of taking turns, giving compliments, or accepting being corrected, in addition to practicing spelling. In this case you would review the social skill in the activity opening and include directions for how and when to use the skill in the activity middle.

Key Planning Considerations

Content Analysis

The content analysis for a social skills lesson includes a task analysis. List the steps for using the social skill, including the steps that involve stopping to think and making decisions. For example, you may plan to teach students to accept *no* for an answer and list the steps as (1) stop and take a deep breath; (2) look at the person; (3) say *ok*; and (4) do not argue. Published social skills programs are good sources of task analyses.

Demonstration

In social skill lessons, demonstration means acting out or modeling the social skill in a scenario that is meaningful to the students. For example, demonstrate the skill of "accepting *no*" in a scenario, in which a teacher refuses to allow a student to sit by a friend in math class.

GUIDELINES FOR DEMONSTRATING (MODELING)

Each step needs to be modeled clearly and correctly, so be sure you and your assistants rehearse in advance. McGinnis and Goldstein (1997) and Sheridan (1995) provide the following guidelines:

- As you act and talk, point to the steps written on a poster.
- Be sure to think aloud.
- Keep it simple. Teach one skill at a time, each step in sequence, without a lot of extra detail.
- Check for understanding by assigning students to watch for different steps and asking them to describe how the step was demonstrated following the modeling.
- You may choose to show a nonexample as well, for clarity.
- Be sure you model the skill working, that is, having a positive outcome: "Thanks for accepting *no* so calmly. You may sit by Ichiro later during lunch." Generalization will be encouraged if you select scenarios relevant to your students and model a variety of scenarios showing different applications, such as accepting *no* at home and at school, from peers and adults, and for major and minor requests.

Supervised Practice

The students practice the skill by role-playing and receiving feedback. You may begin by having them brainstorm scenarios when they will need to use the skill. Then select the first student to take the lead and choose other students for supporting roles.

GUIDELINES FOR SUPERVISED PRACTICE (ROLE-PLAYING)

Each student should have multiple opportunities to play the lead role and to receive feedback. Each student demonstrates asking permission and accepts *no* as an answer, for example. This may mean scheduling the supervised practice over several days. McGinnis and Goldstein (1997) and Sheridan (1995) provide the following guidelines:

- Some students may need scaffolding. They may need to discuss how they will demonstrate each step, or have the opportunity to rehearse with peers first. You may provide support by pointing to the steps on a poster and prompting as they role-play.
- If a student makes an error during the role play, stop him right away, correct the error, and have him redo the role play. You can correct the error through prompting, modeling, or directly telling the student the correct step.
- Assign other students steps to observe and on which to give feedback (active participation).
- Promote generalization by having students provide ideas for scenarios, and by observing them in a variety of settings for scenario ideas. When possible, go to the actual settings to practice, such as going to the playground to practice joining games.
- To prepare students for the real world, include scenarios where the skill does not work, such as when the teasing does not stop, they do not get to join the game, or they do not receive permission. Teach alternatives.
- Provide for cultural diversity by role-playing options and varying scenarios. For example, some students when practicing "dealing with teasing"

will be more comfortable with passive responses such as ignoring the teasing or getting help. Others will be more comfortable with more assertive responses such as telling the person to stop.

- Best practices for teaching social skills such as teaching in the context of real-life scenarios, demonstrating (modeling) the skill, and using role playing with peers are very helpful for English language learners. Pre-teaching vocabulary, incorporating language patterns, and using visual supports will also be beneficial.

Extended Practice

This component is key in promoting generalization. It is essential to provide a great deal of additional practice in real-world applications. Extended practice often takes two forms, homework and follow-up practice at school.

Students may be given homework assignments to use the social skill. Provide a form with a place for the students to list the steps in the skill, to describe where, when, and with whom they used the skill, and to describe the results. The form can also include a place for students to self-evaluate their use of the skill, and a place for others (parents, coaches, day care providers, or peers) to initial that they saw the student use the skill. Homework can incorporate goal-setting or be written in the form of a behavior contract. The purpose is to have the student practice using the skill in a variety of situations.

The teacher can also plan follow-up practice for students to use the skill immediately following the body of the lesson. Depending on the skill, this practice may occur during free time, partner or small-group work, class discussions, centers, recess, lunch, or planned activities in the form of games or projects. Tell the students ahead of time to use the skill ("Remember to practice taking turns while using the computers for your projects"). Coach and prompt the students during the practice situation, and debrief following. Also watch for those unplanned teachable moments.

To summarize, social skills are important for success in school as well as in all other parts of a student's life. Social skills can be taught directly through modeling and role plays. Promoting generalization through well-planned extended practice is very important.

Teaching Learning and Study Strategies

Why teach learning and study strategies? Knowing the expectations for students described in the state standards helps teachers plan what they will teach. Simply knowing the expectations, however, is not very helpful in planning for students who have difficulty learning, remembering, and using information. Students who have effective strategies for learning and studying definitely have an increased chance of performing well on tasks necessary for school success. The learner with missing or ineffective strategies is often at risk for school failure. This is really what strategy instruction is all about, helping students learn and study in more efficient ways so they can be more successful in school.

What are strategies? A strategy is a special kind of procedure, one that is designed to help students become more effective learners. Learning strategies (sometimes called cognitive strategies) and study strategies (sometimes called study skills) are the two basic strategy types.

Learning and study strategies differ in their focus. A learning strategy facilitates the use of higher-level thinking behaviors, such as decision making, self-motivation, and self-monitoring (Deshler, Ellis, and Lenz 1996). For example, using a strategy for finding the main idea requires students to make decisions about what they are reading by asking themselves questions such as, "Does this idea encompass all of the important details in this paragraph?" Therefore, a strategy to find the main idea is an example of a learning strategy.

A study strategy, on the other hand, is more similar to a standard procedure, as described in Chapter 1. The students work through an ordered series of steps that requires limited use of higher-level thinking skills such as decision making or self-monitoring. For example, a proofreading strategy in which students complete steps such as "Check to see that each sentence begins with a capital letter" would be considered a study strategy. The strategy steps can be completed without the use of higher-level thinking skills. Deciding whether a letter is upper- or lowercase is pretty cut and dried. Learning strategies achieve cognitive goals (Arends 2004), whereas study strategies achieve procedural goals, and both are important.

Strategy Purposes

All kinds of strategies can be taught to help students study and learn. Thinking about their purposes can help teachers select appropriate ones. Some strategies are designed to help students gather information from texts and presentations (for example, strategies that teach students how to take notes from a lecture or read for comprehension). Other strategies help students retain information for later use (for example, learning how to use mnemonic strategies or construct concept maps). Still other strategies help students show what they know (learning how to proofread assignments or take multiple-choice tests, for example). One additional group of strategies helps students develop personal organizational habits (learning how to maintain an assignment calendar or complete assignments, for example).

You can decide which strategies to teach your students, by carefully analyzing the trouble spots they encounter when trying to perform school tasks. Information about specific strategies is readily available in journals and texts. (See the resources listed at the end of this chapter for more information.)

Choosing the Lesson Model to Use

Direct instruction is an effective model to use for teaching strategies. Begin the strategy lesson by clearly establishing the value of the strategy and what the students will be expected to know and do. Follow this with the presentation of the strategy steps (developed through a task analysis). Next, explain and demonstrate each step, and finally, give feedback as the students practice. These are key elements for use in teaching strategies.

Key Planning Considerations

Content Analysis

Use a task analysis to organize the content of a strategy. Because strategies are usually written as a series of steps or subskills, the task analysis is already written for you. In addition, the strategy steps almost always include a built-in remembering technique (usually a first-letter mnemonic device), which is very helpful for students when trying to recall the steps. For example, the letters in the RCRC memorization strategy stand for *R*ead, *C*over, *R*ecite, and *C*heck (Archer and Gleason 1990). Each letter represents a step of the task analysis needed to complete the strategy. Note that the task analysis and remembering technique will be used during the presentation of information and demonstration portions of the lesson body.

Opening

The opening of a strategy lesson is a good time to establish the importance of the strategy and the effect its use can have. You could begin by using a technique designed to motivate students, such as by asking a question that describes a problem caused by not using the strategy. You might ask, "How many of you have ever lost points on a writing assignment because it was not complete?" Another important part of the opening is to tell the students the objective ("Today you will learn a technique for checking your written work before you turn it in so that you can be sure that it is complete"). Complete the opening by stating the objective purpose, such as saying, "Using this strategy can help ensure that you receive full credit for your work and can help increase your grade."

Presentation of Information

During the presentation of information section of the lesson body, it is important to explain, tell about, and describe the strategy steps to the students. This is most effective when you show the task analysis (use a transparency or a poster) to the students, and then explain it and give examples of each step. Strategies often have a mnemonic device built in to help students remember the strategy steps. Pointing out and referring to the mnemonic device in the strategy throughout the lesson helps students remember the key steps or subskills.

At some point, students need to memorize the steps of the strategy, so they can be more automatic in using the steps. However, you will need to decide in advance of your lesson whether memorization will be part of the initial lesson or not. If you do not plan for your students to memorize the steps at this point, be sure to provide a visual support of the strategy (a poster of steps, for example) during all phases of your lesson. If you do want your students to memorize the steps, plan ample practice opportunities so students can learn them.

Demonstration

It is also very important to demonstrate or model the use of the strategy after or during the presentation of information portion of the lesson. Using the think-aloud technique is very effective as it allows students to see the steps being used and hear the thinking that is necessary to complete the steps. For example, in the COPS (C = capitalization; O = overall appearance; P = punctuation; S = spelled) error monitoring strategy (Schumaker et al. 1981), the teacher would say, "Let's see, 'C' stands for capitalization. Have I capitalized the first word in every sentence? Yes . . . I capitalized 'The' in the first sentence," and so on.

Be sure that your actions and thoughts during this component of the lesson are obvious (exaggerate if needed), and that students can easily see and recognize what you are doing. Depending on the complexity of the strategy, you may need to model it numerous times before students are ready to try it. In some cases, you may wish to model a number of times over several days.

Extended Practice

The extended practice portion of the strategy lesson is meant to provide opportunities that help students become fluent in their strategy use and to facilitate generalization. These opportunities are often organized as in-class practices, although carefully structured homework assignments can be effective also.

Use in-class practice activities if your goal is to provide frequent, varied practice opportunities so that using the strategy will become a habit. As you work through various content areas, point out when it would be appropriate to use the strategy and then have students practice it. Over time, your role in this area can decrease.

Plan carefully organized homework assignments for students to effectively practice the learned strategies at home. For example, include a strategy check-off sheet with a homework practice assignment. A parent or sibling could check off the steps as the student completes them.

Generalization of strategy use requires special attention. Even though a student may know how to use a strategy, this does not guarantee that the student will use the strategy in various settings. You can increase the likelihood that students will generalize strategy use if you provide practice sessions in a variety of settings, with varied materials, and with prompts to use the strategy. For example, if you have taught a reading comprehension strategy, plan for students to practice the strategy with science, social studies, and other subject matter. In all cases, use interesting materials for practice sessions to help increase a student's interest in using the strategy.

To summarize, strategy instruction provides students with a valuable tool to use in school. Using effective strategies can increase the possibility that students will experience success with school tasks. When strategies become habits, students become more independent, effective learners.

Sample Plans

Look at the framework for diversity responsive teaching (DRT) as you examine the sample plans at the end of this chapter. Ask yourself how the plan incorporates responses to diversity in *what* is taught, *how* it's taught, and the *context* for teaching and learning. We'll give you a start in thinking about how various parts of the plan fit with various components of the framework. We encourage you to look for additional examples of each component and to think about what changes you believe would make this plan even more likely to support all students' involvement and success.

Notice that the social skills lesson "Standing Up for Someone" teaches content that helps prepare students with skills *for a diverse world*. In addition, teachers can use this lesson to create a diversity responsive *social environment* in their classrooms. The lesson "Designing Mnemonic Devices" gives an easy opportunity to respond to diversity in *what* is taught. The content of the lists to be memorized could be based on student interests, for example. Can you think of other ways to use the lists—perhaps to teach *about* diversity?

The "Polygon" lessons illustrate how the same concept can be taught in two different ways. Both lessons include a clear, detailed concept analysis.

The "Standing Up for Someone" lesson includes a number of interesting universal instructional interventions. The extended practice activities are used for the purpose of generalization. Notice that they come after the evaluation for that reason. In addition the supervised practice is unusual in that it extends over two days. This allows each student to role-play more than once.

The social skill lesson is an example of a universal behavioral intervention. Notice that it is part of a series of lessons meant to prevent bullying. Can you think of other universal behavioral interventions for preventing bullying? For example, what classroom rules might you establish? Notice that partner practice is incorporated in the concept lessons "Polygon." If you had a student with serious difficulties paying attention and completing work, how could you use peer support as a selected (antecedent) intervention for him?

References and Suggested Readings for Concepts

Arends, R. I. 2004. *Learning to teach.* 6th ed. San Francisco: McGraw-Hill. (See Chapter 9 in particular.)

Cummings, C. 1990. *Teaching makes a difference.* 2nd ed. Edmonds, WA: Teaching. (See Chapter 11 in particular.)

Eggen, P. D., and D. P. Kauchak. 2006. *Strategies and models for teachers: Teaching content and thinking skills.* 5th ed. Boston: Allyn and Bacon.

Howell, K. W., M. Hosp, and J. Hosp. n.d. *Curriculum-based evaluation: Teaching and decision making.* 4th ed. Belmont, CA: Wadsworth/Thomson Learning. Forthcoming.

Martorella, P. H. 1994. Concept learning and higher-level thinking. In *Classroom teaching skills.* 5th ed., ed. J. M. Cooper, 153–188. Lexington, MA: D.C. Heath.

Sabornie, E., and L. deBetterncourt. 2004. *Teaching students with mild and high-incidence disabilities at the secondary level.* 2nd ed. Upper Saddle River, N.J.: Pearson.

Smith, P. L., and T. J. Ragan. 2004. *Instructional design.* 3rd ed. Columbus, OH: Merrill, an imprint of Prentice Hall. (See Chapter 9 in particular.)

References and Suggested Readings for Social Skills

Allsopp, D., K. Santos, and R. Linn. 2000. Collaborating to teach prosocial skills. *Intervention in School and Clinic* 35 (3): 141–146.

Elksnin, L., and N. Elksnin. 1998. Teaching social skills to students with learning and behavior problems. *Intervention in School and Clinic* 33 (3): 131–140.

Goldstein, A., and E. McGinnis. 1997. *Skillstreaming the adolescent: New strategies and perspectives for teaching prosocial skills.* Rev. ed. Champaign, IL: Research Press.

Gresham, F. 2002. Teaching social skills to high-risk children and youth: Preventive and remedial approaches. In *Interventions for academic and behavior problems II: Preventive and remedial approaches,* eds. M. Shinn, H. Walker, & G. Stoner, 403–432. Bethesda, MD: National Association of School Psychologists.

McGinnis, E., and A. Goldstein. 1997. *Skillstreaming the elementary school child: New strategies and perspectives for teaching prosocial skills.* Rev. ed. Champaign, IL: Research Press.

Sargent, L. 1998. *Social skills for school and community.* Reston, VA: Council for Exceptional Children.

Seattle Committee for Children, 1992. *Second step: A violence prevention curriculum.* Seattle: Seattle Committee for Children.

Sheridan, S. 1995. *The tough kid social skills book.* Longmont, CO: Sopris West.

Smith, S., and D. Gilles. 2003. Using key instructional elements to systematically promote social skill generalization for students with challenging behavior. *Intervention in School and Clinic* 39 (1): 30–37.

Sugai, G., and T. Lewis. 1996. Preferred and promising practices for social skills instruction. *Focus on Exceptional Children* 29 (4): 1–16.

Walker, H., E. Ramsey, and F. Gresham. 2004. *Antisocial behavior in school: Evidence-based practices.* 2nd ed. Belmont, CA: Wadsworth/Thomson Learning.

References and Suggested Readings for Strategies

Archer, A., and M. Gleason. 1990. *Skills for school success.* North Billerica, MA: Curriculum Associates.

Ashton, T. 1999. Spell checking: making writing meaningful in the inclusive classroom. *Teaching Exceptional Children* 32 (2): 24–27. (This title provides a strategy for the effective use of a spell-checker.)

Boyle, J. R. 2001. Enhancing the note-taking skills of students with mild disabilities. *Intervention in School and Clinic* 36 (4): 221–224.

Boyle, J. R., and M. Weishaar. 2001. The effects of strategic note-taking on the recall and comprehension of lecture information for high school students with learning disabilities. *Learning Disabilities Research and Practice* 16 (3): 133–141.

Bryant, D. P., N. Ugel, S. Thompson, and A. Hamff. 1999. Instructional strategies for content-area reading instruction. *Intervention in School and Clinic* 34 (5): 293–302. (This title provides strategies for word identification, vocabulary, and comprehension skills.)

Casteel, C. P., B. A. Isom, and K. F. Jordan. 2000. Creating confident and competent readers: transactional strategies instruction. *Intervention in School and Clinic* 36 (2): 67–74.

Cegelka, P. T., and W. H. Berdine. 1995. *Effective instruction for students with learning difficulties.* Boston: Allyn and Bacon.

Czarnecki, E., D. Rosko, and E. Fine. 1998. How to call up note-taking skills. *Teaching Exceptional Children* 30 (6): 14–19.

DeLaPaz, S. 2001. STOP and DARE: A persuasive writing strategy. *Intervention in School and Clinic* 36 (4): 234–243. (This title provides a strategy for writing persuasive essays.)

Deshler, D., E. S. Ellis, and B. K. Lenz. 1996. *Teaching adolescents with learning disabilities: Strategies and methods.* 2nd ed. Denver: Love Publishing. (See Chapters 3–9 for strategies in reading, writing, test-taking, note-taking, math, and social skills.)

Ellis, E. S., D. D. Deshler, B. K. Lenz, J. B. Schumaker, and F. L. Clark. 1991. An instructional model for teaching learning strategies. *Focus on Exceptional Children* 23: 1–24.

Gleason, M. M., G. Colvin, and A. L. Archer. 1991. Interventions for improving study skills. In *Interventions for achievement and behavior problems,* eds. G. Stoner, M. R. Shinn, and H. M. Walker, 137–160. Silver Spring, MD: National Association of School Psychologists.

Landi, M. 2001. Helping students with learning disabilities make sense of word problems. *Intervention in School and Clinic* 37 (1): 13–18. (This article provides a strategy for solving math word problems.)

Lebzelter, S., and E. Nowacek. 1999. Reading strategies for secondary students with mild disabilities. *Intervention in School and Clinic* 34 (4): 212–219. (This article provides decoding, vocabulary, and comprehension strategies.)

Lewis, R. B., and D. H. Doorlag. 2006. *Teaching special students in general education classrooms.* 7th ed. Upper Saddle River, N.J.: Pearson.

Lovitt, T. C. 1995. *Tactics for teaching.* 2nd ed. Columbus, OH: Merrill, an imprint of Prentice-Hall.

Lovitt, T. C. 2000. *Preventing school failure: Tactics for teaching adolescents.* 2nd ed. Austin, TX: Pro-Ed. (See Chapter 3 on study skills, in particular.)

Mastropieri, M. A., and T. E. Scruggs. 1998. Enhancing school success with mnemonic strategies. *Intervention in School and Clinic* 33 (4): 201–207.

Mastropieri, M. A., and T. E. Scruggs. 2004. *The inclusive classroom: Strategies for effective instruction.* 2nd ed. Upper Saddle River, N.J.: Pearson. (See Chapter 11 on teaching study skills.)

Meltzer, L. J., B. N. Roditi, D. P. Haynes, K. R. Biddle, M. Paster, and S. E. Taber. 1996. *Strategies for success: Classroom teaching techniques for students with learning problems.* Austin, TX: Pro-Ed. (See Chapters 3–6 on strategies for spelling, reading comprehension, written language, and math.)

Mercer, C. D., and A. R. Mercer. 2005. *Teaching students with learning problems.* 7th ed. Upper Saddle River, N.J.: Pearson. (See Chapter 13 in particular.)

Olson, J. L., and J. M. Platt. 2000. *Teaching children and adolescents with special needs.* 3rd ed.

Columbus, OH: Merrill, an imprint of Prentice-Hall. (See Chapters 8 and 9 in particular.)

Polloway, E. A., and J. R. Patton. 2004. *Strategies for teaching learners with special needs.* 8th ed. Columbus, OH: Merrill, an imprint of Prentice-Hall. (See Chapter 13 on study skills.)

Reithaug, D. 1998. *Orchestrating academic success by adapting and modifying programs.* West Vancouver, BC: Stirling Head Enterprises. (This title provides strategies for reading, writing, spelling, and math.)

Ryder, R. J. 1991. The directed questioning activity for subject matter text. *Journal of Reading* 34 (8): 606–612.

Schumaker, J. B., D. D. Deshler, S. Nolan, F. L. Clark, G. R. Alley, and M. M. Warner. 1981. *Error monitoring: A learning strategy for improving academic performance of LD adolescents* (Research Report No. 32). Lawrence, KS: University of Kansas Institute on Learning Disabilities.

Terrill, M., T. Scruggs, and M. Mastropieri. 2004. SAT vocabulary instruction for high school students with learning disabilities. *Intervention in School and Clinic* 39 (5): 288–294.

Vaughn, S, C. Bos, and J. Schumm. 2003. *Teaching exceptional, diverse, and at-risk students in the general education classroom.* Boston: Allyn and Bacon.

Vaughn, S., and J. K. Klinger. 1999. Teaching reading comprehension through collaborative strategic reading. *Intervention in School and Clinic* 34 (5): 284–292.

Wood, D., and A. Frank. 2000. Using memory enhancing strategies to learn multiplication facts. *Teaching Exceptional Children* 32 (5): 78–82.

Polygon: A Direct Instruction Concept Lesson

This is for a large group of students.

I. PREPLANNING TASKS

A. Connection analysis: *State Standard, Mathematics 1.3:* Understand and apply concepts and procedures from geometric sense. *Benchmark 2:* Use multiple attributes to describe geometric shapes.

B. Content analysis

1. Concept analysis

   a. Concept name: Polygon

   b. Definition: A polygon is a two-dimensional, closed figure of three or more sides made by joining line segments, where each line segment intersects with exactly two others at its endpoints.

   c. Critical attributes: Two-dimensional, closed figure with three or more sides, made of joined line segments, each line segment intersects with exactly two others at its endpoints

   d. Noncritical attributes: Size, shape, color, patterns inside or out

   e. Examples: Triangle (three sides), quadrilateral (four sides), pentagon (five sides), or hexagon (six sides). Both regular and irregular polygons need to be included in examples.

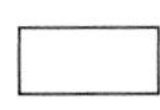

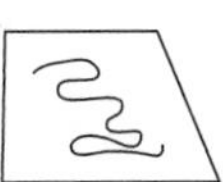

   f. Nonexamples:

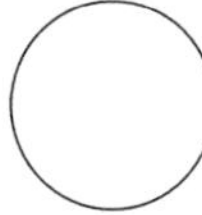

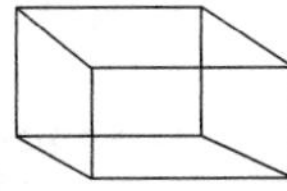
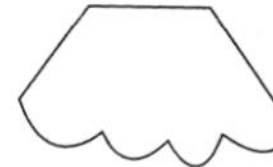

2. Prerequisite Skills or Knowledge: Know how to identify when the endpoints of line segments intersect.

3. Key terms and vocabulary: **Line segment, endpoint, intersect**

C. Objective: Given 12 geometric figures on a worksheet, student will circle (or point to) the seven polygons.

D. Objective rationale: Polygons are basic geometrical shapes and recognizing them is a prerequisite skill for other geometrical concepts, such as regular and irregular polygons.

E. Materials or equipment: three transparencies, math workbooks, worksheet for evaluation.

II. LESSON SETUP

A. Signal for attention: Play musical chords.

B. Behavior expectations: Raise hands to contribute, listen to explanations and comments of teacher and peers, and keep eyes on the speaker.

III. LESSON OPENING

A. Review prior geometry lessons.

   1. Discuss the various shapes ("What are they?") in the current geometry unit.

B. State objective and objective purpose.

   1. Say, "Today you are going to learn how to identify our new shape, polygons. You will learn a definition and the characteristics that make a polygon."

   2. "This lesson will help prepare you for future lessons, such as learning about various types of polygons."

IV. LESSON BODY

A. Presentation of information

   1. Show transparency #1 (concept analysis with polygon definition, list of critical and noncritical attributes, and examples and nonexamples of polygons).

   2. Read the definitions (with students), discuss critical and noncritical attributes, pointing out attributes in the examples, and then point out noncritical attributes.

B. Demonstration

   1. Show transparency #2 (with a list of questions to ask to help decide if shapes are polygons, and more examples and nonexamples).

   2. Think aloud with the first two examples to show how to use questions to analyze shapes (a poster of questions will remain on the whiteboard tray).

      a. Is it two-dimensional?

      b. Is it made of line segments?

      c. Is it a closed shape?

      d. Does each line segment intersect with exactly two others at its endpoints?

      e. Are there at least three sides?

      f. If the answer to all of these questions is yes, the shape is a polygon.

   3. Repeat questions with the next four examples and nonexamples. Ask the students if they agree with my conclusions (have some incorrect ones).

      CFU = Thumbs up/down

C. Supervised practice. (Have students take out their yes and no response cards.)

   1. Partner practice.

      a. Show transparency #3 (list of questions and new examples and nonexamples).

      b. Have students determine whether or not each shape is a polygon (first five shapes). Prompt the use of the five questions.

      AP = Turn to partner

   2. Individual practice.

      CFU = Use response cards.

      a. Point to each of the last five shapes and have students signal. (Have Leah help Molly with reading the questions if needed.)

V. EXTENDED PRACTICE

A. Provide a seatwork assignment. Have students circle the polygons on math workbook page 55, which shows 25 shapes with 15 polygons.

VI. LESSON CLOSING

A. Final review of information learned.

1. Say, "Today we learned . . . ."
2. Quickly review the concept analysis (transparency #1).

B. Pass out and explain the evaluation.

1. Say, "Your ticket to lunch is finding the polygons on the worksheet."
2. Ask questions, such as, "How do you show which are polygons?"

> ***CFU*** = Call on selected nonvolunteers.

VII. EVALUATION

A. Provide a worksheet of 12 geometric figures, seven of which are polygons. Students complete worksheets individually and independently. (Parent volunteer will evaluate Stephan. He will point to the polygons.)

Polygon: A Structured Discovery Concept Lesson

This is for a large group of students.

I. PREPLANNING TASKS

A. Connection analysis: *State Standard, Mathematics 1.3:* Understand and apply concepts and procedures from geometric sense. *Benchmark 2:* Use multiple attributes to describe geometric shapes.

B. Content analysis

1. Concept analysis

   a. Concept name: Polygon

   b. Definition: A polygon is a two-dimensional, closed figure of three or more sides made by joining line segments, where each line segment intersects with exactly two others at its endpoints

   c. Critical attributes: Two-dimensional, closed figure, with three or more sides, made of joined line segments, each line segment intersects with exactly two others at its endpoints

   d. Noncritical attributes: Size, shape, color, patterns inside or out

   e. Examples: Triangle (three sides), quadrilateral (four sides), pentagon (five sides), or hexagon (six sides). Both regular and irregular polygons need to be included in examples.

 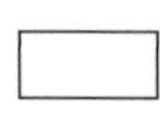 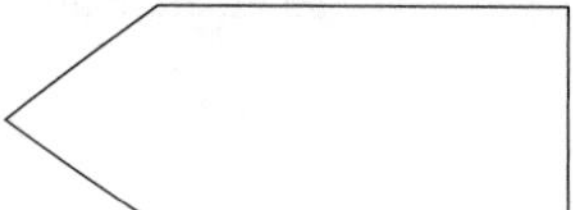  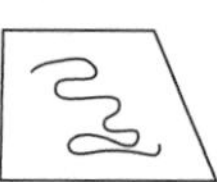

   f. Nonexamples

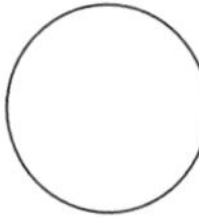  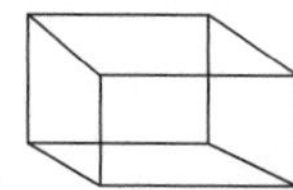 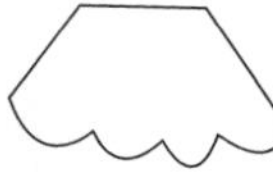

2. Prerequisite skills or knowledge: Know how to identify when the endpoints of line segments intersect.

3. Key terms and vocabulary: **Line segment, endpoint, intersect**

C. Objective: Given 12 geometric figures on a worksheet, student will circle (or point to) the seven polygons.

D. Objective rationale: Polygons are basic geometrical shapes and recognizing them is a prerequisite skill for other geometrical concepts, such as regular and irregular polygons.

E. Materials or equipment: four transparencies, math workbooks, worksheet for evaluation

II. LESSON SETUP

A. Signal for attention: Play musical chords.

B. Behavior expectations: Raise hands to contribute, listen to the explanations and comments of the teacher and peers, and keep eyes on the speaker.

III. LESSON OPENING

A. Review prior geometry lessons.

1. Discuss the various shapes ("What are they?") in the current geometry unit.

AP = Brainstorm

B. State objective and objective purpose.

1. Say, "Today you are going to learn how to identify our new shape, polygons. You will learn a definition and the characteristics that make a polygon."
2. "This lesson will help prepare you for future lessons, such as learning about various types of polygons."

IV. LESSON BODY

A. Set up the discovery.

1. Show transparency #1 (examples and nonexamples of polygons).
2. Say, "Some of these shapes are polygons. Watch me as I circle them" (circle them).
3. Say, "You have five minutes to see if you can figure out how all of the circled shapes are the same."

B. Monitor the discovery.

1. Walk around and prompt as needed, such as, "Are all of the shapes the same color?" "Are the shapes closed?" and so on. Ask questions about both critical and noncritical attributes.

C. Review the discovery.

1. Construct a concept analysis together on transparency #2.
   a. Ask, "In what ways are the circled shapes the same?" (write critical attributes).
   b. Ask, "Can you think of a way to write a definition for a polygon?" (write definition).

CFU = "If this is a complete definition, put thumbs up. If not, put thumbs down."

2. Read definition and critical attributes.
   a. Repeat the procedure with each critical attribute, having students give thumbs up or down.
3. Show transparency #3 (list of questions to ask to help decide if the shape is a polygon and examples and nonexamples of polygons). Explain how to use questions to analyze shapes.
   a. Is it two-dimensional?
   b. Is it made of line segments?
   c. Is it a closed shape?
   d. Does each line segment intersect with exactly two others at its endpoints?
   e. Are there at least three sides?
   f. If the answer to all of these questions is yes, it is a polygon.

D. Supervised practice—Have students take out their yes or no response cards.

1. Partner practice

   a. Show transparency #4 (list of questions and new examples and nonexamples).

   b. Have students determine whether or not each shape is a polygon (first five shapes). Prompt the use of the five questions.

   AP = Turn to partner.

2. Individual practice.

   a. Point to each of the last five shapes and have students signal. (Have Leah help Molly with reading the questions if needed.)

   CFU = Use response cards.

V. EXTENDED PRACTICE

A. Provide a seatwork assignment. Have students circle the polygons, on math workbook page 55, which shows 25 shapes with 15 polygons.

VI. LESSON CLOSING

A. Final review of information learned.

1. Say, "Today we learned . . . ."
2. Quickly review the concept analysis put together as a class (transparency #2).

B. Pass out and explain the evaluation.

1. Say, "Your ticket to lunch is finding the polygons on the worksheet."
2. Ask questions, such as "How do you show which are polygons?"

CFU = Call on selected nonvolunteers.

VII. EVALUATION

A. Provide a worksheet of 12 geometric figures, seven of which are polygons. Students complete worksheets individually and independently. (Parent volunteer will evaluate Stephan. He will point to the polygons.)

Social Skills Lesson: Standing Up for Someone

This is a direct instruction lesson for a small group.

I. PREPLANNING TASKS

A. Connection analysis: This lesson is part of an anti-bullying and acting for social justice program. Related state standard in civics: Understand individual rights and their accompanying responsibilities, explain why democracy requires citizens to exercise their own rights and to respect the rights of others.

B. Content (task) analysis for "standing up for someone" (steps adapted from Goldstein and McGinnis 1997):

   1. Decide if the person is not being treated right by others.
   2. Decide if the person wants you to stand up for him or her.
   3. Decide how to stand up for the person.
   4. Do it.

C. Lesson objective: In a given role play, students will correctly think aloud and demonstrate each step in standing up for someone.

D. Objective rationale: Standing up for someone who is being treated unfairly or unkindly is an important part of friendship and community-building and helps prevent bullying at school. It also has a larger application as part of acting for social justice.

E. Materials: Graphic organizer; poster with steps; homework forms; and backup and evaluation scenarios.

II. LESSON SETUP

A. Initial signal for attention: "Let's get started."

B. Behavior expectations: Listen when others are speaking; contribute ideas.

III. LESSON OPENING

A. Show graphic organizer of components of the anti-bullying program.

B. Remind students of an earlier lesson on standing up for yourself. Ask for key points: using "I" statements, and humor, examples of when to get help.

C. With parent helpers, do a skit in which someone is not being treated right (called a "retard" and excluded from a game), and a bystander does not know how to help.

D. Ask students for examples of when they have needed this skill in their lives.

E. State the objective and rationale (both written on board).

IV. LESSON BODY

A. Presentation of information

1. Show steps written on a big poster. Talk through and add definitions, examples, and questions.

   a. Decide if the person is not being treated right by others. Ask yourself, *Is this person (friend, classmate, stranger) not being treated right (disrespectfully, unfairly, unequally, unkindly) by others (child, adult, group)?*

   b. Decide if the person wants you to stand up for him or her. Ask yourself, *Does this person want my help? How can I find out?* (Ask directly, read body language, or think how you would feel.)

   c. Decide how to stand up for the person. Ask yourself, *What shall I do to help?* (Remember the rules: Do not get hurt and do not make it worse.) Consider the options of telling the other person to stop; explaining why it is unfair; saying something nice to the person not being treated right or walking away with him; and getting help (always use the last two in dangerous situations).

   d. Do it. Use "I" statements in a calm voice. Do not be unkind back.

2. **AP** and **CFU** after each step. **CFU** = call on selected students to paraphrase, repeat, or add examples; or write a definition or example on the whiteboard and hold it up; or **AP** = have students discuss with their partners.

B. Demonstration

1. **AP:** Select students to watch for each step (change for each scenario).

2. With parent volunteers, model three scenarios (demonstrate a student at recess being taunted and pushed around by older kids, the class laughing when a student struggles during oral reading, and a sibling being unfairly accused of breaking a dish and lying). Model each step including think-alouds.

3. **CFU:** After each modeling, call on selected students to describe how each step was used.

C. Supervised practice

1. Have the group brainstorm other scenarios that they have seen (be sure to get at least one from each student).

2. Select Edgar to role-play first, allowing him to choose the scenario. (Parent volunteers will play the roles of "person" and "others.") Leave the poster up for role players to refer to.

3. Ask questions of Edgar to set the scene, such as, "Where is this happening?"

4. Assign steps to watch for to other students.

5. Stop, correct, and redo if errors.

6. Then ask for feedback from peers and adults. "Give feedback politely by referring to the behavior, not the person."

7. Continue until each student has done a role play. (Select Jareese to go second.)

V. LESSON CLOSING

A. Redo skit from the opening; using Think-Pair-Share, ask the students what they think the bystander should do.

B. Tell students we will talk about this skill again as we study civil rights issues in social studies class.

VI. CONTINUATION

A. The next day, model a scenario of a student having his lunch taken and being made fun of for being "foreign," while pointing to each step on poster (review).

B. Then each student will role-play another scenario (continued supervised practice).

VII. EVALUATION

A. The following day, pull students aside, one at a time, to role-play the skill using a new scenario that I provide.

B. Use parent volunteers as "others" and "persons."

VIII. EXTENDED PRACTICE FOR GENERALIZATION

A. Provide homework. "Write the steps on a homework form, noting each time you use the skill this week and how well you do."

B. Have parents initial that they read the homework form.

C. Conduct a follow-up activity, having students videotape themselves role-playing a scenario they create, and then having the class critique.

D. I will explain the skill to the recess supervisor and she will give good-citizen awards to those who use the skill this month. I will do the same in the classroom.

E. Hold a review session in two weeks.

Strategy Lesson: Designing Mnemonic Devices

This is a direct instruction lesson for a large group.

I. PREPLANNING TASKS

A. Connection analysis: This strategy helps students progress successfully toward many state standards, as many require that students have mastered large quantities of information. *IEP objective:* Molly will use memorization strategies as appropriate when preparing for content tests.

B. Content (task) analysis: See lesson body for Designing Mnemonic Devices (steps adapted from Archer and Gleason 1990)

C. Prerequisites: Know the RCRC strategy (Archer and Gleason 1990).

D. Key terms and vocabulary: **strategy**—a plan or method; **Mnemonic devices**—tricks for memorizing

E. Objective and rationale

   1. Given three lists of related items, students will design a word or sentence mnemonic device for each that makes sense.

   2. This will help students organize information to be memorized in preparation for tests and increase scores on tests.

F. Materials and equipment: Transparencies with the last test results, task analysis, lists of related information, and an evaluation worksheet

II. LESSON SETUP

A. Signal for attention: Ring bell.

B. Behavior expectations: Students will look and listen, answer questions, raise hands, and wait to be called on.

III. LESSON OPENING

A. Motivator: Present a list of ten facts and follow with quiz. Then, present another list, tell them a first letter mnemonic, and follow with another quiz. Compare scores.

B. Objective and purpose: "You will be happy to know that today you are going to learn how to create your own memory tricks. They will help you memorize information better and in less time."

C. Review RCRC by having students call out the words in unison.

IV. LESSON BODY

A. Presentation of information and demonstration

   1. Define mnemonic device and strategy.

   2. Explain the steps of the strategies.

      a. Talk through transparency #2, which shows the task analysis below, *and* point out poster of task analysis.

      b. Provide an enlarged version on a handout for Leah.

3. Designing mnemonic devices (task analysis)
    a. Using the word strategy:
        i. Underline the first letter of each item to be memorized (list of words, task parts, steps, and so on). For example: Superior, Huron, Erie, Michigan, Ontario.
        ii. Determine whether a word can be made from the first letters (reorder the letters if necessary): *HOMES*. If the word strategy works, go to (iii). If not, go to (iv).
        iii. Memorize the word and item that goes with each letter of the word using RCRC.
    b. Using the sentence strategy:
        iv. Reorder the first letters of the words and create a sentence (*fruit, meat, vegetable* = the phrase, *very funny man*).
        v. Memorize the sentence and item that goes with each word in the sentence using RCRC.
4. Ask for definitions, paraphrases of steps, and purpose of strategies. Think-Pair-Share (**AP**), then call on selected nonvolunteers (**CFU**).
5. Do a think-aloud of the steps using the following lists of subject matter, which include both word and sentence strategy (five food groups: fruits, vegetables, meat, dairy, fats/oils/sweets; parts of an insect: head, thorax, abdomen).
    a. Pass out whiteboards. (**AP**)
    b. Have students work steps along with me.
    c. Emphasize that there is more than one answer.
6. **CFU:** Provide new content (types of rocks: sedimentary, igneous, metamorphic).
    a. Students will work each step on whiteboards ("Do step one, show me," and so on).
    b. If more instruction is needed, use these examples: Native American chiefs of the nineteenth century, primary colors, exports from California.

B. Supervised practice: Monitor and give feedback.
    1. Partner practice
        a. Give partners two more examples and a checklist of strategy steps.
        b. Have Partner 1 do the first example, while Partner 2 checks it off, and then reverse the roles.
        c. Use the following examples of taproots: carrots, radishes, beets, turnips, and parsnips; parts of a plant: roots, stem, leaves, and sometimes flowers.
        d. Partner Darin with Kristin to help with reading.
    2. Individual supervised practice
        a. Have individuals work two more examples (parts of a volcano: parasitic cone, base, summit, crater, and magma reserve; colors of the rainbow).

V. LESSON CLOSING

A. Go back to transparency #1 of test items. Have partners (**AP**) create mnemonic devices for missed groups of facts. Share with class.

VI. EXTENDED PRACTICE

A. Conduct in-class practice activities (seatwork).

1. During the next two days, we will look for examples of information in various content areas. Students will need to memorize these and develop a mnemonic device for each one, such as the states in the Pacific Northwest region or examples of foods that are low in fat.

VII. EVALUATION

A. Worksheet with three lists of related pieces of information. Students will develop a mnemonic device for each one.

Editing Your Plan

Introduction

Once you have written the first draft of your plan you need to edit it. This is as important for writing lesson and activity plans as it is for any other writing task. There are three main editing tasks for analyzing your plan for completeness and effectiveness. The first editing task is to analyze how to incorporate critical management skills and to write them into the plan. The second editing task is to double-check your plan to make sure that you have used appropriate universal and selected instructional interventions given the content and your students. The third editing task is to examine for congruence so that you can make sure that the various parts of your plan match. These editing tasks will help you increase the chances that your lesson or activity will be successful for all.

This chapter can be used in at least two ways. You can use it as a guide in analyzing your plan to make sure that it is as complete and as carefully thought through as possible. You cannot predict everything that might happen during your lesson or activity, but careful thought can help you predict and prevent many management problems and confusion with content. This chapter (and the following chapter) will also serve as a summary of many of the key ideas in this book, a way for you to review what you have learned.

Following are the three main editing tasks. Each task explanation includes a variety of questions to ask yourself that will provide guidance as you edit your plan. The first two editing tasks also include example plans.

Editing Task #1: Editing for Critical Management Skills

The first editing task is to add in the *critical management skills* that will help your lesson or activity run smoothly. At this point, your plan is pretty much complete in terms of what you'll teach and how you'll teach it. Now it is time to focus on the context for teaching and learning, specifically by adding in strategies for preventing and solving behavior problems. Each of the following critical management skills comes with a set of questions that you can ask yourself to help you select appropriate strategies. Look back at Chapter 11 for a complete description of seven critical management skills.

- Plan the *room arrangement* that will work best for this lesson or activity and write it in your plan. Think carefully about what you and your students will be doing during the various parts of your plan. Remember that the room arrangement needs to match the methods you plan to use and the students' skills and self-control. Ask yourself the following questions:
  - What will students need to be able to see?
  - Will students need to be able to concentrate without distractions?
  - Will students need to work closely with other students?
  - Do students need a writing surface or could they sit on the floor?
  - Will students need to move around? Where? Will I?

- Will any individuals need special seating assignments for this lesson/activity?
- Will I need to make changes in furniture arrangement during the lesson or activity? If so, how will I make those changes and when?

■ Plan the *signals for attention* that would work best for this lesson/activity and write them into the plan where needed. Think about what the students will be doing just before the lesson or activity starts, how interested they are likely to be, and what they will be doing during various parts of the lesson/activity. Ask yourself the following:
- Do I need a strong signal to gain attention at the beginning?
- Will students be working with peers, moving around the room, or engaging in something new and exciting during this lesson/activity? If so, what signal will be best seen or heard?
- Will any individuals need extra support in responding to the signal quickly? How can I provide this?
- Do they need to be reminded how to respond to the signal?

■ Plan how and when you will communicate *behavior expectations* that apply in this lesson or activity and write them into the plan where needed. Look at the various parts of the lesson/activity and analyze the rules, routines, and behavior or social skills required. Ask yourself the following:
- Do I need to communicate expectations regarding rules or routines for making transitions, getting help, what to do when finished, talking, movement, and so on?
- Do I need to remind students to use social or behavior skills such as active listening, sharing materials, following directions independently, disagreeing politely, accepting assigned partner, and so on?
- Will initial expectations need to change as the lesson or activity progresses, for example, change raising hands to calling out?
- Will any individuals need extra support in following these behavior expectations? How and when will I supply that?

■ Plan how and when you will *acknowledge appropriate behavior.* Write reminders into your plan. Ask yourself the following:
- What behaviors will be a challenge to this group?
- What behaviors will be a challenge to individuals?
- What behaviors are essential to the success of this lesson or activity?
- Which students need more acknowledgment than others?
- Have I considered whether students prefer public or private and group or individual acknowledgments?
- Have I planned to use a variety of acknowledgments?
- How strong will the acknowledgments need to be?

■ Think about how and when you should *monitor* students during this lesson or activity. Write reminders into the plan. Ask yourself the following:
- Who will need extra encouragement or prompting (for example, for getting started, sticking with a long task)?
- Will I need to be careful how I position myself when working with individuals or small groups so I can monitor the whole class?
- Will I need to write anything on the board, on transparencies, or on slides in advance so that I will not have my back to my students while I am teaching?
- How and when will I scan the class and move around the room? How will I remind myself to do so?
- Does the activity or lesson include transitions that I need to carefully monitor?
- How can I connect with each student during this lesson or activity?

■ Write in ideas for planning for *logistics.* Ask yourself the following:
- What materials need to be gathered or duplicated?
- Should I list materials needed on the board?
- What equipment needs to be set up or borrowed and checked?
- How will materials be distributed or picked up?
- What is the plan for cleanup, including the time needed?
- Will I have assistants helping with this lesson or activity? If so, what should each do? How and when will I communicate this?

- Think about how to manage *transitions*. Write reminders into the plan. Ask yourself the following:
  - What kinds of directions for transitions are needed? Detailed? Brief?
  - How will I communicate directions and behavior expectations for transitions?
  - How will I communicate behavior expectations for transitions?
  - Will written schedules and time reminders ("three minutes left") be needed to help students prepare for transitions?
  - Could I plan something fun at the beginning of the next activity to encourage quick transitions?
  - Would some of my students benefit from picture schedules or transition buddies?

- Additional things to think about include the following:
  - Have I done everything I can to teach effectively and to make content interesting, clear, personally and culturally relevant, complete, and so on, for all students?
  - Have I used curricular and instructional modifications and accommodations that will help all students be academically successful and thus prevent behavior problems due to frustration, lack of challenge, and so on?
  - Will any students need selected behavioral interventions to be successful in this lesson or activity?

Application of Editing Task #1

Following is an example of a plan (from Chapter 14) with critical management skills written in. It begins, however, with a description of a teacher's thoughts about management issues in this particular activity. You would *not* write these thoughts into a plan but we include them so you see the reasoning that underlies the decisions the teacher makes and understand the notes he writes in the plan.

Tic-Tac-Toe Spelling Activity Plan

Teacher thoughts:

- My students love to play Tic-Tac-Toe so the transition to this activity will be quick and it'll be easy to gain their attention at the beginning of the activity. It won't be so easy later to regain their attention when they are playing.
- Desks are already in pairs facing front and that will work both for giving directions and for playing the game.
- They know the "sit with reading partner routine" so a simple statement will be enough to direct them to the right desks.
- Several students struggle with getting started, even when they really enjoy an activity. I have them sitting in the front of the room near me.
- A variety of behavior and social skills are needed in this activity:
  - Taking turns—Many of my students struggle with this so I'll structure it through partner role descriptions.
  - Giving and receiving feedback—I've recently taught a social skills lesson on this and will remind them just before the game starts and acknowledge polite feedback often.
  - Winning and losing/good sportsmanship—WD really struggles with that. I'll precorrect privately with him before the activity starts by having him tell me and show me what good winners and losers do. Later I'll acknowledge him through our private signal because he doesn't like his friends to notice him being praised.

I. PREPLANNING TASKS

A. Prerequisite skills or knowledge: How to play Tic-Tac-Toe

B. Key terms or vocabulary: NA

C. Long-term objective: Given a list of 15 words that contain one to three syllables and end in "–ing," students will write (or spell orally) all words correctly. Students are given lists that match their skill level (one, two, or three syllables, for example). State writing standard: spell age-level words correctly.

D. Activity description: A Tic-Tac-Toe game where partners quiz each other on their spelling words. Correct responses result in placing an X or O on the Tic-Tac-Toe board.

E. Activity rationale: This game is intended to provide a fun way for students to practice and memorize their spelling words. This format also provides practice in giving and taking constructive feedback.

F. Materials: poster of game directions, transparency of grids and words, worksheets with 25 Tic-Tac-Toe grids on each

[Room arrangement: desks in pairs facing front; Logistics: Ask teaching assistant to help me demonstrate, monitor, and acknowledge polite feedback.]

II. ACTIVITY BEGINNING

[Transition: As students enter the room, remind them to sit in the desks they use for reading partner activities and that we'll be playing Tic-Tac-Toe. Logistics: point to a list on the board of materials needed (pencils, spelling lists).]

A. Setup

1. Signal for attention: "Attention, please."
2. Behavior expectations: "While I'm giving directions, keep eyes on me and raise hands to ask/answer questions unless I ask you to call out."

B. Opening

1. Review: "You are studying words that end with '–ing'. Call out some examples."
2. Motivate: "We're going to play Tic-Tac-Toe Spelling today."
3. Objective and purpose: "Tic-Tac-Toe Spelling will help you memorize correct spelling of words, so you can use these words in your writing; you won't need to look up words in a dictionary."

III. ACTIVITY MIDDLE

A. Post written game directions:

1. Exchange spelling lists with your reading partner.
2. Partner 1 (*X*) asks Partner 2 (*O*) a word from her list.
3. Partner 2 spells. If correct, Partner 2 places an *O* on a Tic-Tac-Toe square.
4. If wrong, Partner 1 says "The word ___is spelled ___. How do you spell ___ ?"
5. Partner 1 places a check if correct or a minus if incorrect by the word spelled.
6. Reverse the roles. Keep playing until time is up.

B. Explain directions for the game using poster and transparency of Tic-Tac-Toe grids and sample word lists.

[Logistics: Make sure I have this with me and that the projector works this time!]

- Demonstrate with teaching assistant as I explain

[Acknowledge eyes on me]

- Explain that checks and minuses are to keep track of words they know and to make sure all words are asked.
- **CFU:** After each step, stop and ask a question and request a unison verbal or signal response ("What would you say if I spelled cat 'kad'?" "What does he write if the word isn't spelled correctly?" and so on.)

[Acknowledge participating]

C. **Check for understanding** of all directions: I choose two students to come to the front and model the game procedure as I ask other selected students specific questions such as "Who goes first? What does the asker do now?"

D. Distribute Tic-Tac-Toe grids.

[Logistics: use this week's paper-passers] "Trade spelling lists with your partner."

[Expectations] "Stay with your partner and use quiet voices. Remember to give each other feedback politely. Who remembers what politely looks like and sounds like? If your partner spells the word correctly, say *you're right* or *good spelling*. If incorrect . . . who remembers what to do?"

E. Play the game: Play for 20 minutes. Complete as many games as possible.

[Acknowledge the three in front if they start quickly, otherwise prompt them. Monitor all pairs often. Acknowledge for following directions (especially MB and FL), taking turns, giving/receiving feedback politely, and good sportsmanship (signal WD).]

[Transition: Warn them when 5 minutes are left, then 1 minute.]

IV. ACTIVITY CLOSING

[Signal: switch lights off/on. Acknowledge for quick response. Acknowledge group if they improved in giving polite feedback.]

A. Preview: "Tomorrow, we'll do another practice activity to help you memorize your spelling words."

B. Practice one final time: "Pick one misspelled word from your list (if no words are misspelled, use "challenge words") and spell it correctly 3 times."

[Logistics: Ask this week's cleanup crew to collect and recycle grid worksheets. I collect their marked spelling lists.]

[Transition: Tell students to quietly and quickly return to their usual desks and get ready for lunch.]

Editing Task #1 involves planning for the use of critical management skills and writing them into the plan. Taking a proactive approach to behavior management and building positive behavior support strategies into your lessons and activities is an important part of planning.

Editing Task #2: Editing for Instructional Interventions (see Chapters 3–9.)

We assume that you used the guides provided in the various lesson and activity plan chapters when you were writing your initial plan. So, the editing task for *instructional interventions* is really just a double-check. This reread of your plan gives you a chance to make any final revisions that you feel are necessary. The following are questions to ask yourself as you double-check your plan for the use of effective instructional interventions:

Focusing Attention (see Chapter 4). Ask yourself the following:

- Is the content or structure of this lesson or activity automatically interesting to my students? Do I need a snappy opening to grab their attention? Is the relevance of the learning obvious?
- Have I written questions to ask my students? Count them. How many are convergent? Divergent? High-level? Low-level? Given the content and objective, does this seem about right?
- How new or complex is the knowledge or skill? Is another review during the closing a good idea? Do my students need some prompts on when to use this content?

Presenting Information (see Chapter 5). Ask yourself the following questions:

- Have I planned to say, write, and show the knowledge or skill?
- Is the new information complex or complicated? Do I need to break it down into smaller portions for presenting?
- Do I have a variety of visual supports? Are they easy to see and appealing to look at? Is the vocabulary I use appropriate for the students?

Promoting Active Participation (see Chapter 6). Ask yourself the following:

- Is the content new or complex? Have I used enough rehearsal strategies and processing strategies?
- Is it a long lesson? Will I be talking a lot? Have I used enough strategies to keep students engaged?
- Have I used a variety of active participation strategies to meet the different individual needs of my students (for example, not just written responses because some struggle with writing)?
- Have I selected strategies that involve every student or just one student at a time?

Planning Practice and Monitoring Progress (see Chapter 7). Ask yourself the following:

- Is the information complicated? If so, am I giving students a chance to practice after each step or two?
- Have I planned opportunities for students to practice with varying degrees of scaffolding, for example, supervised practice or extended practice?
- Do students have an opportunity to practice individually before they are evaluated?
- Have I provided opportunities for students to receive feedback on their performance at various spots during the lesson?
- Have I planned checks for understanding early and often? Am I checking the understanding of all students or just a few?
- In the evaluation section of my plan, am I asking my students to perform the same skill they were taught? Is my evaluation realistic? Is my evaluation relevant? Does my evaluation match my objective?

Planning Partner and Small-Group Work (see Chapter 8). Ask yourself the following:

- Do my students know how to work together, for example, how to cooperate, to share, to listen, to encourage, or to challenge each other? If not, can I teach or review the specific skills they need for this lesson/activity?
- What size groups will work best in this situation?
- How will I decide who is in what group (random selection, reading partners, draw names)?
- How will students share tasks? Shall I assign specific roles?

Selected Interventions (see Chapter 9). Ask yourself the following:

- Do I need any additional universal interventions?
- Are all of my students likely to be successful? Have I considered my students with special needs, my English language learners, cultural variation?
- Are the selected interventions that I have included necessary? Will they meet the needs of the students for whom they were selected? Should any of the selected interventions be built in for everyone rather than added on for some?

Application of Editing Task #2

Remember that editing task #2 is a double-check of the use of universal and selected instructional interventions. The following lesson plan, written by Mr. Curtis Kerce (affectionately known as Mr. K.), shows some of the thoughts that Mr. Kerce had as he read back through his plan. Although you would not write these thoughts into your plan, we provide them simply to show you what Mr. K. thought as he double-checked his lesson for effectiveness.

Multiplication (3-Digit by 1-Digit with Regrouping) Lesson Plan

Setting the scene: In the following example, Mr. K has written a large-group direct instruction lesson plan for his third graders. Here is the information he considered as he wrote his plan. First, two students have difficulty writing—it isn't that they can't write, it is that writing is tedious for them. Next, three of his students are not yet accurate on their multiplication facts. Finally, his class as a whole has trouble sitting and concentrating for long periods of time. When Mr. K wrote his plan in the first place he tried to take into account this information. Now it is time for him to go back and double-check his plan to see if his students' needs are addressed as is or if he needs to revise any part of his plan.

I. PREPLANNING TASKS

A. Connection analysis: State Standard: *Mathematics 1.1:* Understand and apply concepts and procedures from number sense. *Benchmark 1:* -computation: add, subtract, multiply, and divide whole numbers.

B. Content (task) analysis: How to Multiply 3-Digit by 1-Digit Numbers with Regrouping in the Ones and Tens Columns.

1. Multiply the ones, bottom ones by top ones.
2. Write down the ones, "carry" the tens.
3. Multiply diagonally: bottom ones by top tens, add the "carried" tens.
4. Write down the tens, "carry" the hundreds.
5. Multiply diagonally: bottom ones by top hundreds, add the "carried" hundreds.
6. Write down the hundreds and thousands.

[I think my task analysis needs this much detail. My students really benefit from very explicit and detailed directions; it helps prevent confusion. I'm going to leave it as is.]

Note: Write the steps (with an example) on a poster so students can refer to them throughout the lesson.

[Having the steps on a poster for all to see makes it possible for students to focus on how to do each step rather than focus on trying to memorize the steps. On second thought, I think it might be better for Alyssa to have the steps on a card on her desk; it can help her focus.]

C. Prerequisite skills: 1-digit by 2-digit multiplication with regrouping, 1-digit by 3-digit multiplication without regrouping, multiplication facts, place value, [task analysis card for Alyssa]

D. Key terms/vocabulary: NA

E. Objective: Given 15 problems on a worksheet (3-digit by 1-digit with regrouping in the ones and tens columns), students will write the answers with no more than one error.

[Even though students must write answers to the problems, I don't think this will be a problem for Robby. On second thought, the worksheet doesn't have enough space between problems for ease of writing—I'll need to change this. This will help Robby as well as other students.]

F. Objective rationale: This lesson helps prepare students for real-life situations involving this type of problem (for example, store purchases), and provides practice on multiplication facts.

G. Materials: *Worksheets* (evaluation worksheet)—[redo this with more spacing]; *transparencies:* (a) task analysis, (b) 25 problems, (c) dice game rules/partner roles; *dice game*: four 5–10 cubes for each partner group

II. LESSON SETUP

A. Signal for attention: "Let's begin."

B. Behavior Expectations:

1. Look at me while I talk.
2. Raise your hand, wait to be called on before speaking.
3. Respect others (hands to self, listen when someone else is talking).

III. LESSON OPENING

[The students were all successful in yesterday's lesson (a prerequisite to this one), and because they are motivated by success, I think the opening is fine as is—no need to be elaborate.]

A. Review prior learning: Say, "We've been working on multiplication skills and yesterday you learned to multiply a 1-digit number by a 2-digit number with regrouping. Let's review together."

$$\begin{array}{r} 65 \\ \times\ 5 \\ \hline \end{array}$$

1. "What is the first step? Everyone . . ." (5 × 5)
2. "Then what? Everyone . . ." (Carry the 2)
3. Repeat steps and prompts for the following problems:

AP = *Choral responses*

$$\begin{array}{r} 45 \\ \times\ 8 \\ \hline \end{array} \qquad \begin{array}{r} 67 \\ \times\ 4 \\ \hline \end{array} \qquad \begin{array}{r} 18 \\ \times\ 9 \\ \hline \end{array}$$

[On second thought . . . I'm going to have students use their whiteboards at this point, in addition to choral responses. That way I will have a better idea that all of my students are ready for this lesson.]

B. Statement of objective; objective purpose;

1. Say, "Now that we have *reviewed,* we are *ready to start* today's lesson. We will be working with the same type of problem, but instead of multiplying 1 digit by 2 digits, we will multiply 1 digit by 3 digits."
2. This *skill is important*—for a variety of reasons (store purchases, more complicated multiplication, and division problems).

[On second thought, because this type of math isn't really inherently fun and exciting for my students, I think I will use some of their names in the examples I use here, for example, Kelly went to the hardware store to buy three hammers. Each hammer costs $5.38. How much will all three hammers cost? This could increase interest.]

IV. LESSON BODY

A. Presentation of Information *("tell" the task analysis)*

1. Show transparency #1 (shows task analysis and an example problem done in steps).
2. Explain steps and problem. Point out how similar this is to what they've been studying, just adding one more step.

[On second thought, I'm going to make the poster very fancy as a way to interest students. I'll fashion it after a cartoon.]

B. Demonstration *("show" the task analysis)*

1. Show transparency #2 (contains 25 problems to use as needed throughout rest of lesson).
2. Say, "I'll work a few problems. You watch and listen to how I work them."
3. Think aloud each step as I work the problem, for example.

> ***AP*** = Choral responses to facts

$$\begin{array}{r} 73 \\ \underline{\times\ 5} \end{array}$$

   a. "Multiply the ones" (5 × 3) "What's 5 times 3, everyone . . . ?"
   b. "Write down ones" (5), "carry the tens" (1).
   c. "Multiply diagonally—ones times the tens"; "What's 5 times 7, everyone . . . ?"

[The choral response will help students stay with me during my demonstration. I think that is all that is needed here. I'll be checking their understanding later on.]

6. Repeat think-aloud with additional problems; for example, "Let's read the first problem together, everyone . . . Multiply 9 times 2, what's that everyone . . . ?"

> ***AP*** = *Choral read problems, choral respond for facts*

$$\begin{array}{r} 172 \\ \underline{\times\ 9} \end{array} \qquad \begin{array}{r} 229 \\ \underline{\times\ 8} \end{array} \qquad \begin{array}{r} 875 \\ \underline{\times\ 5} \end{array} \qquad \begin{array}{r} 226 \\ \underline{\times\ 7} \end{array}$$

> ***AP*** = *Write answers* on whiteboard.

7. **CFU:** Have students take out individual whiteboards.
8. Show next problem. Have students copy problem.
9. Ask specific questions to review steps, for example, "What should you do first?" Hold up board on signal.

[This type of CFU will give me a good way to make sure that everyone understands the various steps of working these problems.]

[I think my use of active participation is good—lots of variety, lots of opportunities for all students to respond.]

C. Supervised practice (whole group)

> ***AP*** = Write answer, tell a partner, call on nonvolunteers.

1. Say, "Let's work a few problem together." (Ask specific questions to "talk through" the steps, for example, "What do we multiply first?"
2. Work three to five problems with the whole group (partner supervised practice):

$$\begin{array}{r} 129 \\ \underline{\times\ 6} \end{array} \qquad \begin{array}{r} 782 \\ \underline{\times\ 9} \end{array} \qquad \begin{array}{r} 348 \\ \underline{\times\ 5} \end{array}$$

3. Have students put whiteboards away.

[I'm wondering if I really need to include this whole-group supervised practice part. On the one hand, I think they may be getting tired of working the problems, but on the other hand, this is their first chance to work all steps of the problems at once with feedback. I think I should keep this part, but I might be able to cut down on the number of practices prior to this. I also need to really watch carefully for signs of boredom or frustration.]

4. Show transparency and explain games rules for "Four Cube Multiplication Game."

[On second thought . . . I need to demonstrate playing this game. I'm going to select a student who I think may have some trouble getting the idea of the game and that student will play the game with me as a way to demonstrate to all.]

[On second thought, I'm going to assign specific roles because lately, my students have had difficulty dividing tasks and I want to ensure that students have plenty of time to play the game. In the near future, I need to provide some additional practice with dividing up tasks.]

> ***CFU & AP*** *= Ask specific questions about game rules and partner tasks* (for example, "What's the first rule?"). Use *Tell a Partner, then call on selected nonvolunteers.*

5. Form partner groups (*reading partners*) and pass out materials.

[On second thought, I'm going to have them work with their reading partner. I had been thinking that I would have students pick their own partners for this game, but because they are used to working with their reading partner, I won't need to be concerned about them working together cooperatively.]

6. Individual supervised practice
   a. Show the next 5 problems:

354	643	834	795	252
× 5	× 9	× 5	× 2	× 9

   b. Explain that students are to write out complete problems and work them on whiteboards.
   c. As students work, I monitor and give feedback. After checking everyone, have a few students work problem on overhead and have all students check their own problems.

> ***CFU*** = Ask, "Where do you work the problems, everyone . . . ?"

[I think this monitoring plan will work but I'll want to make sure that I check in with Robby and Gail right at the start and that I check in with Alyssa a bit more often than others.]

V. EXTENDED PRACTICE

A. Assign homework if needed. Assign "evens" on page 86, #1–#20 (3-digit by 1-digit multiplication problems with regrouping in the ones and tens column) as homework to be completed before evaluation, if supervised practice results indicate that my students are accurate with this skill, but not fluent. Otherwise the evaluation will come after the supervised practice.

[On second thought, I really need to check for understanding for the directions. I'll have students write down the assignment on their assignment calendar and then I'll go around and check.]

VI. LESSON CLOSING

A. Do a final review of steps; work on more problems

1. Show the transparency of the task analysis.
2. Work one final problem.

[On second thought, I think I need to add in another example to show the value of this skill. This can help students generalize the skill to real life, for example, "Suppose that Alyssa. . . ."]

VII. EVALUATION

A worksheet of 15 problems will be completed at the end of the period (or the following day if extended practice is needed), independently and individually.

Editing Task #2 is a double-check for the use of universal and selected instructional interventions. It is meant to be a quick check, not a time-consuming task. Sometimes just spending a few minutes looking at the plan you have written will help you catch errors that could have adverse effects on student success. It is well worth the few minutes it takes.

Editing Task #3: Evaluate Congruence

Evaluating lesson or activity congruence is the final editing task. As you worked through your initial planning, you undoubtedly thought about the connection between the various plan components. Therefore, this editing task is really just another double-check to ensure that the various pieces match.

How to Determine Congruence

1. Reread or paraphrase the objective.

2. Look at the opening and closing of the lesson or activity and ask:

- Am I telling students about the objective (opening)?
- Am I referring back to the objective (closing)?

3. Look at the main part of the lesson or activity and ask yourself the following questions:

- Am I *explaining* (or *reviewing*) the skill or information described in the objective?
- Am I *demonstrating* the skill or information described in the objective?
- Am I having students *practice* the skill or information stated in the objective?

4. Look at the evaluation section of the plan and ask yourself this question:

- Am I *testing* (or *will I test*) students on the very same thing I explained, demonstrated, and had them practice?

If your answer to all questions is *yes*, then your plan is congruent. If you answered *no* to even one question, revise before completing your final plan.

The following is an example of a lesson/activity in which **none** of the components match:

Objective: Students will write sentences that include adjectives.

Teaching: The teacher shows and tells how to identify adjectives in a sentence.

Practice: Students are asked to list adjectives that describe a given object.

Evaluation: Students write the definition of adjective.

Making your plan congruent helps ensure that students are evaluated on what they were taught and what they practiced.

Summary

The editing tasks component of your lesson and activity planning is a critical one. Here you have an opportunity to write in strategies that impact classroom management and double-check your use of instructional interventions and congruence in your plan. Remember that you cannot predict everything that is going to happen in your lesson or activity, but you may be surprised how much you can predict when you carefully analyze your plan prior to teaching.

Using the Framework for Diversity Responsive Teaching

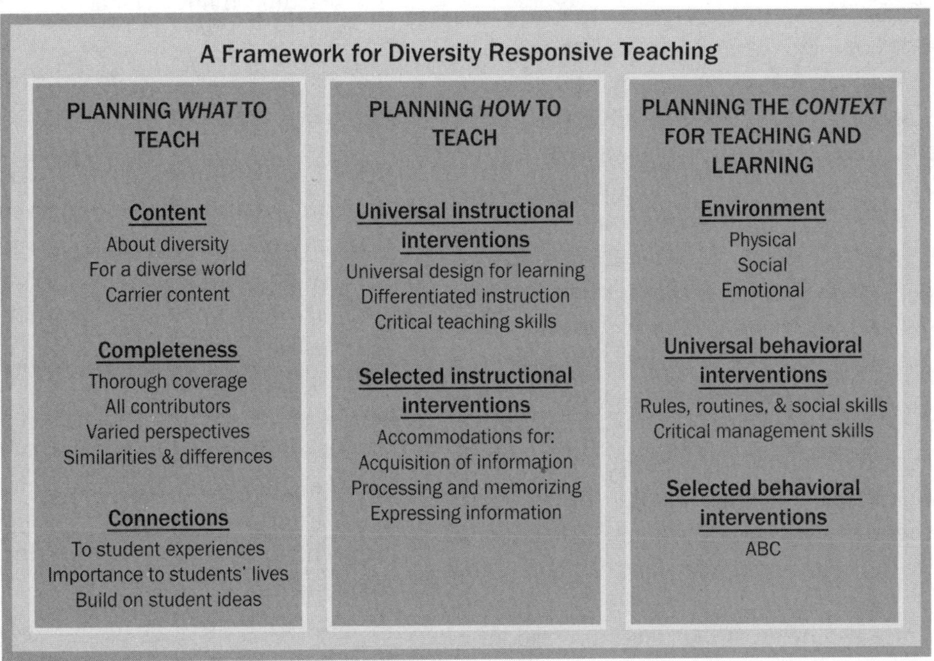

A Framework for Diversity Responsive Teaching
PLANNING WHAT TO TEACH
Content
About diversity
For a diverse world
Carrier content
Completeness
Thorough coverage
All contributors
Varied perspectives
Similarities & differences
Connections
To student experiences
Importance to students' lives
Build on student ideas
PLANNING HOW TO TEACH
Universal instructional interventions
Universal design for learning
Differentiated instruction
Critical teaching skills
Selected instructional interventions
Accommodations for:
Acquisition of information
Processing and memorizing
Expressing information
PLANNING THE CONTEXT FOR TEACHING AND LEARNING
Environment
Physical
Social
Emotional
Universal behavioral interventions
Rules, routines, & social skills
Critical management skills
Selected behavioral interventions
ABC

Introduction

We began our book with the diversity responsive teaching framework, goals for diversity responsive teachers, and a narrative example of diversity responsive teaching (see the Introduction of this book.) The following chapters provided specific information about responding to diversity in what you teach, how you teach, and in planning the context for teaching and learning. We are going to end our book by returning to that framework and those goals with two additional examples. We will show how two teachers use the framework to take a careful look at the "what," "how," and "context" when planning an activity and a lesson. We recognize that it would not be possible, or necessarily even desirable, to respond to diversity in all three of these areas in every lesson and activity that you teach. We do suggest however, that teachers can respond to all three areas in many lessons and activities once they get into the habit of thinking about them as they plan. Using the framework can help develop that habit of mind.

In this chapter we will describe two different ways to use the framework. One way to use the framework is as a support in brainstorming diversity responsive ideas for lessons and activities before writing plans. The other way is to use it as a tool when you want to reflect on your skills as a diversity responsive teacher by examining a lesson or activity plan you've already written.

Using the Framework for Brainstorming

The framework can be useful in helping you generate ideas for diversity responsive strategies to include in lessons, activities, or units of instruction. In this case, you'll use it when you are ready to design learning experiences after consulting state standards, big ideas, and developing measurable objectives.

The procedure to follow in using the framework this way is simply what works best for you. Use it to help you brainstorm as many ideas as possible for diversity responsive teaching in a particular lesson/ activity. Then, when you are ready to write your plan, you'll have lots of ideas to choose from. We suggest that you think about the objective(s), your students, and the three aspects of diversity responsive teaching (what, how, and context) when you begin brainstorming. Keep in mind that your goal is to ensure that all of your students are successful, involved, and challenged by the lesson or activity.

Following is a narrative example of a teacher, Mrs. Choo, using the framework to generate ideas for incorporating diversity responsive teaching into an elaborate activity she is planning for her students. This activity will introduce a unit of instruction about poetry. She predicted a problem—that her students wouldn't be interested in what she was going to teach them over the next few weeks—and wanted to use the framework to try to solve or prevent that problem through this activity. She uses the framework because she believes that diversity responsive teaching strategies work to engage students and to support their success in learning.

Notice as you read this example how Mrs. Choo's thinking reflects the goals of a diversity responsive teacher. We think you'll find that she clearly knows her students as individuals, appreciates their similarities and differences, connects with families and the community, strives to teach so that all her students are challenged and successful, and attempts to prepare them for diversity in the world.

Narrative Example

Mrs. Choo will be teaching a poetry unit. It's part of the curriculum for this grade level. She has developed measurable objectives based on state standards and big ideas and has written a series of lesson and activity plans. However, she is concerned because her students think they don't like poetry. They groaned when she told them they'd be starting the poetry unit next week. From their comments they seem to think that poetry has nothing to do with them, that it's boring, and beyond their understanding and skill.

Mrs. Choo would like to come up with an introductory activity to get her students interested and excited about poetry. She wants an activity that would involve and challenge *all* of her students and convince them that they can be successful in the poetry unit. She decided to use the diversity responsive teaching framework to help generate ideas for this activity.

Planning What *to Teach*

Mrs. Choo began by looking at the "Planning *What* to Teach" component of the framework. She had already carefully considered "content" and "completeness" when writing the unit. For example, she will be teaching about poets from a variety of backgrounds and this will include poets from some of the same cultural backgrounds as her students. Her students have a strong interest in social justice and fairness and she developed a lesson on the poetry of protest. But she thought her students would need to feel a more direct and immediate connection with poetry to get hooked, so she looked at the "connections" component.

Mrs. Choo tried to think what personal experience with poetry her students might have. She considered song lyrics but that theme had just been used in another class. She was thinking about this while walking across the playground. Students in her school are jump rope fanatics. Both boys and girls jump rope and they are extremely competitive. As Mrs. Choo listened to jump rope chants and recognized some from her childhood, she realized she'd found the connection between poetry and the personal experience and interests of her students. She decided the first activity could involve the students collecting jump rope chants. She would have them write down the ones they know and hear in the schoolyard. She would also have the students interview their parents and grandparents about the jump rope chants they remember. Extended families and a strong oral tradition are very important in the community. Mrs. Choo thought this would be another important connection for the students, because one of the big ideas in this unit is that poetry has many purposes and roots. Jump rope chants would be a great example of this.

Planning How *to Teach*

Mrs. Choo next looked at the "Planning *How* to Teach" part of the framework. She thought about how she could use universal design and differentiated instruction in this activity to make sure all her students are successful and challenged. One aspect of universal design is building in options for student responses, that is, how they express their learning. She thought that she wanted all students to collect jump rope chants, to organize them in some way, and to examine their similarities and differences. But students could choose to create books of chants, do an oral presentation, or create a multimedia presentation.

Another aspect of universal design is providing for multiple means of student engagement that involves offering different supports or scaffolds to challenge individuals appropriately. Mrs. Choo thought that having students work in teams could be one way to provide support. She could form teams of students with different strengths (in writing, in using technology, in interpersonal skills for interviewing, and so on). She thought more about the writing aspect of this activity because many of her students struggle with writing. Mrs. Choo decided that providing tape recorders and interview scripts would reduce some of the writing demands.

Next Mrs. Choo thought about selected instructional interventions. Ivan, a student with severe cognitive and physical disabilities, spends some time in her classroom each day. He has been working on his own IEP objective for using assistive technology devices, including various on/off switches. The class will be using quite a few devices with switches, like tape recorders, video cameras, and computers for this project so Ivan will have many opportunities to practice. That made her think of another student who can be very difficult to motivate but loves gadgets and would love to have a chance to use the new digital video camera that Mrs. Choo got through a grant. A third student is very gifted academically and Mrs. Choo has wanted to find more ways to challenge her. This student could benefit from opportunities to take a leadership role. Perhaps she could lead a team that takes on a more elaborate project. Mrs. Choo realized she will need to carefully plan these selected interventions but this gives her some ideas to start with.

Planning the Context *for Teaching and Learning*

For her next step, Mrs. Choo consulted the third part of the framework, the "context for teaching and learning." She began by thinking about how this activity could contribute to creating a diversity responsive environment. She thought she might have the students display photographs and quotations from the interviews on the walls of the classroom. This would certainly be welcoming to families. She next thought about the social environment. She had been looking for more ways to include Ivan socially. Putting him on a team with students who are potential friends and allies will help. Also, his mom and grandma are very fun and great with children. The team would definitely enjoy interviewing them, and that would give Ivan an important role. Mrs. Choo next looked at the emotional environment component. She thought about the varied family structures of her students. It might be a good idea to emphasize interviewing elders in the community rather than just using the words parents and grandparents. As a matter of fact, it would benefit everyone if the interviews went beyond family members. Some cultural groups in the community aren't represented in the class and this could be a way for the students to connect with those groups. In addition, one student recently moved in with a foster family. He's in touch with family members in another part of the state and perhaps could interview them over the phone, as well as interviewing his foster family. That could be emphasized as a strength and an advantage to his team.

Next Mrs. Choo thought about universal behavioral interventions. The class could probably benefit from a social skills lesson focusing on requesting and conducting interviews in a polite way. She could connect that with earlier lessons on polite forms such as saying *please* and *thank you,* starting conversations, and asking for help. She's also using a selected behavioral intervention with one of her students. It's a self-management system for completing assignments on time. Once his team has planned their project, she'll work with him on setting goals for completing his part on time.

Summary

Mrs. Choo has used the framework to brainstorm many ideas for an activity. When she starts writing the activity plan she will probably change or throw out some ideas and add still others. She'll need to get much more specific, of course. When she is done writing and editing the plan she may decide to use the diversity responsive framework one more time to self-evaluate.

Using the Framework as a Tool for Self-Reflection

The second way to use this framework is as a tool for self-reflection about your growth as a diversity responsive teacher. Responding effectively to diversity takes reflective thought, as well as time and practice, and is a process rather than an outcome. Use the framework periodically to analyze a lesson or activity that you have planned. By doing this, you can check up on your use of diversity responsive strategies in general or those particularly useful in addressing specific types of diversity or need. Analysis of your plan will give you information for reflection.

You can work your way through a specific plan using the framework in at least two ways. First, you could work through it component by component, stopping after each component to evaluate your response to diversity in *what* and *how* you taught, and the *context*. Another way would be to look over the whole plan and then evaluate the *what*, the *how*, and the *context*, as well as your response to each. Use whichever way (or a combination of both) is the easiest for you to gather the information you need for self-reflection. The important thing is that you are taking necessary steps to positively impact your skills as a diversity responsive teacher.

Mr. Perez's Lesson Plan

Following is a lesson plan written by Mr. Perez. After he wrote his plan, he used editing tasks to make adjustments that he felt were appropriate and he believed that his plan was now ready to teach. He decided to use the framework for analyzing this particular lesson because he thinks it is fairly representative of the type of lesson he teaches. He plans to assess his overall use of DRT strategies but he really wants to focus on what he has planned for Olga, his new student. He's not sure that he has provided enough support for her. As you read through Mr. Perez's plan, look for examples of strategies that reflect best practice in responding to diversity. Following the lesson plan, you will meet Mr. Perez's students, which will help you determine the potential effectiveness of the strategies he has included. Following the description of the students is Mr. Perez's analysis of his plan.

Lesson Plan

Topic: Teaching the Rule "Include Everyone"

I. PREPLANNING TASKS

A. Connection analysis: This is part of a series of lessons and activities for creating an inclusive social environment in the classroom.

B. Task analysis: How to follow the rule "include everyone" in activities at school:

1. If you see someone alone, invite him or her to join you or your group.
2. If someone asks to join you or your group, say *yes* in a welcoming way.
3. When you are given a partner or group/team member, accept him or her politely.

C. Lesson Objective: Students will apply the rule to include everyone in activities at school by inviting others to join them, saying *yes* to someone who asks to join, and accepting assigned partners/members politely, in three out of three role plays.

D. Rationale: It is important that students learn to work and play with everyone at school to create an inclusive and safe environment and because these are important skills for living in a diverse society.

E. Prerequisite skills/key vocabulary

include: make someone feel invited, welcomed, and accepted

join: become part of an activity or group

invite: ask someone to do something with you

welcoming: acting glad that someone is joining you

accept: taking someone as partner or group/team member

politely: with good manners in words and body language

Note: Introduce these words the day before and create a word bank to post on the wall.

II. LESSON SETUP

A. Signal for attention: Knock on desk.

B. Behavioral expectations: Listen carefully. Say, "Be a polite audience. That means sit quietly and listen carefully without talking so that everyone can see and hear the skit." NOTE: Repeat "sit," "quiet," and "listen" with modeling and gestures.

III. LESSON OPENING

A. Preview: Say, "Remember yesterday when we talked about creating a happy and safe class? A place where feelings don't get hurt? A good place to be? Today we're going to have some sixth graders show us what a class looks like when it is NOT happy, NOT safe, NOT a good place for everyone." Note: Write these three phrases on the board. Use gestures to emphasize "NOT."

B. Begin skit: Sixth graders do a skit of nonexamples of the rule "including everyone": Carlos is not invited to make paper airplanes with other boys; girls refuse Sally when she asks to sit with them during art; kids make rude comments and facial expressions when assigned partners.

[Note: Acknowledge students who followed behavior expectations.]

C. Statement of objective; objective purpose: Say, "We don't want to have a class like the sixth graders showed us—where some kids feel sad and lonely or mad and embarrassed—so we're going to have a rule that says 'Include everyone'. Today you're going to learn how and when to follow that rule at school."

IV. LESSON BODY

A. Presentation of information

Restate behavior expectations: Say, "Participate and follow directions for unison responses and thumbs up."

[Note: Acknowledge students who follow behavior expectations throughout.]

1. Say/write rule (Include Everyone) on board.

   AP = Signal for a unison response.

   a. Ask: "What's the rule?" Repeat.
   b. Say, "Let's study those two words." Point to and say "include."
      i. Call five students up to the front. (Include the two least proficient English language learners.) They hold hands in a circle. Then break hands to include teacher. Say that they included me. Repeat.
      ii. Use *What is it? What is it like? What are some examples?* for defining *include.* If needed, prompt for *invite, welcome,* and *accept.*

      ***AP** = Brainstorm*

      iii. Point to word bank. Remind students of the definition of *include* (invite, welcome, accept all kids)

   ***AP** = Choral read*

2. Summarize: "Include everyone," means welcome and accept *all* kids. Point to the rule and ask them to say it in unison.
3. Show task analysis:

   How to Follow the Rule "Include Everyone" in Activities at School

   a. If you see someone alone, invite him or her to join you.
   b. If someone asks to join you, say *yes.*
   c. When you're given a partner, accept him or her politely.
4. Uncover/show posters: Each poster has a photograph of class members acting out one of the three aspects of the rule along with the words they use. Each poster includes titles and pictures and pattern sentences.

   Say, "We are going to practice three ways to include everyone. These are (show with fingers) (1) when you see someone alone, (2) when someone asks to join you, and (3) when you are given partners."
5. Review each poster.

   ***AP** = Unison reading*

   a. Point to poster #1. Read title, for example, "When you see someone alone. . . . "
   b. Discuss the picture: Two kids are working on their spelling words and they see a girl who is alone. . . .

c. Read the pattern sentence under the photo: "Come and *work* with us." (Insert the *work* word card.) She says, "Okay. Thanks." Have students read the pattern.

AP = *Unison reading*

d. Model another example of inviting (sitting with friends at lunch) while thinking out loud ("That girl is standing there alone with her tray. . . ."). End by reading the pattern sentence and filling in *sit* with the word card. Have them repeat. Again point to *sitting* and *sit*.

6. Repeat review (#5) for the other two posters.

B. Demonstration (with assistant)

1. Explain/model: "Watch and think if I follow the rule." Model inviting (playing with friends at recess) while thinking out loud ("That girl is standing there alone with her jumprope. . . ."), and say "Come and *play* with us."

AP = *Thumbs up* (if I followed it)

2. Demonstrate examples and nonexamples, using welcoming and polite acceptance voice tone and body language.

AP = *Tell a partner*

3. Repeat with saying *yes* to assistant who asks to sit by you on bus and with accepting assigned basketball team member.

C. CFU: Remind them of Carlos in the first scene of the skit (playing with paper airplanes). Ask, "What could the boys have said to Carlos to include him? Write it on your scratch paper." Monitor. Repeat for other scenes. Call on nonvolunteers to say out loud with friendly tones and body language. **(AP)**

D. Supervised Practice (individual practice with a partner; use desk partners)

1. Show/say directions for practice (on board). "You'll be taking turns being the inviters and accepters."

   a. Find partner. Decide who is A and who is B.

   b. Collect six scenario cards.

   c. Partner A reads scenario 1 and both act.

   d. Decide if both agree rule was followed. Redo if necessary.

   e. Switch. Partner B reads scenario 2.

   f. Continue with scenario 3, and so on.

2. Demonstrate following directions (with assistant).

   Example scenario cards: "Partner A is playing kickball with other kids at recess and sees Partner B alone"; "Partner B and classmates are working on their science reports and see that Partner A is alone." Reading level of scenarios vary per desk partner group.

3. CFU: Signal with fingers when we are following step #1, #2, and so on.

4. Explain and show partner list: "You will work with your desk partner" (show partner list).

5. Explain behavior expectations: Say, "Stay on task; give each other polite feedback as you've learned."

6. Monitor and ask questions, give feedback. [Acknowledge students following directions.]

V. LESSON CLOSING

A. Summarize: Say, "You have learned three ways to include everyone so the class is a happy and safe place to be. I will leave these posters up to remind you."

B. Prompt generalization: Hand out cards. Say, "Write one way you plan to follow the rule today at recess. Tape it to your desk."

VI. EXTENDED PRACTICE

A. Assign partners/groups several times tomorrow and prompt.

B. Precorrect before recess and lunch for the rest of the week.

C. Reward "including" with good citizen certificates.

VII. EVALUATION

Pull each student aside over next few days and give scenarios to role-play.

Mr. Perez's Students

Now you will meet Mr. Perez's students. This will help you better understand Mr. Perez's analysis of his use of diversity responsive teaching DRT strategies and ideas. Mr. Perez has a fairly typical mix of students and he really enjoys all of them. His students display a range of skill levels, for example, some of his students are reading below their grade level, while three read above grade level. As a whole group, they are active yet focused, but have difficulty sitting for long periods of time. Four of his students are English language learners. Both of his Spanish speakers (Carlos and Rosa), and one of his Russian students (Mikhail) are fairly fluent in English, but his new student, another Russian speaker (Olga) speaks very little English. One student (Julia) spends part of the day in a special program for gifted learners and has definite strengths in creative writing, language, and drama. Two of Mr. Perez's students, Jimmy and Jake, receive special education services because of disabilities. Jimmy has significant skill deficits in reading and writing due to a learning disability. Jake displays many acting-out behaviors (name-calling, noncompliance with following directions, for example) and consequently has had some difficulty establishing relationships with the other students. The class is made up of 23 students, 12 boys, and 11 girls. The students who speak Spanish come from families who make their living by following the farm harvest and working throughout several states. Consequently, they are in Mr. Perez's room for just the next few months. The occupations of the parents of his other students vary from professional (for example, teacher) to retail sales positions.

Narrative Example

The following is Mr. Perez's analysis of his lesson plan using the framework as his guide. He considered his response to diversity in *what* he taught, *how* he taught it, and the *context* for teaching and learning that he created. As you read through Mr. Perez's thoughts, see what additional ideas you have.

Planning What *to Teach*

Mr. Perez began by looking carefully at the first component of the framework and thought about the content he selected, the specifics of the content to be taught, and what connections he had made to his students' lives. He really didn't think that the issue of completeness applied to this lesson, but he saw that he did address the areas of content and connections. Here are some examples:

- Mr. Perez deliberately selected the "Including Everyone" rule for this lesson because it is a skill that his students need both in the classroom and in society at large (for a diverse world). He wants all of his students to be accepting and tolerant of all people. He also thought about the couple of students in his class who have difficulty establishing relationships with others. For example, his students from migrant families will only be in school for a short amount of time and he recognizes that it is hard, especially for the shy one (Rosa), to develop friendships in this context. His student with social challenges (Jake) displays behaviors that have led to some isolation. He thought this lesson could be of extra help for these students.

- He included a number of strategies to try to connect this lesson to the experiences and interests of his students. He selected real-life scenarios that he saw happen in his own class and in other settings, since the beginning of the school year. These scenarios are directly connected to his students' own experiences and they will help students see how important the skill is to learn. These connections to real life can help make content meaningful to students.

- The skit during the opening also provides common experience and background knowledge so students have something with which to connect the new learning. It should grab their attention and be memorable and motivating, especially when acted by older students. Because of the context, Mr. Perez determined a skit would be easier to follow than just describing situations or reading scenarios.

Planning How *to Teach*

Next Mr. Perez moves on and consults the next component of the framework. This component causes him to carefully think through his use of universal and selected instructional interventions. Here are some specific examples:

- Various strategies in this lesson reflected general approaches to universal interventions such as the universal design and differentiated instruction. In numerous places throughout the plan for example, Mr. Perez planned to say, write and show the information he was teaching, such as when he explained how the supervised practice portion of the lesson would work. He also emphasized the lesson information in a variety of ways such as through the skit, a variety of visual supports, partner practice, modeling, and so forth.

- Mr. Perez's plan included numerous critical teaching skills. For example, when he gave directions, he wrote, said, and demonstrated them. He used checks for understanding (monitoring) throughout his lesson that allowed him to check the understanding of every student (for example, when he had students hold up the number of fingers that represented the step number). He also incorporated numerous types of opportunities to respond, that is for active participation (choral responses, turning to partners, and so on). Mr. Perez carefully monitored students at each step of the way as they worked toward the objective. When students worked in partners, he moved around the classroom to make sure that each partner group was practicing correct information.

- He included numerous opportunities for choral responses and choral reading (active participation strategies) because they would help keep all of his students engaged. They also provided valuable, comfortable practice of information for his students who are learning English, which was additionally beneficial.

Mr. Perez originally included a selected intervention that turned out to be a universal intervention. When he completed editing tasks however, he thought again about his students and he decided that the strategy he selected would actually benefit many students. He built in the following rather than adding it on:

- He used actions to help clarify word meaning, thereby benefitting all the students, including English language learners. For example, acting out the term *include* could be better for everyone than simply saying a dictionary definition, especially for such an abstract term.

After thinking about universal design, differentiated instruction, and critical teaching skills, Mr. Perez knew that several of his students would need additional support. He included the following selected interventions for those students:

- He planned to pre-teach vocabulary to his English language learners. He thought about pre-teaching the words to all students but decided that it was not necessary or appropriate to do so.
- When Mr. Perez wrote up the scenarios, he simplified the vocabulary in those to be used by Jimmy and his English language learners. This accomplished two things. First, Jimmy could work independently with his reading and the students learning English could practice their reading in a comfortable way. Julia helped write the scenarios that she and her partner used. Julia's strength in writing, and her flair for the dramatic made for some interesting dramatics. It wouldn't have been appropriate to simplify the vocabulary for everyone.

Planning the Context *for Teaching and Learning*

The final component of the framework helped Mr. Perez examine his setup of the classroom environment as well as his use of universal and selected behavioral interventions. The following are examples:

- Mr. Perez took great care to set up desk partners so that everyone would feel supported. For the English language learners he assigned desk partners who are good language models and who will help, but not do it all. He partnered Olga with Mikhail, who is a more fluent speaker. Mr. Perez then considered the compatibility of all the desk partner groupings. For instance, he matched Jimmy with Michael who is friendly, supportive, and a great role model.
- He used the "turn to your partner" strategy for the partner practice. Using desk partners in this way was an advantage because his students were familiar with this process.
- Mr. Perez wrote reminders to acknowledge appropriate behavior right into his plan. He knows this strategy is very effective in supporting students who are following behavior expectations. It also serves as a reminder to those students who may have difficulty.
- He used simplified language for giving behavior expectations. He explained some words, such as *sit, quiet,* and *listen,* with modeling and gestures. This especially helps Jimmy and the students who are learning English, but it is a good reminder for many of the students.
- Changing behavior expectations throughout the lesson helped ensure that students were following them. Mr. Perez recognized that expectations change with the flow of the lesson. For example, at times, he wanted students to raise their hands and wait to be called on. At other times, he wanted students to call out answers. It was important that Mr. Perez communicated these changes to his students so they understand his expectations at all times and. He doesn't want to appear to say one thing and allow another, such as saying to raise hands and then accepting call-outs.

After reviewing all of the strategies to use with the whole class, Mr. Perez decided that Jimmy could benefit from an additional selected behavior intervention:

- Jimmy is learning how to manage his own behavior through self-monitoring. Mr. Perez thought that this particular lesson could be one where

Jimmy had some difficulty with compliance. Mr. Perez gave Jimmy a self-monitoring chart to tape on his desk so that he can track his compliance with directions. Mr. Perez also made sure that he provided Jimmy with the support that he needed by increasing the amount of attention he gave to Jimmy for following directions.

Mr. Perez's Reflection

Once Mr. Perez worked his way through the diversity responsive teaching framework, he thought about areas he considered strengths and those areas where he felt he needed more information. Here are a couple of his conclusions:

- Use of gestures, pictures, and so forth are helpful for his English language learners who speak some English, but he wasn't sure they were enough for Olga. He has been told she is in the early production stage. As he thinks through this lesson, it occurs to him that he really isn't sure that she is progressing as fast as she could. He notes that he needs to gather more information about additional strategies that might benefit her. Perhaps he can talk with the teacher who works with English language learners and get more ideas for strategies and resource materials.

- He thought he had included a wide variety of active participation techniques. He was pleased about this and really feels like he has a great repertoire of strategies.

- The behavior system that has been set up for Jimmy just doesn't seem to work as well as he'd like. He needs to set aside some time to really study the system to see if he can figure out why it isn't all that effective. He likes the idea of self-monitoring but it just isn't working as well as he had hoped. Mr. Perez thinks perhaps he'll ask other teachers at the next grade-level meeting and get their ideas and opinions.

These are some of the ideas that Mr. Perez had as he reflected on the information he had gathered. Can you identify other strength areas for reflection?

Summary

Mr. Perez used the diversity responsive teaching framework as a way to gather information for self-reflection about his growth as a diversity responsive teacher. This is not something that he does after every lesson, but he does it regularly. He considers the needs of his students, the goals of the diversity responsive teacher, and all elements reflected in the diversity framework. This provides him with important food for thought.

Final Thoughts

Teachers need to be aware of the diversity in their classroom and respond to it effectively if all students are to be successful in school. We recognize that this can seem like a daunting task at first, and many teachers may feel that they do not know where or how to begin. We have found that this feeling is not an unusual one among teachers. We hope that our framework has helped break down this task into manageable parts that will help you in your pursuit of creating a diversity responsive classroom. Remember that responding to diversity is a process that evolves over time, not something that happens overnight.

We think that one important factor in the professional growth process of diversity responsive teaching is the development of habits. It is probably unrealistic to think that you can respond to all diversity, all of the time. It is realistic though, to respond to much diversity, much of the time. The framework we have presented to you and all of the information that fits into it, gives you many places to begin developing the habit of being responsive to diversity. Our challenge to you is to select an idea that you haven't tried before: try it, see how it works, then try something else, and so on. We wish you the best!

TO THE OWNER OF THIS BOOK:

I hope that you have found *Planning Effective Instruction,* Third Edition, useful. So that this book can be improved in a future edition, would you take the time to complete this sheet and return it? Thank you.

School and address: ______________________________

____

Department: ______________________________

Instructor's name: ______________________________

1. What I like most about this book is: ______________________________

____

____

2. What I like least about this book is: ______________________________

____

____

3. My general reaction to this book is: ______________________________

____

____

4. The name of the course in which I used this book is: ______________________________

____

5. Were all of the chapters of the book assigned for you to read? ______________________________

   If not, which ones weren't? ______________________________

6. In the space below, or on a separate sheet of paper, please write specific suggestions for improving this book and anything else you'd care to share about your experience in using this book.

____

____

____

____

____

____

____

DO NOT STAPLE. TAPE HERE.

DO NOT STAPLE. TAPE HERE.

FOLD HERE

NO POSTAGE NECESSARY IF MAILED IN THE UNITED STATES

BUSINESS REPLY MAIL

FIRST-CLASS MAIL PERMIT NO. 34 BELMONT CA

POSTAGE WILL BE PAID BY ADDRESSEE

Attn: *Dan Alpert, Education Editor*

Wadsworth/Thomson Learning
10 Davis Dr
Belmont CA 94002-9801

FOLD HERE

OPTIONAL:

Your name:____________________________________ Date:____________________

May we quote you, either in promotion for *Planning Effective Instruction,* Third Edition, or in future publishing ventures?

Yes: __________ No: __________

Sincerely yours,

Kay M. Price and Karna L. Nelson